20TH Century PAPER DOLLS

Identification & Values

Mary Young

COLLECTOR BOOKS

A Division of Schroeder Publishing Co., Inc.

Front cover: Little Miss Lady, p. 161; Miss Hollywood, p. 181; Miss Silver Screen, p. 181; Let's Play Paper Dolls, p. 198; Best of Friends, p. 136; Teeny Weeny Dolls, p. 155; Tiny Twinkle, p. 151; Dolly's Kut-Out Klothes, p. 28.

Back cover: Ideal Doll Book, p. 192; Dennison's Doll Outfit, p. 76; Dainty Dollies, p. 100.

Other books by this author:
Paper Dolls and Their Artists — Book One; Paper Dolls and Their Artists — Book Two; A Collector's Guide to Paper Dolls — Saalfield, Lowe, Merrill; A Collector's Guide to Paper Dolls — Second Series; A Collector's Guide to Magazine Paper Dolls; Paper Dolls and Their Artists — Revised Edition; Tomart's Price Guide to Lowe and Whitman Paper Dolls; Tomart's Price Guide to Saalfield and Merrill Paper Dolls.

Cover design by Beth Summers

Book design and layout by Mary Ann Hudson

Photographs by Mary Young

COLLECTOR BOOKS
P.O. Box 3009
Paducah, Kentucky 42002-3009
www.collectorbooks.com

Copyright © 2006 Mary Young
P.O. Box 9244
Dayton, OH 45409

Searching For A Publisher?

We are always looking for people knowledgeable within their fields. If you feel that there is a real need for a book on your collectible subject and have a large comprehensive collection, contact Collector Books.

The current values in this book should be used only as a guide. They are not intended to set prices, which vary from one section of the country to another. Auction prices as well as dealer prices vary greatly and are affected by condition as well as demand. Neither the author nor the publisher assumes responsibility for any losses that might be incurred as a result of consulting this guide.

Contents

Dedication

To our four terrific sons-in-law, Larry, Dave, Guy, and Manny, and our two newest grandchildren, adorable grandsons Scott and David.

Acknowledgments

I wish to thank the following, who have given so generously of their time and effort by either lending their paper dolls or sending information without which this book could not have been possible: Norene Allen, Marlene Brenner, Edna Corbett, Rosemary Davidson, Barbara Faber, Patti Fertel, Wilma Goss, Mary Herzog, Lynne Hough, Pam Hunter, Jayne Keller, Judy Lawson, Jo Anne McCleary, Betty McConnell, Jan McKay, Carole Morgan, Jane Razor, Audrey Sepponen, Betsy Slap, Karla Steger, Mary Stuecher, Jean Sullivan, Judy Waldmann, and Wynn Yusas.

Extra special thanks to Peggy Ell, Virginia Crossley, Rosalie Eppert, Ruth Morrison, Elaine Price, Betsy Addison, Louise Leek, Joe Golembieski, and Shirley Fischer.

To my husband, George, many thanks for all your support and understanding.

Introduction

This book is a revised edition of my book that was published by Collector Books in 1984 with the title *A Collector's Guide To Paper Dolls — Second Series*. The book was often referred to by collectors as the Blue Guide or Blue Book.

This revised edition will cover many additional companies and their paper dolls, plus many additional paper dolls that have been found for many of the original companies. Over 150 publishing companies that produced paper dolls are covered in this expanded edition. Some companies produced only a few paper dolls, while others produced quite a few. This book, as before, will cover paper dolls produced in the twentieth century. In a few cases, some paper dolls are shown that were published in the 1890s but were still being produced in the early 1900s. At the back of the book is a list of even more companies that have produced paper dolls.

The paper dolls pictured are copyrighted by the company in whose section they appear, unless otherwise stated. All photographs, unless stated otherwise, are by the author.

Price Guide

The prices in this book are based on mint, uncut original paper dolls. Cut sets are usually half the price, providing all the dolls and outfits are included and the pieces are in very good condition. Otherwise the prices decrease accordingly. Some of the older paper dolls covered in this book were produced in die-cut form (packaged with the dolls and outfits already cut). In these cases, the prices shown are for die-cut sets in mint condition and with all costumes and accessories.

A.T. Co.

No information has been found to indicate what the initials *A* and *T* in A.T. Co. stand for.

There were two different styles of Our Favorite Dolls. One style has the boy in short hair and the girl in long hair parted in the center. The dolls pictured came with outfits reading "A.T. Co." on their backs. This set has also been found to say "A.T. Co." on the back of the dolls. The folders pictured came with these two A.T. Co. dolls and are not marked with the company name.

The second style of Our Favorite Dolls has the boy in long hair and the girl in long hair with bangs. This pair was published by Selchow and Righter and also by the Amlico Company. Those companies are pictured in their own sections in this book. Notice that the boy dolls are the same from the neck down, and likewise the girl dolls. Both Selchow and Righter and Amlico put their company names on their folders.

Each doll came with five costumes and hats, for a total of ten outfits for the pair. The ten outfits came in six paper doll sets, all of which were described on the back of each A.T. Co. outfit and sometimes on the backs of the dolls. The following description is quoted exactly as it is written on the dolls and outfits:

Set No. 1 consists of Girl Doll, Girl's Turquoise Blue Dress, with Hat to match. Set No. 2 consists of One Girl's Pink Dress, with Hat to match. One Girl's Plaid Dress, with Hat to match. Set No. 3 consists of One Girl's Old Rose figured Dress, Apron filled with Flowers, and hat to match. One Girl's Royal Blue defender Sailor Dress, with hat to match. Set No. 4 consists of Boy Doll, Red Newport Sailor Suit with Cap to match. Set No. 5 consists of One Boy's Suit American Guard, Army Blue Uniform, with Cap to match. One Boy's Suit, Scotch Highland costume, complete, with Cap to match. Set No. 6 consists of One Boy's Suit, Zouave Uniform, with Cap to match. One Boy's Suit, Prince Charles costume, complete, with Cap to match.

 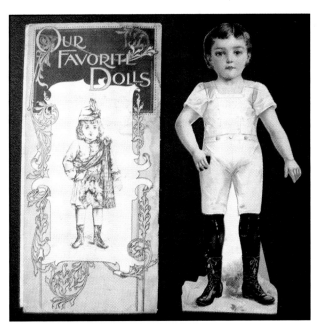

Our Favorite Dolls, $125.00 each with folder.

A.T.R. Publishing Corp.

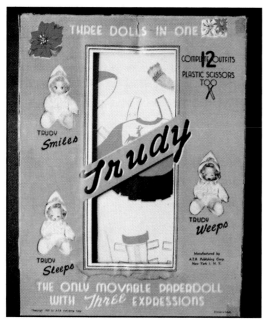

Trudy, Three Dolls in One, 1947, $30.00.

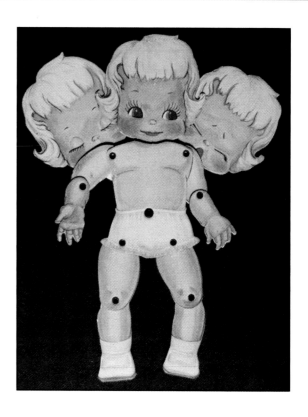

The Abingdon Press

Items not pictured:

China, 1923
Japan, 1923
Korea, 1923

Twin Travelogues, India, 1923, $25.00.

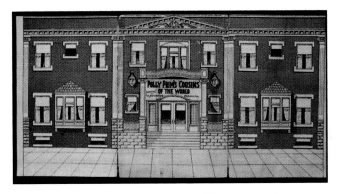

Polly Prim's Cousins of the World, 1911, a three-part house folder to hold the sheets of paper dolls, $60.00.

Polly Prim and Brother Billy.

Nanki Poo and Pitti Sing of Japan.

Hans and Gretchen of Holland.

Alphonse and Isabella of Spain.

Donald from the Highlands of Scotland and Noreen from County Kildare, Ireland.

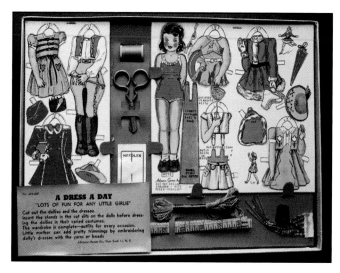

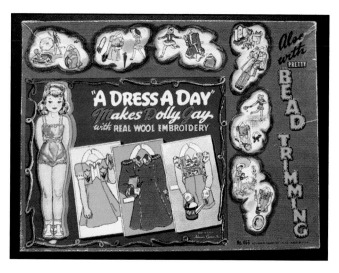

466 A Dress a Day. This set contains three dolls (only one doll is shown), $40.00.

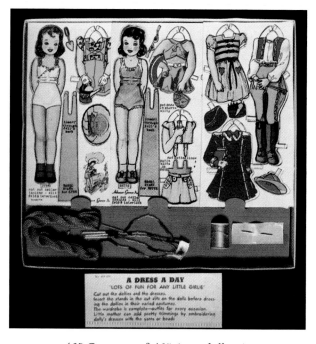

465 A Dress a Day, 1942, $35.00.

465 Contents of 465 (two-doll set).

Nursery Rhyme Theater, Little Red Riding Hood #1126 was also produced by the company but did not contain outfits for the characters.

New Laurie, $18.00.

201 Plastic Cut-Outs, Susie, Judy, Laura, and Annie, $40.00.

101 Laura and Annie
101 Annette and Zorro
102 Annette (Disney)
103 Walt Disney's Formed Plastic Cut-outs, two sheets of cut-outs: Donald and Daisy Duck on one sheet, Disney Stand-ups on the other.
201 Susie, Judy, Laura, and Annie (pictured)
201 Formed Plastic Doll Cut-outs (includes New Judy, New Laurie, and New Susie)
203 Walt Disney's Cut-outs: Annette, Cinderella, Snow White and Zorro

The following sets either did not have numbers or the numbers are not available:

New Judy
New Laurie (pictured)
New Susie
Mickey Mouse and His Pals
Sleeping Beauty
Cinderella
Zorro
Darlene
Popeye Thimble Theater
Peter Pan
Tinker Bell
Alice In Wonderland
Mighty Mouse
Heckle and Jeckle
My Fair Lady (pictured)
Snow White
Donald Duck

My Fair Lady, $30.00.

American Colortype Company

Most of the paper dolls printed by American Colortype were done in the early 1900s through the first World War. Many of the dolls were also printed with advertising for various companies. Bakeries especially used these paper dolls to advertise their bakery goods on the backs of the dolls.

In 1927, six books of paper dolls were printed by the American Colortype Company and were completely different from earlier paper dolls. They came in two sets of three books each, two dolls to a book. Set 1 contained books 25, 26, and 27, and the dolls were marked "copyright A.C. Co." On the next set of three books, 101, 102, and 103, the company name is spelled out completely, "c. American Colortype Co."

Some paper doll boxes or envelopes have been found with a trademark logo of "Cut Craft Cut Outs" in addition to the "American Colortype Co., Chi." (Chicago) imprint on the box or envelope.

Folder for set 1.

Folder for sets 101, 102, and 103.

25 Patsy Ann and Marie, 1927, $40.00.

26 Jane and Betty Lou, 1927, $40.00.

The folder for the books 101, 102, and 103 is the same as the folder for books 25, 26, and 27, except it doesn't say "Set No. 1" at the bottom.

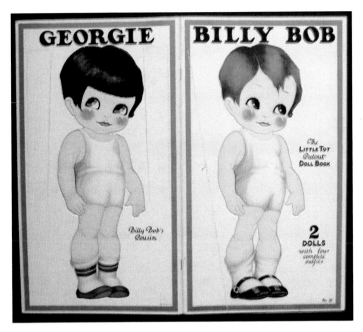

27 Georgie and Billy Bob, 1927, $40.00.

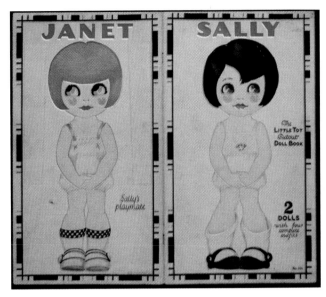

101 Janet and Sally, 1927, $40.00.

102 Mildred and Margy, 1927, $40.00.

103 Jack and Jimmy, 1927, $40.00.

The following paper dolls were found intact in a salesman's sample case and provide invaluable information as to the name and stock number of each doll. All American Colortype paper dolls listed with a 600 number are 6½" tall.

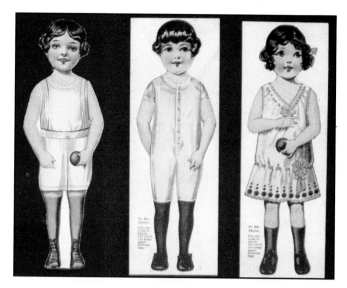

Left to right: 600 John, 601 Henry, 602 Pearl. $18.00 each.

Left to right: 603 Martha, 604 Nancy, 605 Ruth. $18.00 each.

Left to right: 606 Anna, 607 Peter, 608 Janet. $18.00 each.

Left to right: 609 Laurette, 610 Grace, 611 Andrew. $18.00 each.

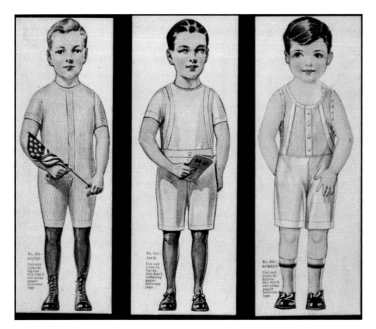

Left to right: 612 David, 613 Jack, 614 Robert. $18.00 each.

Left to right: 615 Catherine, 616 Betty, 617 Gladys. $18.00 each.

Left to right: 618 Dorothy, 619 Arthur, 620 Howard. $18.00 each.

Left to right: 621 Charles, 622 William, 623 Frederick. $18.00 each.

Other small boxes of the dolls in this series of box sets have also been found, including another set of Little Alice Busy Bee with just three dolls.

Little Alice Busy Bee, $70.00. The six dolls in this box are 7⅜". Besides Little Alice Busy Bee, the dolls include Little Polly Dress-up (p. 16), and the dolls on this page and the next.

Little Betty Gad-About, $70.00. The four dolls in this box are 7⅜". They can vary between Little Polly Dress-up (p. 16) and the dolls shown on this page and the next.

624 Little Betty Gad-About, $60.00. Envelope and outfit sheets 909, 910, and 911.

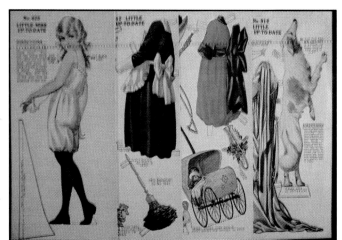

625 Little Miss Up-to-Date, $60.00. With outfit sheets 912, 913, and 914.

626 Little Alice Busy Bee, $60.00. Outfit sheets 915, 916, and 917.

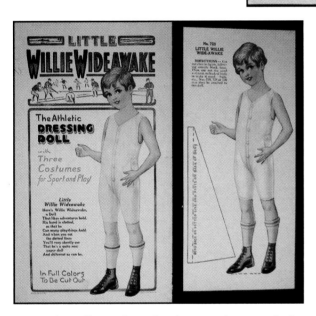

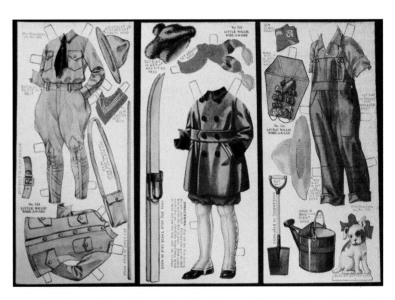

723 Little Willie Wideawake, $85.00. Shown is the large 13" set of Willie Wideawake and outfits sheets of 724, 725, and 726. The doll and outfits are identical to the smaller doll 627 and outfit sheets 918, 919, and 920.

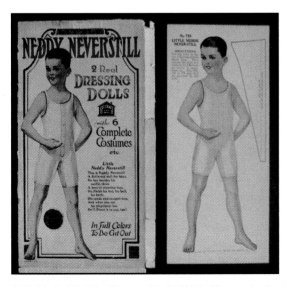

735 Little Neddy Neverstill, $85.00. Shown is the large set of Neddy Neverstill. This is a box set and includes two dolls of Neddy and three outfits — 736, 737, 738 — in color and the same three outfits in black and white, to be colored. The doll and outfits in color are the same as the smaller doll 628 and outfits 921, 922, and 923.

629 Little Polly Dress Up, $60.00.
Outfit sheets 924, 925, and 926.

My Favorite Dressing Dolls, Laurette, 13"
doll with outfits 700, 701, and 702. $60.00.

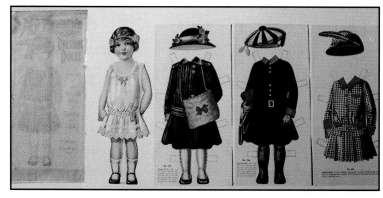

My Favorite Dressing Dolls, Corinne, 13" doll with
outfits 703, 704, and 705. $60.00. Corinne has also
been found in an envelope titled Little Sunbeam,
My Favorite Dressing Dolls.

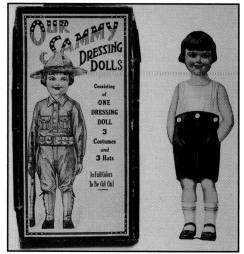

Our Sammy, box and 13" doll, $75.00. With outfits 710, 711, and 712.

Liberty Fair, 13" doll with outfits 713, 714, and 715. $75.00.

13" doll with outfits 716, 717, and 718. $75.00.

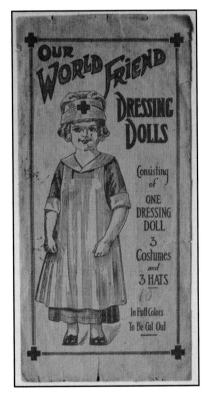

Our World Friend, $75.00. Doll is same as Liberty Fair. The outfits are 714, 715, and 717.

This doll and her outfits were used to advertise Bond Bread. There are no identifying numbers on the sheets. $35.00. Although not marked these outfits are 821, 829, and 830. The name of the doll is unknown.

My Favorite Dressing Dolls, Richard, with outfits 706, 707, and 708. $75.00. Shown is the envelope set. The box set is identical but has the doll's name under the doll's feet. Another set has been found with the "Cut Craft Cut Outs" logo. It has an identical doll of Richard and identical outfits, and the cover is also the same, except the words "My Favorite" have been left out.

The following are just a few examples of the many American Colortype paper dolls that were used for advertising by companies in the early 1900s.

Bond Bread doll and outfits, $35.00. Although not marked, this doll is Anna, and the outfits are 814, 808, and 813.

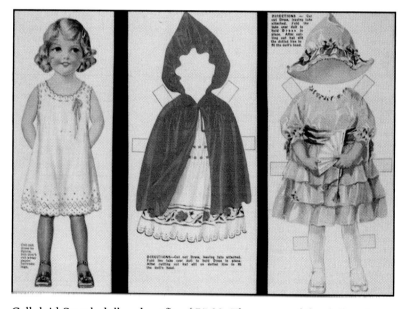

Celluloid Starch doll and outfits, $35.00. The names of the doll and outfits are unknown. The backs of the doll and outfits have the advertising for Celluloid Starch, and in small print at the bottom is "American Colortype Co. Chicago."

All 800 numbers are outfits for the 6½" dolls. The outfit's number is given under each picture. For information about the outfit, consult the list of American Colortype paper dolls on pages 25 and 26. Outfits are $15.00 each.

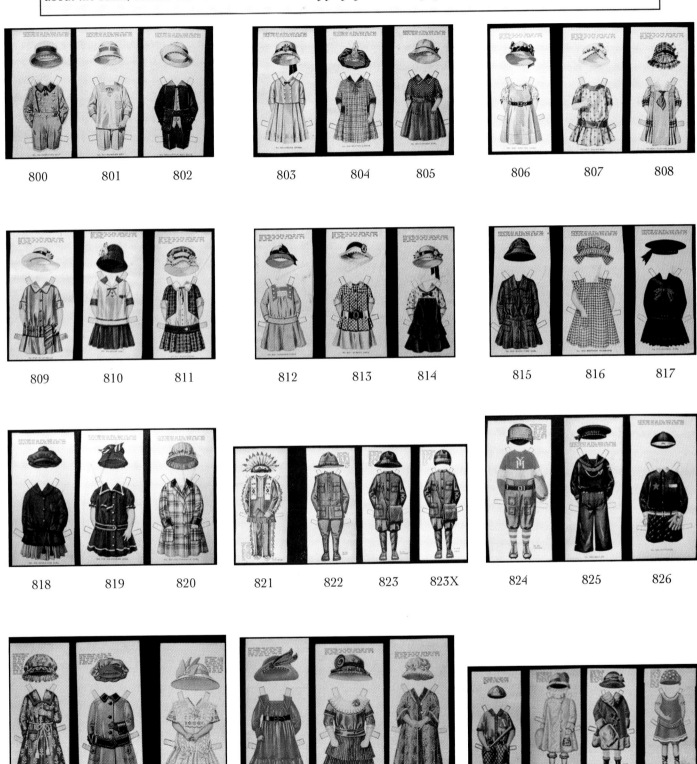

800   801   802   803   804   805   806   807   808

809   810   811   812   813   814   815   816   817

818   819   820   821   822   823   823X   824   825   826

827   828   829   830   831   832   833   834   835   836

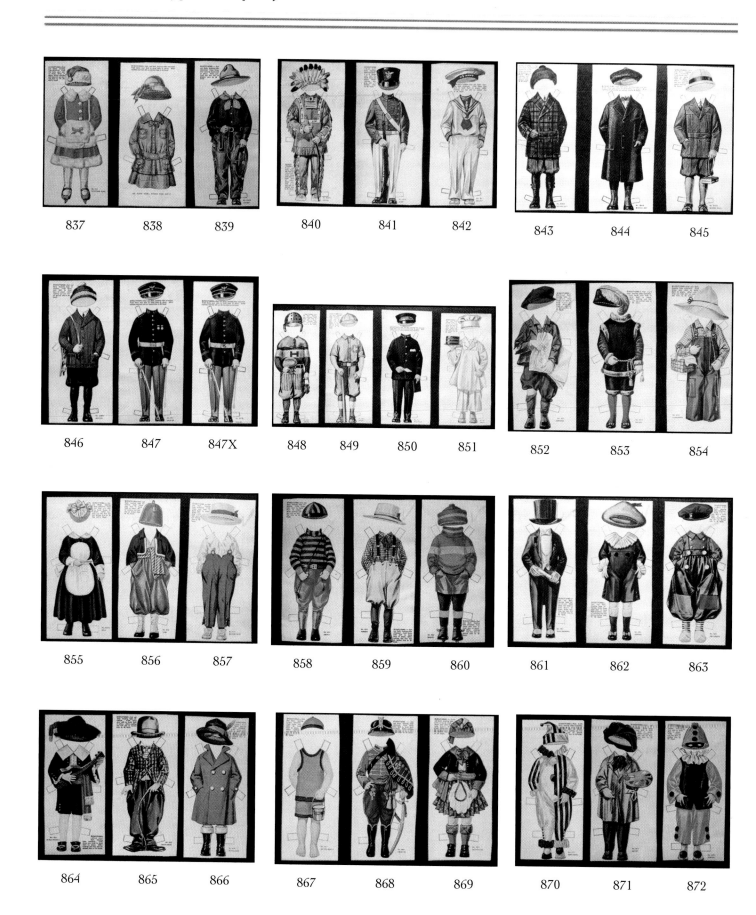

837   838   839

840   841   842

843   844   845

846   847   847X

848   849   850   851

852   853   854

855   856   857

858   859   860

861   862   863

864   865   866

867   868   869

870   871   872

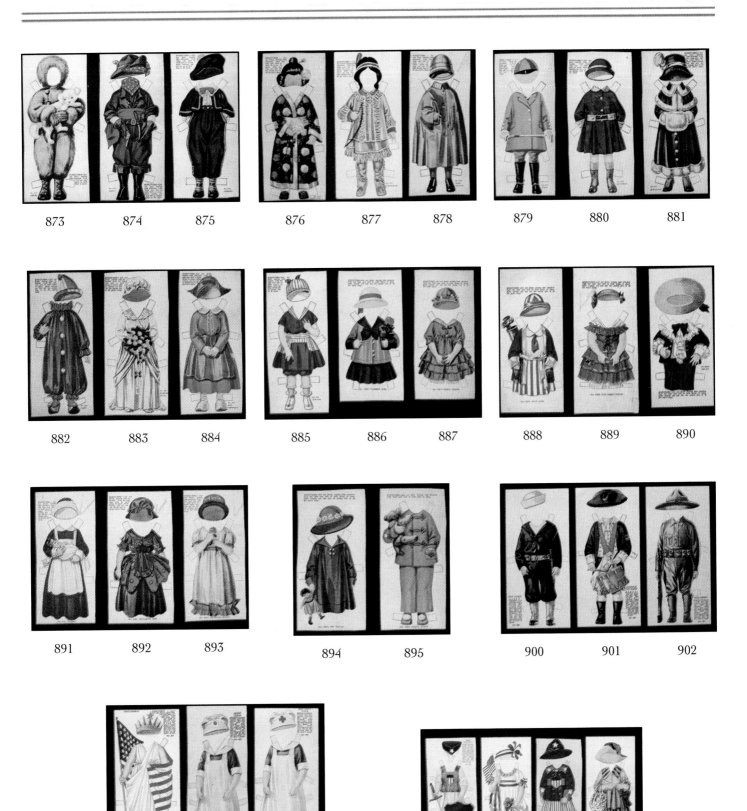

873   874   875   876   877   878   879   880   881

882   883   884   885   886   887   888   889   890

891   892   893   894   895   900   901   902

903   904   904   905   906   907   908

Dolly's Home, $100.00. Dolly's Home is a cardboard dollhouse to put together, plus two dolls and 10 outfits. The dolls and outfits can vary. This set was also sold by the Fair Store in Chicago. That set contained two dolls and 15 outfits.

Little Darling Dressing Dolls, with two 6½" dolls. Dolls can vary from set to set. $50.00.

Little Darling Dressing Dolls, with four 6½" dolls, $65.00.

The Little Darling, the My Pet, and the Patriotic Dressing Doll Series were all produced in two-, four-, and six-doll sets.

My Pet Dressing Dolls, box set with four 6½" dolls. Dolls can vary from set to set. $65.00.

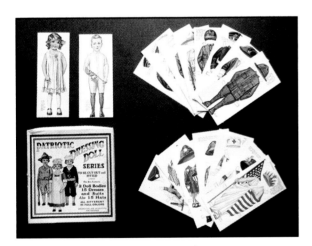

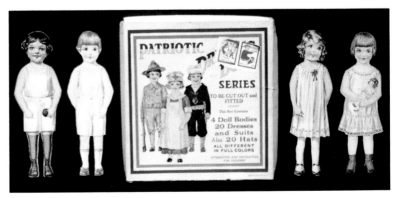

Patriotic Dressing Doll Series, box set with two 6½" dolls. Dolls can vary from set to set. $65.00.

Patriotic Dressing Doll Series, box set with four 6½" dolls. Dolls can vary from set to set. $65.00.

23

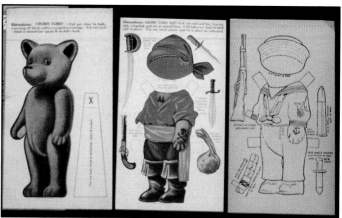

Pretty Kitty, $75.00.

Chubby Cubby, $75.00.

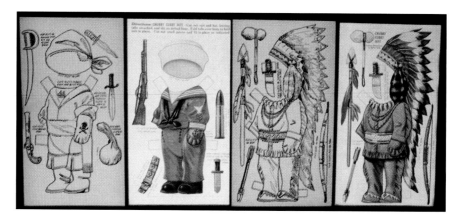

Chubby Cubby, outfits in color and to be colored.

Dandy Doggie, $75.00.

Little Kitty Cut-up and Her Playmates, $80.00. Little Kitty Cut-Up and her playmates is a small box set containing Pretty Kitty, Chubby Cubby, and Dandy Doggie in miniature. They range in size from 4¾" for Chubby Cubby to 5¼" for Dandy Doggie. The outfits for the three dolls are the same as in the larger sets pictured.

Dressing Dolls (Aunt Sally Bread) small 5¼" size of Pretty Kitty. $30.00. These small envelopes included one doll, one dress, and one hat with every wrapped loaf of Aunt Sally Bread. The name of the bakery is printed on the envelope. At the bottom of the envelope is printed "American Colortype Co. Chicago." This is another example of how the American Colortype dolls were used for advertising.

25 Marie and Patsy Ann, 1927	Numbers 700 to 717 are outfits for the 13" dolls.	736 Outfit for Little Neddie Neverstill
26 Betty Lou and Jane, 1927		737 Outfit for Little Neddie Neverstill
27 Billy Bob and Georgie, 1927		738 Outfit for Little Neddie Neverstill
101 Janet and Sally, 1927	700 Dress	739 Little Alice Busy-Bee 13" Doll
102 Margy and Mildred, 1927	701 Dress	740 Outfit for Little Alice Busy-Bee
103 Jimmy and Jack, 1927	702 Coat	741 Outfit for Little Alice Busy-Bee
	703 Coat	742 Outfit for Little Alice Busy-Bee
All 600 numbers are for 6½" dolls.	704 Suit	
	705 Dress	All 800 numbers are outfits for the 6½" dolls.
600 John	706 Sailor Suit	
601 Henry	707 Soldier Suit	800 Morning Suit
602 Pearl	708 Coat	801 Summer Boy
603 Martha	709	802 Little Boy Blue
604 Nancy	710 Our Jackie	803 House Dress
605 Ruth	711 Colonial Drummer	804 Scotch Lassie
606 Anna	712 Our Sammy	805 Cowboy Girl
607 Peter	713 Miss Liberty	806 Pink Tea Dress
608 Janet	714 Army Nurse	807 Calico Girl
609 Laurette	715 Miss Columbia	808 Playtime Dress
610 Grace	716 Miss Patriot	809 Blue Bells
611 Andrew	717 Glory on Parade	810 Sailor Girl
612 David	718 Miss Knitting	811 Plaid Dress
613 Jack	719 Little Betty Gad-About 13" Doll	812 Gingham Dress
614 Robert	720 Outfit for Little Betty Gad-About	813 School Days
615 Catherine	721 Outfit for Little Betty Gad-About	814 Outing Dress
616 Betty	722 Outfit for Little Betty Gad-About	815 Camp Fire Girl
617 Gladys	723 Little Willie Wide-Awake 13" Doll	816 Mother Hubbard
618 Dorothy	724 Outfit for Little Willie Wide-Awake	817 School Girl
619 Arthur	725 Outfit for Little Willie Wide-Awake	818 Sweater Girl
620 Howard	726 Outfit for Little Willie Wide-Awake	819 Seashore Girl
621 Charles	727 Little Miss Up-to-Date 13" Doll	820 Automobile Girl
622 William	728 Outfit for Little Miss Up-to-Date	821 Sioux Indian
623 Frederick	729 Outfit for Little Miss Up-to-Date	822 Scout
624 Little Betty Gad-About	730 Outfit for Little Miss Up-to-Date	823 Boy Scout
625 Little Miss Up-to-Date	731 Little Polly Dress-up 13" Doll	823-X Aviator
626 Little Alice Busy-Bee	732 Outfit for Little Polly Dress-up	824 Captain
627 Little Willie Wide-Awake	733 Outfit for Little Polly Dress-up	825 Sailor
628 Little Neddie Neverstill	734 Outfit for Little Polly Dress-up	826 Catcher
629 Little Polly Dress-Up	735 Little Neddie Neverstill 13" Doll	827 Bathrobe

828 Matinee Girl
829 Party Dress
830 Evening Dress (two versions)
831 Afternoon Dress
832 Kimono
833 Baseball
834 Snow Girl
835 Winter Girl
836 Bathing Girl
837 Skating Girl
838 Girl from the West
839 Cowboy
840 Indian Boy
841 Cadet
842 Sailor
843 Outing suit
844 Winter Boy
845 School days
846 Skating
847 Soldier
847-X Marine
848 Captain
849 Batter
850 Messenger
851 Baker
852 News Boy
853 Knight
854 Fisherman
855 Maid
856 Turk
857 Oliver Twist
858 Jockey
859 Farmer
860 Skater
861 Beau Brummel
862 Domino
863 Hollander
864 In Old Madrid
865 Guess Who?
866 Riding Suit
867 On the Beach
868 Cavalier
869 Scotch Lad
870 Yama-Yama
871 Artist
872 Domino
873 Eskimo
874 Bandit
875 Spaniard
876 Geisha Girl
877 Pocohontas
878 Rainy Weather
879 Jockey

880 On Parade
881 Winter Girl
882 Clown
883 Wedding Bells
884 Miss Normandie
885 Surf Girl
886 Flower Girl
887 Party Dress
888 Golf Girl
889 Tea Party Dress
890 Rob Roy
891 Nurse
892 Holland Girl
893 Morning Glory
894 My Dolly
895 Good Night

All 900 numbers are outfits for 6½" dolls.

900 Our Jackie
901 Colonial Drummer
902 Our Sammy
903 Miss Liberty
904 Army Nurse
904 Red Cross Nurse
905 Miss Columbia
906 Miss Patriot
907 Glory on Parade
908 Miss Knitting
909 Little Betty Gad-About outfit to fit doll 624
910 Little Betty Gad-About outfit to fit doll 624
911 Little Betty Gad-About outfit to fit doll 624
912 Little Miss Up-to-Date outfit to fit doll 625
913 Little Miss Up-to-Date outfit to fit doll 625
914 Little Miss Up-to-Date outfit to fit doll 625
915 Little Alice Busy-Bee outfit to fit doll 626
916 Little Alice Busy-Bee outfit to fit doll 626
917 Little Alice Busy-Bee outfit to fit doll 626
918 Little Willie Wide-Awake outfit to fit doll 627
919 Little Willie Wide-Awake outfit to fit doll 627
920 Little Willie Wide-Awake outfit to fit doll 627

921 Little Neddie Never-still outfit to fit doll 628
922 Little Neddie Never-still outfit to fit doll 628
923 Little Neddie Never-still outfit to fit doll 628
924 Little Polly Dress-up outfit to fit doll 629
925 Little Polly Dress-up outfit to fit doll 629
926 Little Polly Dress-up outfit to fit doll 629

The following paper dolls by American Colortype did not have a number:

Chubby Cubby, envelope set
Dandy Doggie, envelope
Little Kitty Cut-up and Her Playmates, box set (Chubby Cubby, Dandy Doggie and Pretty Kitty in miniature)
Our Sammy Dressing Doll-Box with outfits 710, 711, and 712
Pretty Kitty, envelope set
My Favorite Dressing Dolls, Richard, with outfits 706, 707, and 708
My Favorite Dressing Dolls, Corinne, with outfits 703, 704, and 705
My Favorite Dressing Dolls, Laurette, with outfits 700, 701, and 702
Our Dainty Dressing Dolls (doll and outfits same as Laurette)
My Pet Dressing Dolls (sets with two, four, and six dolls)
Patriotic Dressing Dolls Series (sets with two, four, and six dolls)
Liberty Fair Dressing Doll with outfits 713, 714, and 715
Little Darling Dressing Dolls (sets with two, four, and six dolls)
Dolly's Home with two paper dolls and 10 outfits. Some box covers also have a trademark of "Cut Craft Cut-Outs." Another set is in a large envelope with the same picture as the box sets and was sold by the Fair Store in Chicago. The store name is printed on the front of the envelope. This set has two paper dolls and 15 outfits.
Our Hero Dressing Dolls (doll and outfits same as Our Sammy)
Our World Friend Dressing Dolls with outfits 714, 715, and 717

American Crayon Co.

The American Crayon Company was located in Sandusky, Ohio. These dolls and clothes were also sold by the American Colortype Company.

 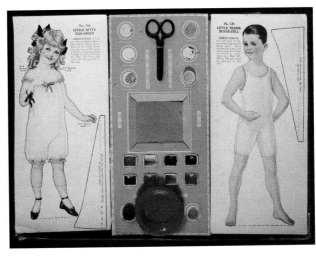

Betty Gad About–Alice Busy Bee Dressing Dolls, $80.00.

American Toy Works

The American Toy Works was founded in 1896. It was known for producing badges, toys, and novelties. In 1931, its address was 7 & 8 Chatham Square, New York.

The American Toy Works participated in the American Toy Fair from 1932 to 1936. At that time, it produced toy money sets, paint sets, sewing and embroidery sets, paper doll outfits, Santa Claus surprise packages, ring toss, duck pins, hammer and nail sets, chalk and slate sets, clay sets, tapestry sets, and garden sets.

Paper Doll Outfit, view 1, $45.00. This is a complete set and contains one older-style jointed doll that is like the jointed dolls that the Dennison Co. used in its early sets.

Paper Doll Outfit, view 2, $50.00. This contains the two jointed dolls listed on the envelope. The contents also state there is "one sheet colored cut out doll." This could very well be the same sheet shown in view 3. There is also evidence that the sheet could be one of the Universal Toy paper doll sheets.

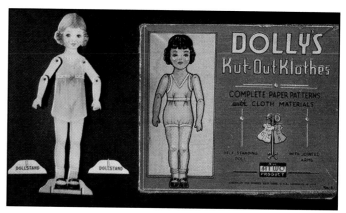

4 Dolly's Kut-Out Klothes, $20.00.

Paper Doll Outfit, view 3, $50.00. This set used the newer style jointed dolls and is a newer version of the set seen in view 2. Both envelopes have the same contents listed in the same exact order.

100 Paper Doll Outfit, $35.00.

102 Paper Doll Outfit, $50.00.

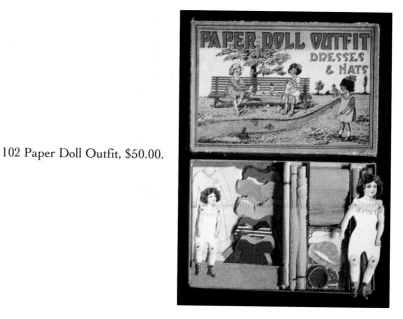

50 Little Folks Cut Outs, $50.00.

These sets of 50, 100, and 102 have been found to contain either the older-style jointed dolls like those used in the older Dennison Co. sets or the newer-style dolls like those in the 900 series by American Toy Works.

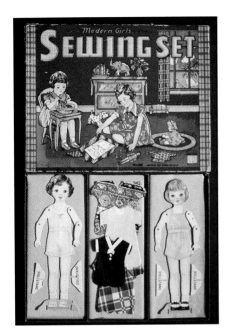

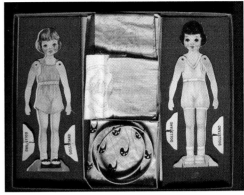

417 Moderne Sewing for Little Girls, $35.00.

301 Modern Girls Sewing Set, $35.00.

400 Modern Girls Sewing Set, $35.00.

528 Sewing for Girls, Stitchart, $35.00.

901 Little Folks Crepe Paper Doll Outfit, $30.00.

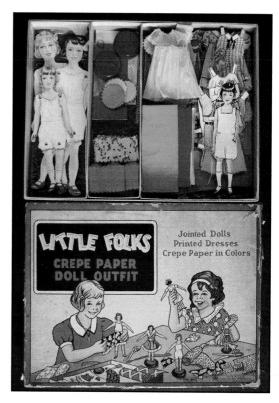

902 Little Folks Crepe Paper Doll Outfit, $50.00.

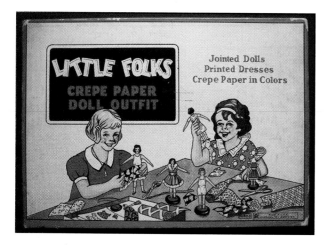

903 Little Folks Crepe Paper Doll Outfit, $75.00.

903 inside contents. The dolls in this nice hinged box are held in with ribbons.

904 Little Folks Crepe Paper Doll Outfit, $40.00.

905 Crepe Paper Doll Cut-Outs, $30.00.

1000 Every Day Play Set, $50.00. This set includes two front and back paper dolls. Their feet have shoes that fold to make stands. The paper doll clothes are printed on crepe paper.

1000 inside contents.

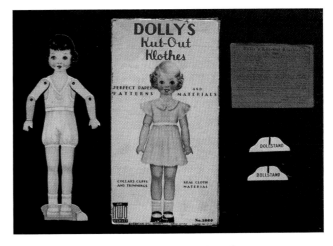

3080 Dolly's Kut-out Klothes, $30.00.

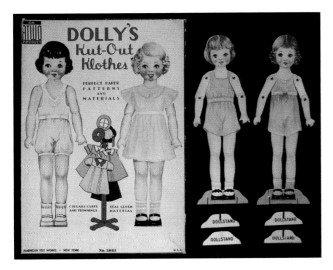

3081 Dolly's Kut-Out Klothes, $35.00.

Many of the American Toy Works paper doll sets were produced with dolls that could vary from set to set.

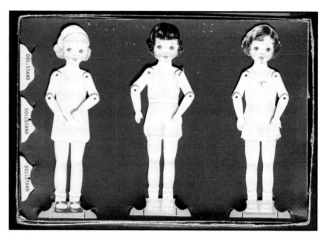

3083 Make Dolly's Wardrobe, $50.00.

4022 Stitchart, 1937, $50.00.

4   Dolly's Kut-Out Klothes, one doll (doll can vary)
40   Dolly's Kut-Out Klothes, one doll (not pictured, same set as 4 above)
50   Little Folks Cut-Outs, one doll (has also been found with two dolls)
100 Paper Doll Outfit, one doll
101 Paper Doll Outfit, one doll (not pictured; same box cover as 100 and 102)
102 Paper Doll Outfit, two dolls
300 Modern Girls Sewing Set. (Not pictured; box has same picture and is same size as 301.)
301 Modern Girls Sewing Set, two dolls
400 Modern Girls Sewing Set, three dolls
417 Moderne Sewing For Little Girls, two dolls
528 Sewing For Girls, Stitchart
901 Little Folks Crepe Paper Doll Outfit, two dolls
902 Little Folks Crepe Paper Doll Outfit, three dolls and one smaller doll on clothes page
903 Little Folks Crepe Paper Doll Outfit, six dolls
904 Little Folks Crepe Paper Doll Outfit, three dolls
905 Crepe Paper Doll Cut-Outs
1000 Every Day Play Set, two dolls
3080 Dolly's Kut-Out Klothes, one doll
3081 Dolly's Kut-Out Klothes, two dolls
3082 Make Dolly's Wardrobe, three dolls (not pictured, same box cover as 3083)
3083 Make Dolly's Wardrobe, three dolls
4022 Stitchart, 1937
Paper Doll Outfit (view 1) in glassine envelope
Paper Doll Outfit (view 2) in glassine envelope
Paper Doll Outfit (view 3) in glassine envelope

Our Favorite Dolls, $125.00. No date, but research has shown that these were being sold as late as 1907. Pictured is the 16½" girl and her folder. A 17" boy was also published. Please see the Selchow and Righter and A.T. Co. sections for further information on these dolls.

Hello, I'm Adeline, 1944, $35.00. A spiral paper doll storybook, plus words and music to ten songs.

Art Award Company

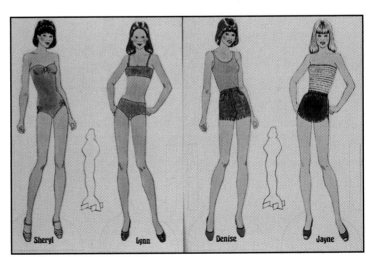

6000 Fashion Art Dolls, $12.00.

8950 Mickey & Minnie's Cut n' Color Costume Party box set, no date

Daintee Doll Series 1, Lynn, $12.00.

Daintee Doll Series 2, Terry, $12.00.

Daintee Doll Series 3, Kent, $12.00.

Daintee Doll Series 4, Karen, $12.00.

Daintee Doll Series 5, Dennis, and Series 6, Steve, $12.00 each.

Daintee Doll Cut-Outs (Kent, Karen, and Terry), $25.00.

Stock Med-1, Katrine from Holland, $25.00.

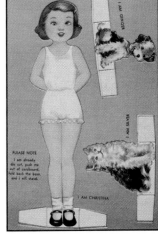

Stock Med-2, Rosetta from Mexico, $25.00.

Stock Med-3, Christina from Sweden, $25.00.

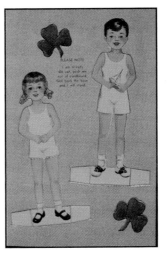

Stock Med-4, Pat and Patty from Ireland, $25.00.

Avalon Industries/Standard Toykraft

Avalon Industries, formerly known as Standard Toykraft, was founded by brothers Nathan and Louis Ullman. They began as box manufacturers for toy companies on Long Island. In 1887, after extensive research, Standard Toykraft began manufacturing toys of its own. Its first products were crayon/watercolor sets and stitchery sets.

Just prior to World War I, a young European engineer, Soloman Luber, joined the firm. With the addition of Mr. Luber, the company began to grow and prosper. Eventually Mr. Luber acquired control of Standard Toykraft, which later became Avalon Industries, Inc.

Paper dolls through the mid-1960s were marked "Standard Toykraft" on the boxes. By the late 1960s, the name Avalon appeared and from then on, the boxes had either "Avalon Industries, Inc. — Standard Toycraft Div." or "Avalon Industries, Inc.— Toycraft Division." Notice the *Toykraft* was spelled with a *k* until the late 1960s, when it was changed to *Toycraft*.

D100 Betty and Dick Tour the U.S.A., 1940, Standard Toykraft, $50.00.

D100 box contents.

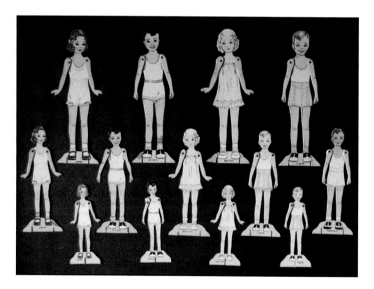

Even though the title on the boxes state "Betty and Dick Tour the U.S.A.," some sets include other dolls (Jane, Tom, or Harry). In an early 1940s catalog, these extra dolls are referred to as Betty and Dick's brothers and sisters.

The Betty and Dick series of paper dolls published by Standard Toykraft in 1940 had many different sizes of box sets. The known sets are listed here. The dolls were in three sizes; 6¼", 8¼", and 10". The boxes contained cloth clothes to sew and paper outfits to cut out. All boxes have the same picture on the box cover.

D-10 Betty and Dick Tour the U.S.A., small box size 8" x 11" with two 6¼" dolls (dolls can vary).

D-25 Betty and Dick Tour the U.S.A. Small medium box 9¼" x 13½" with two 8¼" dolls. (sets have also been found with dolls of Jane, Tom or Harry, so dolls can vary.)

D-25-S Betty and Dick Tour the U.S.A., medium box size 10" x 15" with four dolls (two 8¼" and two 6¼" dolls; dolls can vary.

D-50 Betty and Dick Tour the U.S.A., larger size box 10½" x 16" with four dolls (two 8¼" and two 10" dolls; dolls can vary.)

D-100 Betty and Dick Tour the U.S.A., large size box 13¼" x 17¼" with six dolls (two 8¼" and four 10" dolls; dolls can vary and some sets only contain the four 10" dolls.

Betty and Dick Tour the U.S.A., A suitcase style box with handle & clasp and four 6¼" dolls.

D-10 Betty and Dick Tour the U.S.A., $20.00. This is the smallest set.

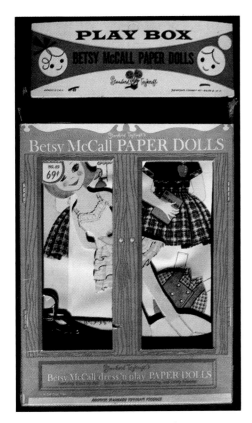

85 Betsy McCall, 1960, $35.00.

193 Snap-On Fashion Boutique, 1982, $18.00.

401 Betsy McCall's Fashion Shop, 1959, $35.00.

402 Betsy McCall's Fashion Shop, 1959, $50.00.

403 Betsy McCall's Fashion Shop, 1959, $55.00.

403 Betsy McCall's Fashion Shop, inside contents.

401 My Fair Lady, $50.00.

401 My Fair Lady (newer edition), $50.00.

301 Petticoat Junction ©Wayfilms, $50.00. There are three different sets of Petticoat Junction. All sets have this same box cover and number. Each box contains either Bobbie Jo, Billie Jo, or Betty Jo. All are in the same pose but with different hair color and swimsuits. Set shown here is Billie Jo.

501 Barbie Fashion Embroidery Set, 1962, $50.00. There is a second version of this Barbie Fashion Embroidery Set. In that set Barbie is in the same pose but is wearing a red swimsuit. The box cover is the same, but the cloth costumes are different.

502 Barbie and Ken Fashion Embroidery Set, 1962, $50.00.

601 Gidget, 1965, $50.00.

640 Cabbage Patch Kids, 1983, $12.00.

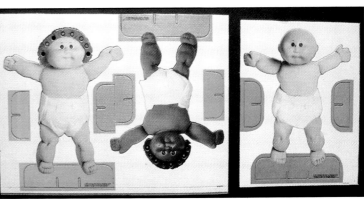

641 Cabbage Patch Kids Deluxe, inside contents.

641 Cabbage Patch Kids Deluxe, 1984, $15.00.

645 Cabbage Patch Kids Preemie, 1984, $12.00.

701-1 Susie, $15.00.

701-1 Linda the Ballerina, $15.00.

701-2 Teena the Teenager, $15.00.

701-2 Debbie, $15.00.

701-3 Sandra the Bride, $15.00 each.

701-3 Connie, $15.00.

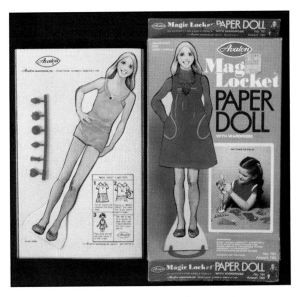

761 Magic Locket Paper Doll, 1978, $15.00.

762 Magic Touch Paper Doll, 1978, $15.00.

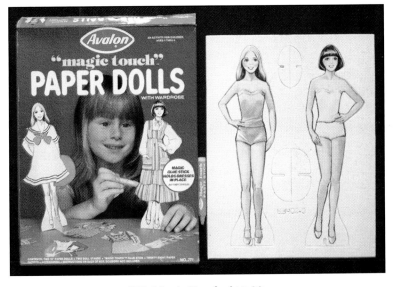

771 Magic Touch, $15.00.

801 Betsy McCall Dress 'n Play, 1963, ©The McCall
Publishing Co., $45.00. Box cover was produced in
two versions, inside contents the same.

801 Betsy McCall, $45.00. (This is the second version of the Betsy McCall 801 box.)

801-1 Linda the Ballerina, 1969, $15.00.

702 Betsy McCall Around the World, $70.00 (includes five sheets of dresses, and scissors, comb, and mirror).

702 Betsy McCall Around the World, inside contents.

801-3 Sandra the Bride, 1969, $15.00.

802 Betsy McCall Dress 'n Play, 1963, $80.00. This is the largest set of Betsy McCall and includes seven sheets of clothes. (A mirror, comb, brush, and scissors belong with, but are missing from, this set.)

802 Betsy McCall Dress 'n Play, inside contents.

811 Margie, $50.00.

The following sets are not pictured:

52R Willie the Weatherman

191 Fashion Design Center, 1979

378 Shirt Tales Playhouse, 1984, five dolls.

601 Teena the Teenager Magic Paper Doll (reprint of #601 Gidget)

701 Betsy McCall Around the World (slightly smaller box than 702; same dolls and three clothes sheets.) The dolls do not have the "real hair," and the box cover was produced in two versions.

801-2 Teena the Teenager, Magnetic Paper Doll, 1969 (see 701-2)

6212 Wendy the Weather Girl

80-50 Build-Your-Own U.S. Defense, 1941, box set of military figures to color (includes crayons and stands)

1000 Cleopatra, 1963, $25.00.

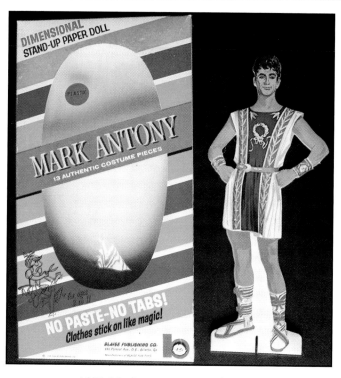

1001 Mark Antony, 1963, $25.00.

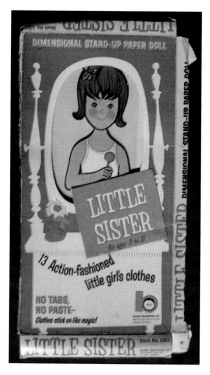

1003 Little Sister, 1963, $12.00.

1004, Tommie Lea, 1963, $18.00.

Gertrude Breed

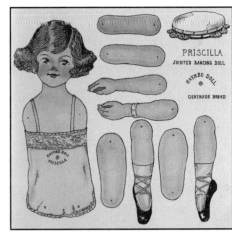

Dancing Priscilla, 1927, $20.00.

Baby Jane, 1927, $20.00.

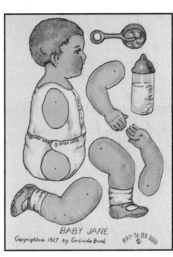

Baby Jane, inside contents.

L.J. Bullard Co.

This company operated in Cleveland, Ohio.

Play Time, 1948, $20.00. This is a folder-type box with 54 activity booklets in color. Two of the booklets are paper dolls of the Lynn family.

Burton Playthings, Inc.

Children's books by Burton Playthings, Inc., published from 1933 through 1935, have been found. Most, if not all, carried the logo "Happy Kids." The company produced storybooks, coloring books, and paper doll books. The coloring books have small boxes of crayons attached to the covers, and the paper doll books have small pairs of scissors attached to the covers.

275 Your Own Quintuplets, 1935, $75.00.

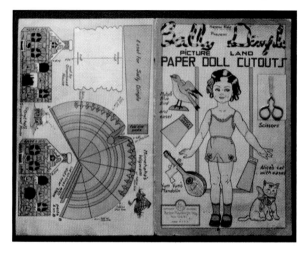

975 Sally Dimple, 1935, $75.00.

875 Dotty and Danny on Parade, 1935, $75.00.

550 Bobby and Betty, 1934, $75.00.

675 Jean and Jack, 1935, $75.00.

275 Your Own Quintuplets, 1935
550 Bobby and Betty, 1934
675 Jean and Jack, 1935
775 Circus is in Town Cut-Outs, 1935 (stand-ups; not pictured)
850 Farmyard Cut-Outs, 1934 (stand-ups; not pictured)
875 Dotty and Danny on Parade, 1935
925 Jack and the Beanstalk, 1934 (stand-ups; not pictured)
975 Sally Dimple, 1935

Western Gal, Pat, $15.00.

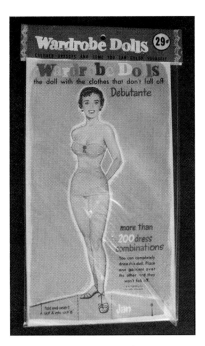

Debutante, Jan, $15.00.

Big Sister, Jean, $15.00.

Little Sister, Jane, $15.00.

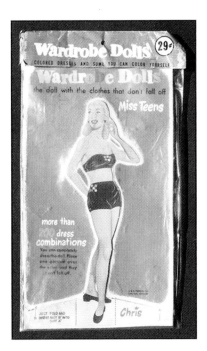

Miss Teens, Chris, $15.00.

Sports Gal, Michele, $15.00.

PP-105 Doll 'n Dresses, 1959, "a pocket playbox," $15.00.

3 in 1 Home Kit for Her, 1961, paper doll same as PP-105, plus sewing items, $25.00.

Cardinal Games

501 Sewing Set, Dolls to Dress, 35.00.

Inside contents of box 501.

502 Sewing Set, $35.00.

502 Sewing Set, inside contents.

Happi Time Dressmaker Kit, $35.00. There is no identification of any kind as to publisher, date, or number for this set. The three dolls are the same type used in the Cardinal sets, and the paper doll of Joan in this set is the same Joan paper doll found in the Cardinal set 502. "Happi Time" is a logo Sears uses on many of its toy items, so this set most likely was manufactured by Cardinal Games and sold by Sears.

Carol Toys and Novelties

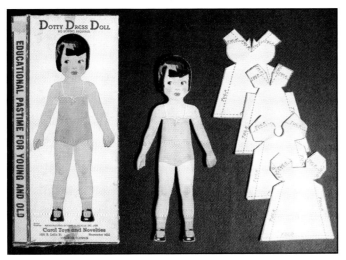

Dotty Dress Doll, $25.00. Statuette doll with paper patterns and cloth clothes. Box set, additional information on box says "Manufactured by Gaul and Ingalls, Inc. for Carol Toys and Novelties." No date.

Celco Corporation

Celco was known to be in business in the late 1940s. A catalog from the company shows that it had box sets of paper dolls, put-together toy animals sets called Knock-Outs, and coloring sets that included the company's brand of crayons, called Crayoffs, which were new soap-based washable crayons. It also produced "white" blackboards and other toys.

Color and Re-Color Cut-Out Dolls, the Holiday Twins, 1948, $15.00, (no number on box, but shown as 71 in catalog).

Central Committee on United Study of Foreign Missions

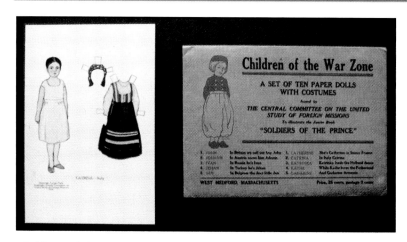

Children of the War Zone, 1916, $20.00. Set of ten paper dolls with costumes.

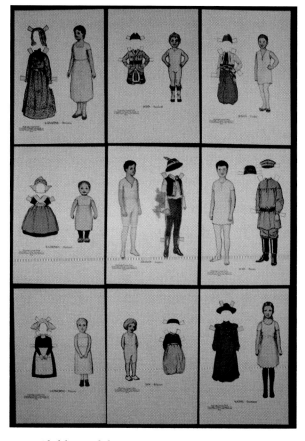

Children of the War Zone, inside contents.

This was a New York company.

Double Date and Family
Fun, both 1989, $10.00 each.

Friends at School and Fashion
Fun, both 1989, $10.00 each.

Glamour World and School
Fun, both 1990, $10.00 each.

Party Time and Action Club, both 1990, $10.00 each.

Child Art Productions

Amy, 1977, $15.00.

Denim Dolls, 1977, $15.00.

Fashion Parade Dolls Book, 1977, $15.00.

Little Ladies, 1977, $15.00.

Childrens Press, Inc.

R1006 Toy Parade, $15.00.

3000 Around the World with Bob and Barbara, 1946, 30.00.

3001 Country Weekend with Kathy and Jill, 1946, $30.00.

3002 Patsy, 1946, $30.00.

3003 Mother and Daughter (for picture of this book, see Lilja 914).

Star Bright Classics Records with Stand-up Figures and Paper Dolls (not pictured):

R400 The 3 Pigs, 1949
R401 The 3 Bears, 1949
R402 The Shoemaker and the Elves, 1949
R403 Snow White and the 7 Dwarfs, 1949
R404 Gingerbread Boy, 1949
R405 Old MacDonald, 1949
R406 Hansel and Gretel, 1949
R407 Pinocchio, 1949
R408 Little Red Riding Hood, 1949
R409 Cinderella, 1959
R410 Little Red Hen
R411 3 Little Kittens
R413 Peter Rabbit
R415 House That Jack Built
R1000 Nursery Rhymes, 1950
R1001 Nursery Games, 1950
R1002 Nursery Lullabies, 1950
R1003 Cowboy Roundup, 1950
R1004 Farmyard Fun, 1950
R1005 Oh, Susanna! 1950
R1006 Toy Parade, 1950 (pictured)
R1007 Sleigh Bells Ring
R1008 Silent Night
R1009 Happy Birthday
R1010 Hurdy Gurdy Tunes
R1011 Let's Play School, 1951
R1012 Play Boat
R1013 Play Train
R1014 Play Airplane

101 Miss Airlanes, $35.00, Pat Kennelly of TWA, no date.

Magna Magic Sue, 1954, $25.00, no number.

Colorforms®

Colorforms® was founded in 1952 by Harry Kislevitz in the basement of his home. The first Colorforms® were simply thin flat pieces of shiny plastic cut into the basic shapes. The child would then create pictures with the shapes on a special playboard included in the set. The plastic pieces would peel right off when the child wanted to change the picture. In a short while, these basic sets gave way to more elaborate play sets. The plastic pieces took the form of characters from stories and TV shows. Children could spend many happy hours creating scenes from their favorite TV shows or storybooks.

Dress Designer and Dress-up sets have been very popular. These sets contain costumes for a doll or dolls, and the costumes cling to the doll and easily peel off when a new outfit is wanted.

The following is a list of the known Colorforms® paper doll sets:

104 Junior Dress Designer Kit
105 Johnny Dress-up Kit (pictured)
117 Popeye the Weatherman, 1959
150 Sleeping Beauty Dress Designer Kit, 1959
1952 Debbie Reynolds Dress Designer Kit, 1960
1955 Shari Lewis Dress-up Set, 1963
160 Dale Evans Western Dress-up Set, 1959
175 Betsy McCall's Garden Dress Kit, 1960
176 My Baby Dress-up Kit, 1964
182 Annette Dress Designer Kit, 1961
199 Miss Ballerina Dress-up Kit, 1962
234 Bride Dress-up Kit, 1963 (pictured)
250 Tammy dress-up Set, 1964
300 Mary Poppins dress-up Kit
302 Mork from Ork Dress-up Set, 1979
333 Three Stooges Slap-Stick-On, 1969, includes outfits

345 Curley McDimple Dress-up Kit, circa 1972
350 Little Orphan Annie Dress-up Kit, 1968
355 Julia Dress-up Kit, 1969
361 Barbie Dress-up (Travel Pak), 1989
400 Miss Weather Dress-up Kit, 1966
408 Miss Nurse Dress-up Kit, circa 1972 (pictured)
460 Twiggy Dress-up Kit, 1967
480 Raggedy Ann Dress-up Kit, 1967
495 Liddle Kiddles Dress-up Kit, 1968
510 Barbie Dress-up Set, 1970
510 Barbie Dress-up Kit, 1977
525 The Old Fashioned Doll, 1970 (pictured)
581 Smile Dress-up Set, 1971 (pictured)
583 Miss America Dress-up Set, 1972
585 Mary Poppins Dress-up Set
587 David Cassidy Dress-up Set, 1972
589 Little Lulu Dress-up Set, 1974
597 Holly Hobbie Dress-up Set, 1975
604 Heather Dress-up Set, circa 1976

616 Ballerina Barbie Dress-up Kit, 1977
628 Baby Holly Hobbie Dress-up Set, 1978
639 Sindy Dress-up Set, 1979
644 Miss Piggy Dress-up Set, 1980
647 Darci, Cover Girl, Disco Dress-up Set, 1980
653 Monchhichi Dress-up Set, 1981
657 Western Barbie Dress-up Set, 1982
662 Smurfette Dress-up Set, 1982
664 Cabbage Patch Kids Dress-up Set, 1983
665 Barbie, 1983
666 Barbie Dress-up Set, 1983
671 Rainbow Brite Dress-up Set, 1983
671 Gremlins Play Set, 1984, includes a few outfits
675 Michael Jackson Dress-up Set, 1984
683 Barbie and the Rockers Dress-up Set, 1986
710 Dress-up Totally Minnie Fashion Show, 1987
713 Raggedy Ann Dress-up Set, 1988
716 Barbie & the Sensations Dress-up Dolls, 1988
724 Super Star Barbie Dress-up Dolls, 1989
729 Cabbage Patch Kids Dress-up Set, 1990
730 Barbie, Dance Magic, 1990, includes outfits
734 Minnie 'N Me Dress-up Set
740 Barbie, All American Dress-up Set
741 Barbie Costume Ball Dress-up Set, 1991
742 Barbie Private Collection
752 How's the Weather, Lucy? Dress-up Set, 1972
761 Barbie Secret Hearts Dress-up Set
762 Snoopy and Belle Dress-up Set (circa 1983)
777 Minnie Mouse Dress-up Play Set
782 Glitter Hair Barbie Dress-up Set, 1994
793 Baywatch Barbie playset, 1995, includes a few outfits
795 Ballerina Barbie Dress-up Set, 1995
801 Miss Piggy, 1989 (same doll and clothes as 991)
802 Hollywood Minnie Paper Doll
803 Minnie Paper Doll
804 Norfin Troll Paper Doll, 1992
805 Shari Lewis' Lamb Chop & Friends Paper Dolls, 1993
910A Mickey Mouse Sew-ons, circa 1975
910B Popeye Sew-ons, circa 1975
910C Raggedy Ann Sew-ons, 1974
910D Holly Hobbie, Sew-ons, 1975
920A Barbie Color 'N' Play, 1974, dolls but no outfits
930A Raggedy Ann Lace and Dress Dancing Doll, 1975
930B Barbie Lace 'N' Dress Dancing Doll, 1975
930C Raggedy Ann Surprise Package, 1975, includes a dress-up doll
952 Baby Miss Piggy Muppet Babies Sew-ons, 1989

991 Miss Piggy Paper Doll, 1980
1504 Dress Designer Kit, 1955 (pictured)
1933 Betty Boop Dress-up Set, circa 1975
2109 Romper Room, Willie the Weatherman, 1957
2117 Popeye the Weatherman, 1959
2150 Sleeping Beauty Dress-up Kit, 1959
2152 Debbie Reynolds Dress Designer Kit, 1960
2155 Shari Lewis Dress-up Kit, 1963
2160 Roy Rogers and Dale Evans Western Dress-up Set, 1959
2175 Betsy McCall's Garden Dress-up Set, 1960
2176 My Baby Dress-up Set, 1964
2182 Walt Disney's Babes In Toyland, Annette Dress Designer Kit, 1961
2199 Miss Ballerina Dress-up Set, 1962
2234 Bride Dress-up Set, 1963
2301 Crissy Dress-up Set, 1970
2341 Dawn Dress-up Set, 1970
2352 Barbie Sport Fashion Set, 1975
2354 Donny and Marie Dress-up Set, 1977
2356 Super Star Barbie Dress-up Set, 1978
2362 Snoopy How's the Weather? Dress-up Set, circa 1981
2363 Barbie and Beauty Dress-up Set, 1981
2369 Michael Jackson Deluxe Set, 1984
2376 Barbie and the Rockers Deluxe Dress-up Set, 1986
2500 Tammy Dress-up Set
2503 Miss Weather Dress-up Set
2708 Walt Disney's Cinderella — the Perfect Dress, 1992
2808 Disney's Dress-up Pocahontas, 1995
4098 Jim Henson's Muppet Show, 1980, includes outfits
4108 Snoopy's Beagle Scouts Play Set, 1965, includes outfit
4109 Holly Hobbie General Store Stand-up Play Set, 1976, includes costumes
4117 Cabbage Patch Kids Playhouse, 1983, includes a couple of outfits
4300 Mickey Mouse Puppetforms, circa 1972, includes outfits
4301 Popeye Puppetforms, includes outfits
4307 Snoopy, You're a Star, 1971, includes outfits
4310 Raggey Ann Puppet Show, 1975, includes outfits
4350 Barbie 3-D Fashion Theater, 1972, includes a couple of outfits
5550 Tina the Talking Paper Doll
6000 E.T. Dress-up Set, 1982
7956 Dress-up Barbie, 1980, game with outfits

No number Puzzleforms Michael Jackson, 1984, includes outfits
Number not available Raggedy Ann Dress-up Set, 1988
No number Vanna's Villa, 1992, includes a few outfits

408 Miss Nurse Dress-up Kit, $25.00.

525 The Old Fashioned Doll, 1970, $18.00.

581 Smile Dress-up Set, 1971, $12.00.

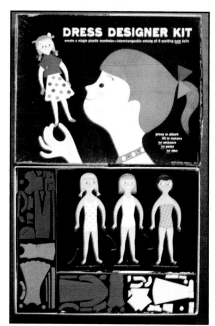

1504 Dress Designer
Kit, 1955, $35.00.

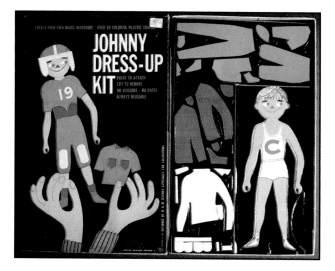

105 Johnny Dress-up Kit, $25.00.

234 The Bride Dress-up Kit, 1963, $25.00.

Concord Toy Company

This company manufactured children's embroidery and sewing sets, and also cardboard doll houses.

209 Stitchcraft Sewing Set, $20.00.

215 Stitchcraft Sewing Set, $35.00.

215 box contents (doll on the left is on paper).

235 Mayflower Sewing Set, $30.00.

202 Stitchcraft Sewing Set, $25.00.

201 Stitchcraft Sewing Set (with one paper doll; same box cover as 209)
202 Stitchcraft Sewing Set (with one paper doll; same box cover as 209)
202 Stitchcraft Sewing Set (different from above set 202; pictured)
204 Stitchcraft Sewing Set (with one paper doll; same box cover as 215)
209 Stitchcraft Sewing Set (pictured)
215 Stitchcraft Sewing Set (pictured)
214 Stitchcraft Sewing Set (with two paper dolls; same box cover as 215)
235 Mayflower Sewing Set (pictured)

David C. Cook Publishing Company

Each of the nine sheets pictured measures 11¼" x 16¼". Each sheet contains a story from the Bible and paper dolls to let a child act out the story. 1933. $25.00 for set of nine sheets.

Robert J. Crombie Company

Around the World with Dorothy Dot, 1910, box set with 12 different sheets. $85.00 complete.

The Dandyline Company

Little Sister, 1918, $25.00.

Elsie Dinsmore, Spring 1917, $25.00.

> Not Pictured:
> Elsie Dinsmore, Spring 1916
> Little Sister, 1921

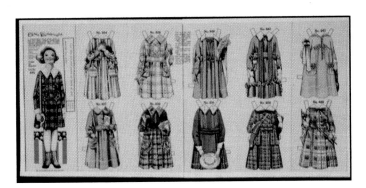

Elsie Dinsmore, 1918, $25.00.

Elsie Dinsmore, 1919, $25.00.

Little Sister, 1919, $25.00.

H. Davis Toy Corporation

The H. Davis Toy Corporation produced weaving looms, sewing cards, pot holder sets, lacing sets, flannel boards, and other items besides the paper doll sets pictured below.

Not Pictured:
414 Ballet Doll Costume Designer Set.

242 Town and Country, "to dress and to embroider," $25.00. The paper doll is of heavy cardboard and has a special surface that allows cloth clothes to cling to the doll.

240 On Stage Cut-Outs (Ballet), $25.00.

Decalco Litho. Company

This company operated in Hoboken, New Jersey.

Doll Cut-Outs Set 1, $15.00.

Not pictured:
Set 2 A lady and a little girl
Set 3 Two ladies

Decro Plaks, Inc.

Decro Plaks, Inc., produced pin-up wall plaques, Mother Goose nursery plaques, and T.V. cartoon plaques. Its only known paper doll is pictured.

Life size doll, $20.00. No date, but from the late 1950s or early 1960s.

The DeJournette Mfg. Company

It was in the late 1930s when a paper doll company called the Paper Doll House was formed in Atlanta, Georgia. When the company expanded, it was renamed after its paper doll designer, Alma DeJournette, and it was incorporated in 1946. The company was sold in 1962 to Merry Manufacturing Company of Cincinnati. That company is covered later in this book.

The first paper doll was Curly Top, a paper doll with "real" hair. She was patented in 1938, when the company was still known as the Paper Doll House. This paper doll and variations of the doll were sold for many years. In the 1950s, the paper dolls had many added features that were not like your run-of-the-mill paper dolls. A doll might come in a box that converted to a trunk or a house. Another would have paper clothes that were washable or have eyes that blinked or, if a baby paper doll, come with a cloth diaper and bottle and actually drink water! The "real" hair feature was carried over to many of these later paper dolls as well.

Following the DeJournette list are pictures of the paper dolls. The pictures and list will give you some hint as to some of the ingenuity that went into the DeJournette paper doll sets to give them a certain quality of distinction.

The following is a list of all the known DeJournette paper dolls:	R-55 Shoo-Shoo Shirley
	R-56 Mommee and Her Little Girl
22 Claire. (Doll and clothes same as Jill 711, but this doll is smaller and hair is shorter.)	60 Mother Daughter Dolls
23 World's First Paper Doll to Drink (see 222)	65 Tracy (see 711)
R-30 Blondie (R-90)	R-69 Travel Kit
35 Froggie Went a Courting	72 Claire. (Same doll and outfits as Jill 711, but this doll is smaller and her hair has been shortened.)
R-50 Honey Bun	R-75 Masquerade Party. (This has the same dolls and outfits as 2202.)

R-80 Gina (800)

85 Bright Eyes the Winking Blinking Doll

R-90 Penny and Her Dolly. This doll has "real" hair in a choice of three colors.

91 Goldilocks and the Three Bears

P-100 My Name is Marian

100 Bride. (Doll is the same as 1350 and 911.)

150 Bobbie Girls. (Set of twins, includes crayons and soap.)

198 3 Big Dolls. (Dolls are the same as Gina R-80. Each of the three dolls has a different hair color.)

200 Heidi, Pocket Book Doll

200 Kathy

222 Littlest Darling

300 Pam. (Same as R-55, but Pam's shoes are attached with a chain.)

500 The Dolly Twins. (Dolls same as R-90.)

701 7 Dolls in One

711 Jill

725 Wooden Soldier, "Dress Parade of the American Army"

777 New! Becky

800 Playmate, 22" tall

899 Curly Top and Her Own Little Dolly Topsy

899 Miss Candy and Her Dolly — World's Largest Real Hair Doll

901 Little Red Riding Hood

902 Little Miss Muffet

903 Little Bo Peep

911 Jayne, 1961

1000 Glendora Paper Doll with Curly Locks

1350 Dottie with the Snap-on Dresses.

1440 Hansel and Gretel. Box becomes Gingerbread House.

1600 Caroline Kay

2200 Mimi the French Model Paper Doll

2201 Miss Holly Day. Box is fitted suitcase.

2202 Sleeping Beauty and Prince Charming. Box becomes four-poster bed.

2500 Story Land Dolls (box set with dolls from 901, 902, and 903)

11-946 Single Girl Scout paper doll, sold for 20¢

11-947 Single Girl Scout paper doll, sold for 20¢

11-947 Brownie Scout Paper Doll

11-948 Single Girl Scout paper doll, sold for 20¢

11-949 Girl Scout Paper Doll

11-950 Girl Scout Paper Doll

11-950 Brownie Paper Doll

11-951 Girl Scout Paper Doll

11-951 Brownie Scout Paper Doll

11-952 Girl Scout Paper Doll

11-953 Brownie Paper Doll

11-954 Single Girl Scout paper doll, sold for 20¢

The following paper dolls have no stock numbers:

Betsy Ballerina. Includes stage, scenery changes, and stage settings.

Bobbie

Bobbie Twins. (Same as 150, but has new box cover and includes crayons and soap.)

Brownie Scout Paper Doll

Cindy

Curly Top. Earliest set; box is fastened with staples in illustration #1.

Curly Top. Like above, but with newer box and choice of hair color. "Made in U.S.A." now printed on bottom in illustration #2.

Curly Top Triplets. (Three dolls like doll in illustration #4. Each doll has different color hair.)

Curly Top, illustration #3.

Curly Top, 1947, illustration #4

Curly Top, with washable dresses in illustration #5

Curly Top Doll and Color Set, illustration #6

Curly Top Deluxe Set

Curly Top Visits the Holy Land. (This was also published by the Cross Publishing Co.)

Design-ette Set with Gingham Girl, 1948

Gingham Girl

Gingham Girl Doll box set

Girl Scout Paper Doll

Little Mike

Lone Ranger (stand-ups)

Mammy and Kinky Top

My Baby. This is a flat rubber doll with a complete layette of paper outfits.

Nancy Eddicoat. (Doll is like Gingham Girl.)

Poky Hontas

The Young Designer, Draw Dresses on Me, 1940. There is a type of magic slate dress on the doll that can be colored over and over.

Publisher name not given:

Festival Fun. This box just reads "Atlanta, Georgia," which is where DeJournette was located. The doll is the same as the Curly Top doll in illustration #5. Jewish festival outfits, songs, and handicrafts are included in the set.

35 Froggie Went A Courting, $25.00.

R-30 Blondie, $18.00.

22 Claire, $30.00.

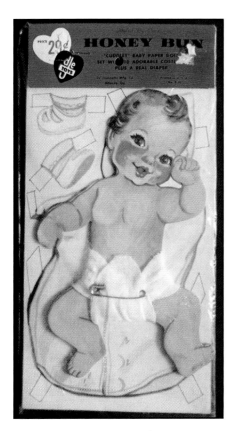

R-55 "Shoo-Shoo" Shirley, $25.00.

R-50 Honey Bun, $18.00.

R-56 Mommee & Her Little Girl, $20.00

60 Mother Daughter Dolls, $20.00.

R-69 Travel Kit, $25.00.

R-80 Gina, $15.00 each.

85 Bright Eyes, $15.00.

R-90 Penny, $18.00.

91 Goldilocks and the Three Bears, $18.00.

100 Bride, $30.00.

P-100 My Name is Marian, $18.00.

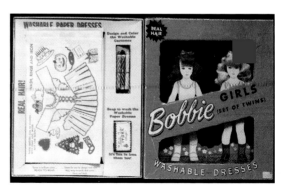

150 Bobbie Girls, $18.00.

198 3 Big Dolls, box contents.

198 3 Big Dolls, $20.00. This set has also been found with a different box cover.

200 Kathy, $18.00.

200 Heidi, $18.00.

500 The Dolly Twins, $25.00.

222 Littlest Darling, $20.00.

500 The Dolly Twins, $20.00.

500 The Dolly Twins, box contents.

701 *7 Dolls in 1*, $18.00.

711 Jill, $40.00.

725 Wooden Soldier, "Dress Parade of the American Army," $100.00.

777 New! Becky, $25.00.

800 Playmate, $16.00.

899 Curly Top and Her Own Little Dolly Topsy, $20.00.

899 Miss Candy, $20.00. This set is the Canadian version of 899. It has the same contents as the U.S. set.

901 Little Red Riding Hood, $22.00.

902 Little Miss Muffet, $22.00.

903 Little Bo Peep, $22.00.

911 Jayne, $20.00.

911 Jayne, $25.00. This is a different version of Jayne.

1000 Glendora, $20.00.

1350 Dottie with the Snap-on Dresses, $18.00.

1440 Hansel and Gretel, $35.00.

1600 Caroline Kay, $20.00.

The DeJournette Mfg. Company

2200 Mimi the French Model, $35.00.

2201 Miss Holly Day, $35.00.

2202 Sleeping Beauty, $50.00.

2500 Story Land Dolls, $30.00.

2500 Story Land Dolls, box contents.

Bobbie, $15.00.

Betsy Ballerina, $40.00.

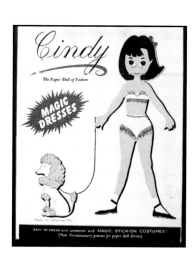

68   Betsy Ballerina, box contents.   Poky-Hontas, $10.00.   Cindy, $22.00.

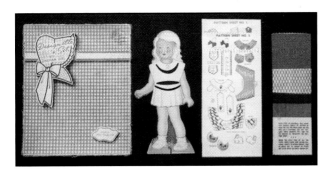

Design-ette Set with Gingham Girl, 1948, $22.00.

Festival Fun, $35.00. This doll is the same as the Curly Top doll in illustration #5 (page 71).

Gingham Girl, $18.00 each.

Little Mike, a Luvable Little Stinker, $25.00.

Mammy and Kinky Top, $300.00.

Mammy and Kinky Top, box cover and contents.

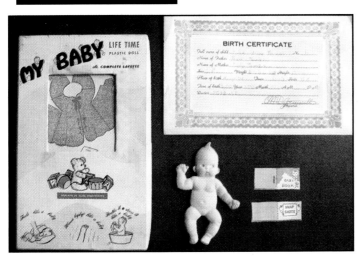

My Baby, $25.00.

The Young Designer, 1940, $20.00.

Curly Top

The Curly Top paper doll was designed by Alma DeJournette. The first patent was filed in December 1936, but was not issued until June 1938. Alma applied for a second patent in March 1937, and it was issued in October 1939. This second patent covered improvements for attaching the hair to the doll's head. Shortly after the second patent was issued, Alma moved to Atlanta and formed a company to sell the paper dolls. It was known as the Paper Doll House. The third and last patent for the Curly Top doll was filed in February 1942 and issued in July 1943. This patent also dealt with an improved way of attaching the hair to the doll. Since these Curly Top paper dolls do not have a number on the box to identify them, they will have an illustration number.

Illustration #1 is the very first Curly Top. (In the earlier version of this book, she had not been found yet.) The very first patent number, D110044, appears on the box lid. The box lid was made with staples. The box states "The Paper Doll House, Atlanta, Ga."

Illustration #2 is of a later edition that has the same box cover but one that is not stapled. "Made in USA" and the hair color of the doll are now printed on the side of the box.

Illustration #3 shows the next Curly Top. She has the first and second patent dates printed on the box lid. This doll now has a base/stand attached at her feet. She was sold in the early 1940s. (After July 1943 the third patent number, 2323522, began to appear on the stands of the dolls.)

Illustration #4 shows the next version of the doll. She is basically the same doll as the one in illustration #3, but has new outfits and a new box cover, and a date of 1947. Another set with this doll and these clothes has a date on the box of 1946. It is the same size box but is plainer, without the edge designs in dark green.

Illustration #5 has a new doll and new dresses that can be washed.

Illustration #6 has an even later doll. When she is used in the Brownie sets, her hairbow, shoes, and socks are brown.

Illustration #1, Curly Top, $25.00.

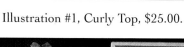

Illustration #1A, side of box.

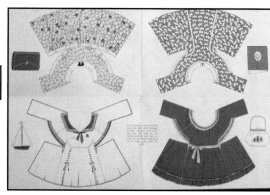

Illustration #1B, dresses.

Illustration #2A, side of box.

Illustration #2, Curly Top, $25.00.

Illustration #3, Curly Top, $20.00.

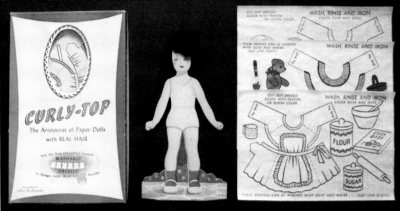

Illustration #4, Curly Top, 1947, $20.00.

Illustration #5, Curly Top with washable dresses, $20.00.

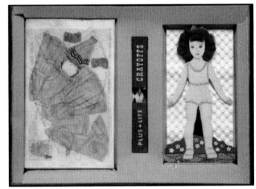

Illustration #6, Curly Top Doll and Color Set, $25.00. The box cover is faded.

We Are the Curly Top Triplets, $25.00. These dolls are like Curly Top in illustration #4.

Curly Top De Luxe Set, $25.00. These dolls are like those in illustration #6 and have washable dresses. This set has also been found with the dolls from illustration #5.

Curly Top Goes to the Holy Land, $30.00.

Brownie and Girl Scout Paper Dolls

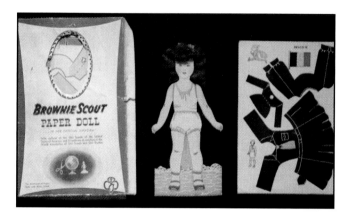

Brownie Scout, $25.00. This is the earliest Brownie Scout paper doll. She is shown in the 1950 Girl Scout catalog and she is like the Curly Top in illustration #4. The box has no number, but the catalog lists her as 11-947.

Brownie Scout, $25.00. This is the second Brownie Scout. She is like the Curly Top in illustration #5. She is shown in the 1951 Girl Scout catalog and is listed as 11-947.

Brownie Scout 11-947, $25.00. The number 11-947 is printed on the box now. The doll is like illustration #6 Curly Top, but her shoes, socks, and hair bow are now brown.

Brownie Scout 11-951, $20.00. Shown in the 1958 Girl Scout catalog. Same doll as 11-947 on the left, but her uniforms are different and do not wrap around.

Brownie 11-953, $20.00. Shown in the 1960 and 1966 Girl Scout catalogs. The set includes 44 uniforms.

Brownie 11-950, $20.00. Shown in the 1970 Girl Scout catalog. Included in the set are 78 World Association uniforms. Brownie pins, instead of flags, are shown on the uniform pages now.

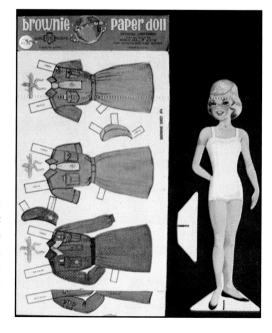

Girl Scout, $25.00. The doll is like Curly Top in illustration #5. She is shown in the 1951 Girl Scout catalog. There is no number on the box, but in the catalog the set is listed as 11-949. An extra paper doll with the number 11-948 could also be purchased for 20¢.

Girl Scout 11-950, $25.00. This is a new doll. She has white shoes and socks, and her eyes glance to the left. This set is shown in the 1958 catalog. Extra dolls could also be purchased for 20¢. The price and the number 11-948 were printed on the backs of these extra dolls.

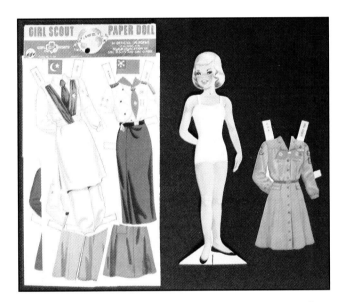

Girl Scout 11-952, $20.00. Shown in the 1960 catalog. The set includes 44 World Association uniforms.

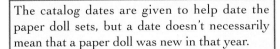

The catalog dates are given to help date the paper doll sets, but a date doesn't necessarily mean that a paper doll was new in that year.

Girl Scout 11-952, $20.00. Shown in the 1966 catalog. This is a later set of 11-952. The U.S.A. uniform is now a newer style, with short sleeves and has a sash for the badges. Forty-four uniforms are included.

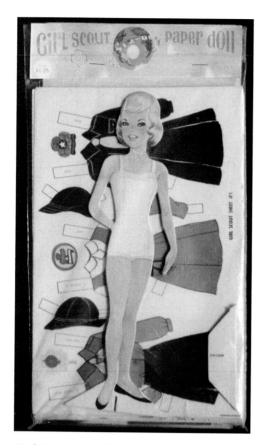

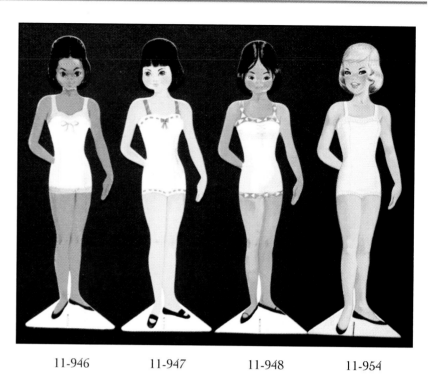

11-946 11-947 11-948 11-954

These four dolls were sold separately in the 1970 Girl Scout equipment catalog. The number printed on the back of each doll is shown under each paper doll in the above picture. The price of 20¢ is also printed on the back of each doll.

Girl Scout 11-951, $20.00. Shown in the 1970 Girl Scout equipment catalog, which states there are 81 uniforms. The uniform pages show Girl Scout pins instead of the country flags now.

Dennison Manufacturing Company

The Dennison Manufacturing Company is known worldwide for its paper products. The company was established in 1843 in the state of Maine. The first items produced by the company were jewelry boxes. By the time of the Civil War, the company was producing shipping tags, which became one of its mainstays. Late in the nineteenth century the firm moved to Boston, and then moved from there to Framingham, Massachusetts, in the very early 1900s.

In the 1870s, Dennison introduced colored tissue paper to its line of products, and by 1905 it offered 130 different shades of tissue paper. It was in about 1890 when crepe paper was introduced into its line, as its 1896 *Art and Decoration* catalog mentions that it introduced crepe paper six years before. By the time the 1905 *Art and Decoration* catalog was published, it listed 31 shades of the company's Imperial brand of crepe paper, and the decorated crepe paper could be bought in over 40 styles. It was during the later 1800s that Dennison also began to sell paper dolls. Some were sold in box sets or envelopes, which included tissue and crepe paper to make clothes for the dolls. The early paper dolls were beautiful embossed dolls and were printed in Germany by K & B (Kutzner & Berger) or L & B (Littauer and Bauer or Littauer and Boysen). After World War I, the paper dolls were printed in the United States. Catalogs from 1895 to 1907 list individual jointed doll forms that ranged in price from 5¢ for a small size doll to 15¢ for the tall 16¾" Prima-Donna. The early paper dolls were of babies, children, ballet dancers, and Prima-Donnas. By 1905, two Indians and four African babies had also been added to the catalog lists. The dolls could be bought in different sizes and designs. The two Indians were only of the 10" size. By 1909, only children dolls were being sold in the catalogs.

Dennison sold a set of paper dolls in the 1890s called Dennison's Nursery Outfit (pictured). The dolls in this set were not the jointed type of paper doll. Instead, the outfit came with four paper doll body forms — four paper doll head pieces, combination upper body and arm pieces, and separate legs that could be glued to the body forms. A larger set, titled Dennison's Complete Outfit, was also sold in the 1890s and is found for sale in the 1901 and 1905 catalogs as well. It has the same type of paper dolls as the Nursery Outfit, and both sets have the same picture on the box cover. At first the sets contained tissue paper, but at least by the 1896 catalog, crepe paper was also included in the sets. The Complete Outfit box was larger and sold for 75¢, while the Nursery Outfit set cost only 25¢. Both sets had the makings for four paper dolls, but the Complete Outfit set contained more tissue paper (36 sheets) and crepe paper (8 sheets), plus extra supplies to make paper flowers and other items. The Nursery Outfit contained six sheets of tissue paper and four sheets of crepe paper. The "Complete Outfit" has a new picture on the box cover in the 1905 catalog. The size and contents of the box are the same. A supplementary envelope set with a dozen heads, legs, body, and dress forms is shown in the 1896 and 1901 catalogs. It has the same picture on the envelope as the Nursery and Complete Outfits. This supplementary envelope was also listed in the 1905 catalog, but was not pictured.

The 1896 catalog listed a "new tissue paper outfit" called the Little Mother's Outfit of Crepe and Tissue Paper. This set contained two jointed paper dolls, tissue and crepe paper, four dress forms, a *Little Mother's Fashion Book*, and trimmings for decorating the dresses. This set was also sold in the 1901 catalog with the same title and two jointed paper dolls, but the box had a new picture cover. By 1905 the set had a new title: Dennison's Crepe and Tissue Paper Doll Outfit. The contents were basically the same as the Little Mother set, with two jointed dolls, tissue and crepe paper, etc. In the 1907/08 catalog, this set was offered with either a plain box cover or with a holly print (pictured). The 1909 catalog showed the set still being sold; it was now given a catalog number of 8. In the 1913 catalog it had a new box cover and the number 31.

Dennison also sold individual paper dolls already dressed in crepe paper dresses. Its 1896 catalog has a long list of paper dolls ranging in price from 25¢ to 75¢ each and including babies, children, ballet dancers, and bloomers (Prima-Donnas). Dennison continued to sell the dressed dolls in the early 1900s, but the number of dolls was reduced.

It's not known when the first *Art and Decoration* catalog was published, but the 1896 catalog is referred to as the 10th edition on the introduction page of the catalog. The 1901 catalog is referred to as the 13th edition, and the 1905 catalog as the 16th edition. So the catalog was not published annually, but maybe every 15 or 16 months.

In 1990 Dennison merged with Avery Products Corporation (founded in 1935), and it is now known as Avery Dennison.

11 Design-A-Doll Carol, circa 1950
11 Design-A-Doll Joan, circa 1950
11 Design-A-Doll Betti, circa 1950
11 Design-A-Doll Nancy, circa 1950
16 Dennison's Dressed Doll Set, circa 1905, 9" doll and three dresses and hats (not pictured)
17 Dennison's Dressed Doll Set, circa 1905, 7" doll and three dresses and hats (not pictured)
18 Doll House Outfit 1909 catalog (includes two paper dolls, not pictured)
21 Design-A-Doll Carol and Betti, circa 1950 (not pictured)
21 Design-A-Doll Joan and Nancy, circa 1950 (not pictured)
31 Dennison's Crepe and Tissue Paper Doll Outfit, 1913 catalog
33 Dennison's Crepe and Tissue Paper Doll, 1916
33 Dennison's Crepe Paper Doll Outfit, 1919
34 Dennison's Dolls and Dresses, 1916
34 Dennison's Dolls and Dresses, 1919
34 Dennison's Dolls and Dresses, 1922
36 Crepe Paper Doll Outfit (some sets are titled Little Tot's Crepe Paper Doll Outfit), circa 1930
37 Dennison's Dolls and Dresses, circa 1930
38 Nancy Crepe Paper Doll Outfit, circa 1930
512 Dress-A-Doll, Bud and Babs, circa 1950
512 Dress-A-Doll, Pat and Bunny, circa 1950
513 Dress-A-Doll; Bud, Babs, and Bunny; circa 1950
522 Dennison TV Playhouse, circa 1950. (Dolls are Pat and Bunny from 512.)

Dennison's Nursery Outfit, $100.00. Sold in the 1890s to early 1900s. These dolls are not the jointed type. (See Dennison introduction for details).

Dennison's Crepe and Tissue Paper Doll Outfit, $100.00. Shown in catalogs of 1905 to 1909. The 1907 catalog states the box could be bought in either white or with a holly print as pictured here. In the 1909 catalog the set is No. 8.

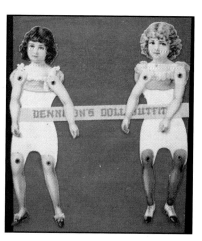

The dolls in the Dennison Doll Outfit set.

Dennison's Crepe and Tissue Paper Doll Outfit No. 31, $100.00.

Dennison's Crepe and Tissue Paper Doll Outfit No. 31 box, dolls, and contents.

Doll Outfit No. 31 is pictured in the 1913 catalog. The contents include two jointed paper dolls, small rolls of crepe paper in assorted colors, colored tissue paper, gold and silver paper, gold and silver stars, crepe paper ribbon, paper lace, strips of decorated paper, dress and hat forms, and a fashion booklet with dressmaking instructions.

Many of the jointed paper dolls have a patent date of August 24, 1880. A patent search was done, and the patent was issued for toy figures using eyelets in the arms and legs. McLoughlin Brothers also had jointed paper dolls with this same patent date. The patent was not issued to either the McLoughlin or Dennison companies. However, the patent could be leased to companies to use on their paper figures. The patent date printed on the dolls is when the patent was issued and does not mean the dolls were published at that time.

Dennison's Jointed Paper Doll Prima Donnas and Ballerinas

These paper dolls can be found in four sizes: 5¼", 9¾", 13¾", and 16¾". Sizes may vary slightly. The doll's heads are the same for the Prima Donnas and the Ballerinas.

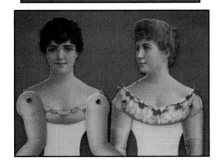

Ballerina (unpunched), $35.00.

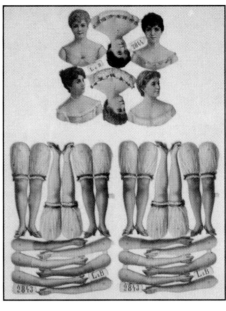

Prima Donna's arms, legs, and heads (un-punched), $100.00.

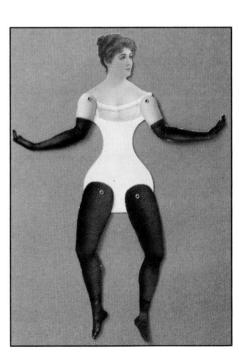

Prima Donna, $25.00.

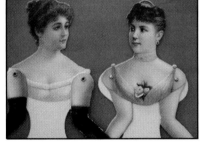

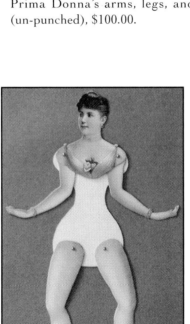

Ballerina, $25.00.

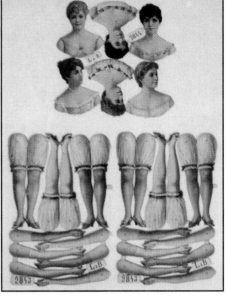

Ballerina, $25.00.

Dennison's Jointed Paper Doll African Babies

The African babies were issued in one 9" size.

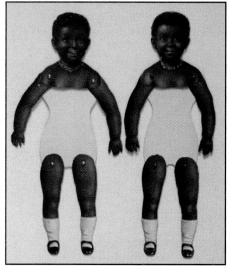

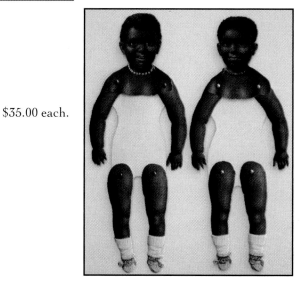

$35.00 each.

$35.00 each.

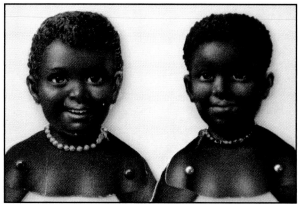

Dennison's Jointed Paper Doll Children

The children were available in 7" and 9¼" sizes. Sizes could vary slightly.

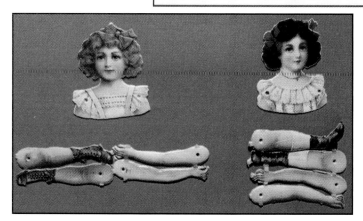

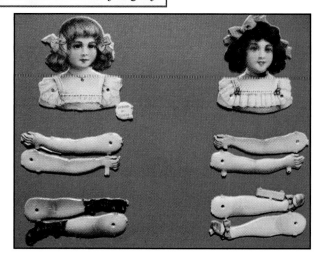

An example of two doll's head pieces and their legs and arms, which are still joined, $30.00 each.

Another example of two doll's head pieces with legs and arms still joined, $30.00 each.

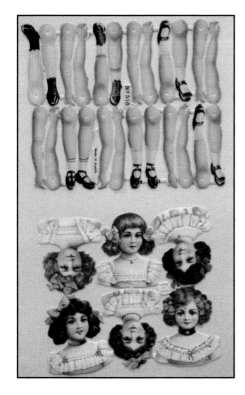

Six more embossed paper doll head pieces, still joined, $60.00.

Example of two versions of the same girl, in two different sizes, $25.00 each.

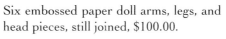

Six embossed paper doll arms, legs, and head pieces, still joined, $100.00.

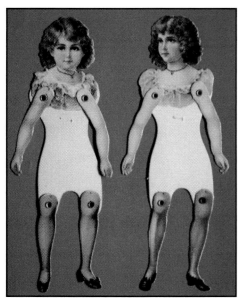

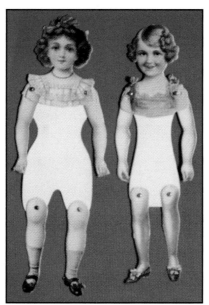

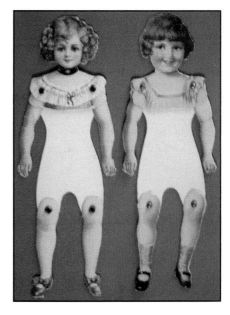

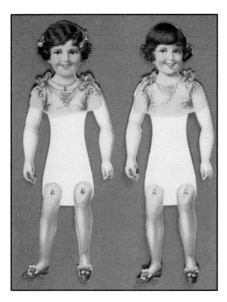

Two girls almost alike at first glance, but notice the differences (see close-up). $25.00 each.

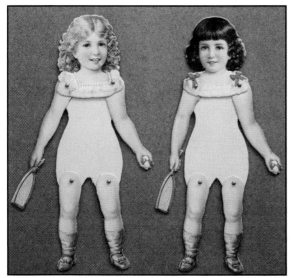

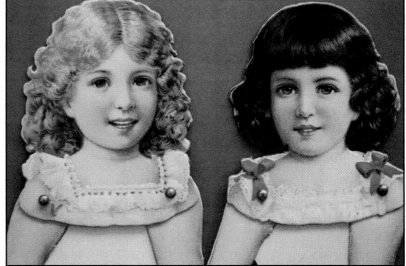

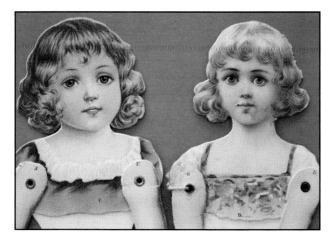

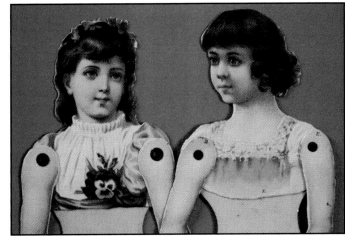

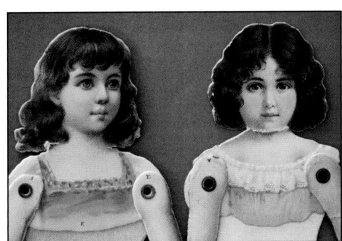

Doll dressed in crepe paper, $25.00.

Doll with pink body form, $25.00.

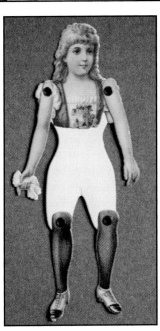

Doll holding handkerchief, $25.00.

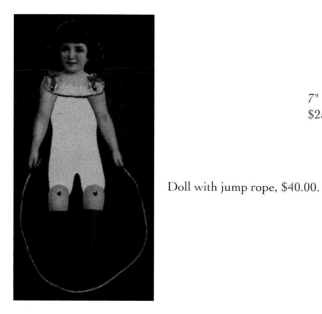

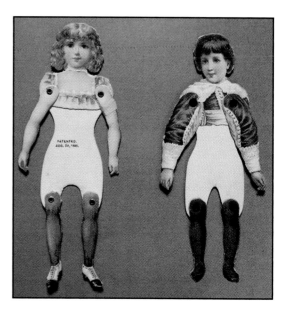

7" size girl and boy, $25.00 each.

Doll with jump rope, $40.00.

Two 9¼" boys, $25.00 each.

$25.00.

Dennison's Jointed Paper Doll Babies

The babies were issued in two sizes, 6½" and 8½". Sizes could vary slightly.

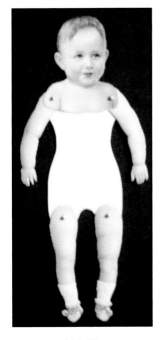

$25.00.

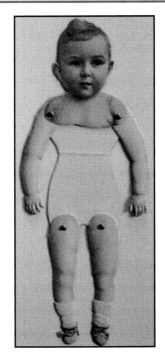

$25.00.

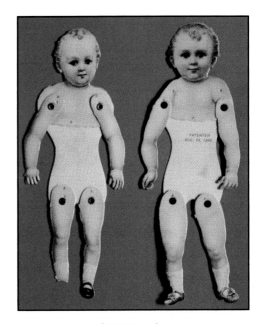

$25.00 each.

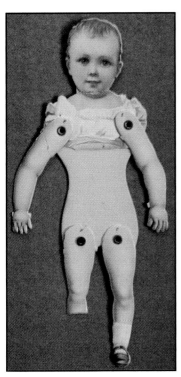

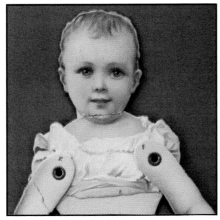

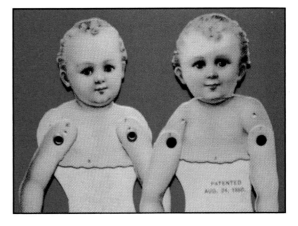

$25.00.

Dennison's Jointed Paper Doll Indians

There were two Indians published; both were the 10" size.

Indian with peace pipe and rattle, $40.00.

Indian with tomahawk and shield (missing top part of tomahawk), $40.00.

33 Dennison's Crepe and Tissue Paper Doll Outfit, 1916, $75.00.

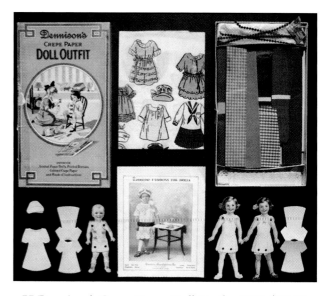

33 Dennison's Crepe Paper Doll Outfit, 1919, $75.00.

Shown are the 1916 and 1919 number 33 sets. The boxes have the same picture on the cover, but in 1919 the word *tissue* was dropped from the title and the set was called Dennison's Crepe Paper Doll Outfit. The dolls remained the same but the printed clothes pages changed. The baby came dressed in either pink or blue. Set 33 continued to be sold in the 1920s.

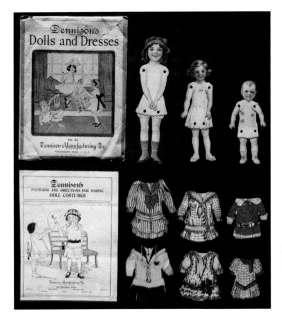

The Dennison 34 sets are in envelopes. This is the 1916 edition and the dolls are in three different sizes. The girl dolls could be either blonde or brunette and the baby was dressed in either pink or blue. The 1922 edition of set 34 is pictured below. There was also a 1919 edition. The dolls are the same in all editions. The envelope for the 1919 edition is the same as the 1922 edition, but the instruction booklet is like the 1916 edition booklet except Berlin is not included in the list of cities printed at the bottom of the 1919 front cover.

34 Dennison's Dolls and Dresses, 1916, $75.00.

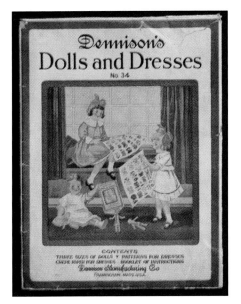

34 Dennison's Dolls and Dresses, 1922, $75.00.

The three dolls and instruction booklet for the 1922 set of 34.

37 Dennison Dolls and Dresses, circa 1930, $75.00. This is an envelope set.

36 Crepe Paper Doll Outfit, circa 1930, $75.00.

July 1931 ad in *Home Circle Magazine* for paper doll Nancy Lee, which is the same doll as 38 Nancy.

38 Nancy Crepe Paper Doll Outfit, circa 1930, $45.00. Notice that Nancy is the same doll as the middle-size doll in sets 36 and 37.

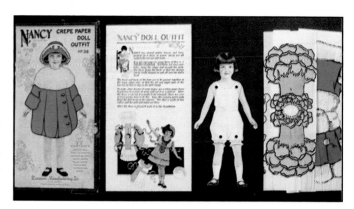

Dennison Paper Dolls from the 1950s

11 Design-A-Doll Joan, circa 1950, $20.00.

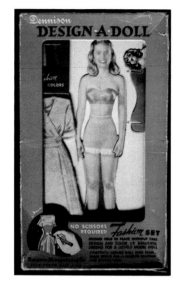

11 Design-A-Doll Betti, circa 1950, $20.00.

11 Design-A-Doll Nancy, circa 1950, $20.00.

11 Design-A-Doll Carol, circa 1950, $20.00.

513 Dress-a-Doll Bud, Babs, and Bunny, circa 1950, $25.00.

513 Dress-a-Doll box contents.

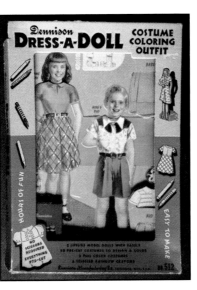

522 Dennison TV Playhouse, circa 1950, $30.00.

512 Dress-a-Doll Pat and Bunny, circa 1950, $20.00.

512 Dress-a-Doll Bud and Babs, circa 1950, $20.00.

Determined Productions, Inc.

Wolfit Enterprises, Inc., and Boucher Associates are subsidiaries of Determined Productions, Inc.

Lisa Your Paper Doll Playmate and Her Clothes Closet, 1961, large 20" jointed doll, $18.00.

A Friend Paper Doll©, 1967, $18.00. Boucher Associates.

Love Paper Doll©, 1975, $18.00. Wolfpit Enterprises, Inc.

Snoopy Paper Doll Peanuts Character©, 1958, 1965 United Feature Syndicate, Inc. (not pictured)

M.A. Donohue and Company

60 Daisy Dimple and her Playmates, $75.00. Box set, dolls, and clothes from 85B.

80A Bob and Nan, $60.00.

80C Ann and Joe, $60.00.

81C Ted and Bob, $60.00.

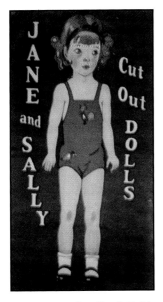

81A Jane and Sally, $60.00.

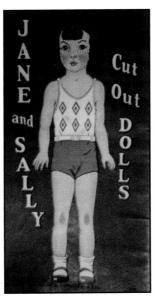

Jane and Sally, back cover.

85B Tiny Tiptoe and Her Neighbors, $75.00.

85B Tiny Tiptoe, inside pages.

85B Tiny Tiptoe, inside pages.

85B Tiny Tiptoe, inside pages.

85B Tiny Tiptoe, inside pages.

85B Tiny Tiptoe, inside pages.

671 Fairy Favorite, 1913, $75.00.

672 The Nursery Favorite, 1913, $75.00.

675 Fairy-Tale and Flower Paper-Dolls, 1913, $100.00.
This book combines 671 and 672.

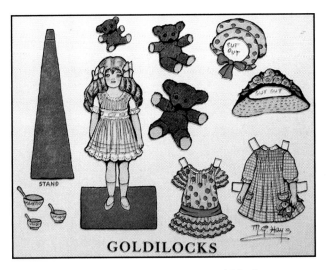

675 Fairy-Tale and Flower, Goldilocks.

675 Fairy-Tale and Flower, Sleeping Beauty.

675 Fairy-Tale and Flower, Cinderella.

675 Fairy-Tale and Flower, Fatima.

675 Fairy-Tale and Flower, Bo-Peep.

675 Fairy-Tale and Flower, Red Riding Hood.

675 Fairy-Tale and Flower, Daisy.

675 Fairy-Tale and Flower, Forget-Me-Not.

675 Fairy-Tale and Flower, Pansy.

675 Fairy-Tale and Flower, Poppy.

675 Fairy-Tale and Flower, Lily of the Valley.

675 Fairy-Tale and Flower, Rose.

610 Paper Cut-Out Dolls, $35.00.

610 Paper Cut-Out Dolls, inside pages.

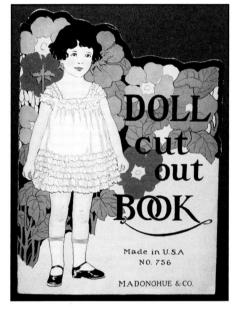

756 Doll Cut Out Book, $35.00. The little girl on the front cover is not a paper doll. The paper dolls inside the book are from 675.

756 Doll Cut Out Book, inside contents.

60 Daisy Dimple and Her Playmates, box set (dolls from 85B)
80A Bob and Nan
80C Ann and Joe
81A Jane and Sally
81C Ted and Bob
85B Tiny Tiptoe and Her Neighbors
86B Johnny Jones (same as 2005 Goldsmith Pub. Co.)
86B Pretty Polly (same as 2005 Goldsmith Pub. Co.)
610 Paper Cut-Out Dolls (two paper dolls from 675)
655 Paper Doll Cut-Outs (four paper dolls from 675; picture not available)
671 Fairy Favorite, 1913
672 The Nursery Favorite, 1913
673 Bob and Nan (not pictured, see 80A)
674 Ann and Joe (not pictured, see 80C)
675 Fairy-Tale and Flower Paper Dolls, 1913
756 Doll Cut-Out Book (dolls from 675)

Dot and Peg Productions

Dot and Peg Productions was founded in 1941 by the sister team of Mrs. Dorothy Hedges (Dot) and Mrs. Margaret Lamb (Peg).

Dot designed the first paper dolls as a result of making handmade paper dolls for her two young daughters. Seeing the possibility of interesting other children, Dot asked Peg to collaborate with her in making a set for the public.

In the summer of 1941, Dot took the handmade paper doll sample of Young American Designer to New York and was led to the *Good Housekeeping* magazine editor. It was wartime, and the importation of toys had stopped, so there was a big demand for original American toys. *Good Housekeeping* had a department promoting the best American-made toys of the year. The editor was so enthusiastic over Young American Designer that a contract was immediately signed. This was all done in a day's work, and Dot returned home to Chattanooga informing Peg that they were in business! Orders began pouring in from all over the country. Marshall Field and Company alone bought 10,000 sets that first year.

The Christmas issue of *Good Housekeeping* that year not only gave Young American Designer the seal of approval, but featured the set as the best American toy of the year. The set contained two paper dolls, named Peg and Dot, seven basic patterns, and 18 sheets of "material" made of paper that resembled velvet, gingham, wool, tweed, prints, polka dots, etc. There were eight gummed sheets with trim for the dresses. Real veiling to trim the hats was also included. Also included was an illustrated booklet of instructions, plus wooden stands for the dolls, a pencil, and even an automatic "hydraulic" (with sponge tip) that could be filled with water for moistening the gummed pieces.

This was the beginning of a 20-year business that progressed into business ventures other than paper dolls. When paper became scarce near the end of the war, the company decided to produce a shell craft kit for making shell jewelry and ornaments. Its last paper doll set was produced in 1950, and its toy line was discontinued, as by this time the company had entered into a new venture — manufacturing ladies' scuffs and accessories. The scuffs were so elegant that all the large stores in the country were ordering in great quantities. Stores like Bonwits in New York, Marshall Field in Chicago, and I. Magnin in California. Saks Fifth Avenue liked the scuffs so much, it had its own label sewn into them. In addition to scuffs, bed jackets and sleepwear were also added to the line.

By 1962 Dot and Peg Productions had grown so large the sisters decided it was time to retire and sell their business, which they did.

Young American Designer, 1941, $50.00.

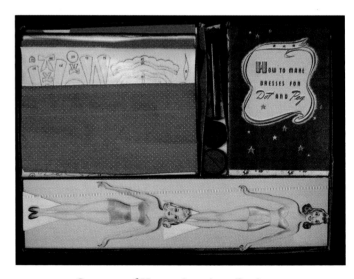

Contents of Young American Designer.

Mother and Daughter Dresses, 1943, $35.00.

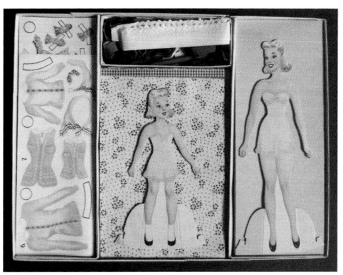

Contents of Mother and Daughter Dresses.

Wedding Belles, 1945, $50.00.

Dottie Dress-Up, 1950, $25.00.

Dottie Dress-Up, inside contents.

E.P. Dutton and Company

Many of the E.P. Dutton paper dolls were imported from the color printing and publishing firm of Ernest Nister in Nuremberg, Germany. Dutton was the sole distributor in the U.S. of the internationally famous firm's products from the middle-1880s until the outbreak of World War I, which ended the association. Besides Nister's paper dolls, Dutton distributed the beautiful Nister calendars, cards, valentines, and children's books during that time period.

The Dutton Co. also carried in its line a series of "Model" books that were also published by the McLoughlin Publishing Co. Examples are *The Model Book of Trains*, *The Model Book of Soldiers*, and *The Animal Model Book*. See the McLoughlin section for a more complete list of these books.

The Ernest Nister firm also had a branch in London, England.

878 The Model Book of Dolls, $100.00.

878 Two inside pages from The Model Book of Dolls.

2739 Dolly Darling, $100.00.

2739 Dolly Darling, inside page.

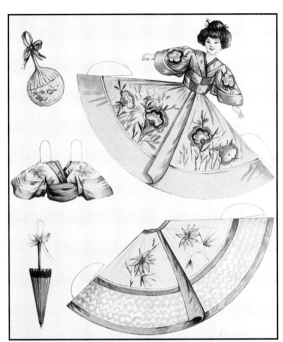

2739 Dolly Darling, inside pages (not all pages shown).

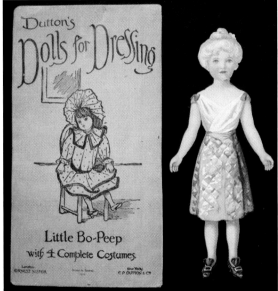

1312 Dutton's Dolls for Dressing, Little Bo-Peep, $100.00.

1129 Dutton's Dolls for Dressing, Dolly Dear, $90.00.

1311 Dutton's Dolls for Dressing, Little Red Riding Hood, $100.00.

1310 Dutton's Dolls for Dressing, Little Polly Flinders, $100.00 if complete.

1309 Little Miss Muffet, $25.00 for doll alone.

3915 Lettie Lane's Sister's Children, $100.00.

3915 Lettie Lane's Sister's Children, inside pages.

3915 Lettie Lane's Sister's Children, inside pages.

3916 Lettie Lane's Great Grandparents, $100.00.

3916 Lettie Lane's Great Grandparents, inside pages.

3916 Lettie Lane's Great Grandparents, inside pages.

3159 Dainty Dollies and Their Dresses, $80.00.

3159 Dainty Dollies, inside page.

3159 Dainty Dollies, inside page.

4309 Pretty Paper Pets, $80.00.

4309 Pretty Pets, inside page.

4309 Pretty Pets, inside page.

4309 Pretty Pets, inside page.

4309 Pretty Pets, inside page.

John H. Eggers Co., Inc.

This New York company was well known for publishing children's books and small miniature books on birds, animals, etc. A logo it used called the company "the house of little books." In the 1920s, it reprinted many of the Dolly Dingle paper dolls that appeared in the popular magazine *Pictorial Review*. The paper dolls were drawn by Grace Drayton and were a monthly feature in the magazine for many years. The Dolly Dingle pages that the John Eggers Company reprinted were printed on lightweight cardboard. Some were single sheets, and others were joined together in groups of three or more sheets.

Dolly Dingle's Travels, Series 2, 1921, $75.00. Pictured are the front and back pages of a four-page set. (There was also a Series 1 and a series called Dolly Dingle's Operas). The paper dolls on the front page are two Dolly Dingles that didn't appear in *Pictorial Review*. The other three pages appeared in 1917 issues of *Pictorial Review*. Included with this set is a page on paper that has four miniature books for the child to cut out and put together. They are *Dolly Dingle in Holland, Spain, Italy*, and *Switzerland*. (These are the same countries that the Dolly Dingle paper dolls visit in this set.) These little books are © 1922 by the John H. Eggers Co.

Dolly Dingle at Play, 1927, $65.00. This is the front page of a four-sheet set. Other series were called Dolly Dingle and Her Friends, Dolly Dingle and her Pals and Dolly Dingle's Parties.

Dolly Dingle at Play, inside pages.

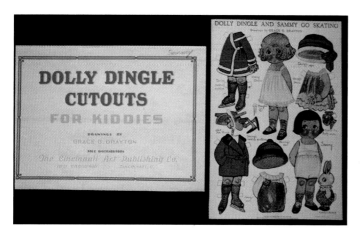

Dolly Dingle Cutouts for Kiddies, 1927, $25.00. This Dolly Dingle page is dated "1927 by the Eggers Co." and was in an envelope distributed by the Cincinnati Art Publishing Company of Cincinnati, Ohio. The page originally appeared in the Jan. 1922 issue of *Pictorial Review*. The paper doll pages in the envelopes could vary.

Dolly Dingle Travel Series No. 130-B, 1929, $65.00. This is a three-page folder. At the bottom of the front page, there is an added story with pictures by Grace Drayton. The paper doll is from the April 1928 issue of *Pictorial Review*. The other two pages are from 1924. An interesting feature of this series and series 130-C is the black and white drawings on the backs of the pages. Each illustration has "© J.H.E." (John H. Eggers).

Dolly Dingle Travel Series No. 130-C, 1929, $65.00. This is a three-page folder. At the bottom of the front page, there is an added story with pictures by Grace Drayton. The paper doll is from the July 1928 issue of *Pictorial Review*. The other two pages are from 1917 and 1918.

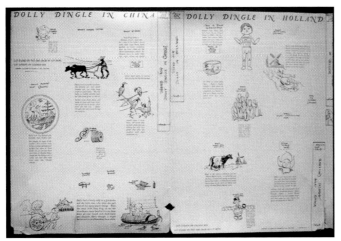

These pages are the back of series 130-C.

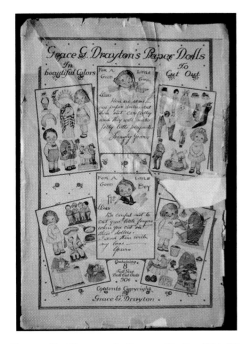

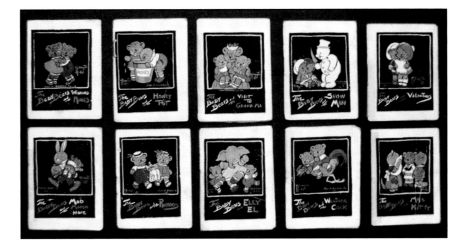

Grace G. Drayton's Paper Dolls, $85.00. This set of eight Dolly Dingle pages may also be attributed to the Eggers Co., but there is no publisher given on the envelope or on the pages. The envelope states "Contents Copyright by Grace G. Drayton." The pages are on paper and are blank on the back. These Dolly Dingle pages originally appeared in 1918 issues of *Pictorial Review*.

As mentioned in the introduction, the John H. Eggers company was known for its miniature books. Grace Drayton drew the Baby Bears, a series of 12 miniature booklets. Each little book is marked "copyright 1913, 1914 The Century Co." and "copyright 1920 John H. Eggers." They measure 2¼" x 2¾" and have eight pages, including the covers. Ten of the books are pictured here.

Another set of six Dolly Dingle pages, "© 1927 by John H. Eggers," was sent out by the magazine *Woman's World*. The paper dolls may have been a subscription premium given with a new subscription, as the six Dolly Dingle sheets were in an envelope mailed from *Woman's World* in Chicago, Illinois. These paper dolls are on heavy paper and not cardboard and are blank on the back. They originally appeared in *Pictorial Review* in 1922 and 1924.

Eilert

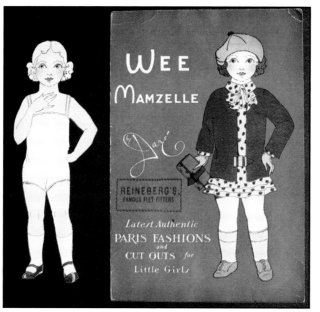

Wee Mamzelle, $60.00.

Einson Freeman Company, Inc.

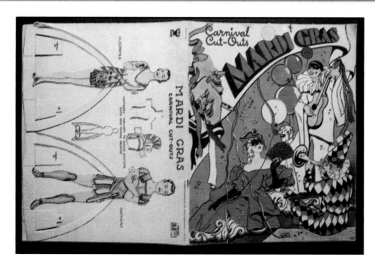

432 Mardi Gras, 1935, $75.00.

Rosemary the Roundabout Doll, 1932, $60.00.
No number (sold in glassine envelope).

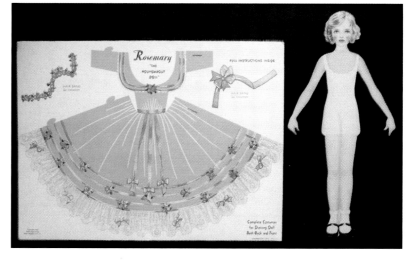

Emmylou Specialties

Emmylou Specialties produced 12 different styles of cloth dresses to be sewn for a large cardboard doll that was jointed at the shoulders. The outfits came in envelopes for the price of 60¢ each, and the dolls were sold separately at 30¢ each. There were at least four different dolls; three are pictured here. The name "Charles Bloom, Inc." appears at the bottom of the instruction sheet. Karl Gut Litho. Co. also used these dolls for its paper doll sets, but the clothes were on paper.

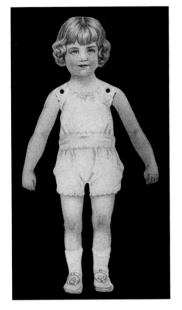

Girl doll, $15.00.

Emmylou Specialties, $40.00.

Boy doll, $15.00.

Estelle Ansley Worrell

Country Music Star Dottie West Paper Dolls, 1973, $35.00.

Fish-Lyman Company

In September 1922, the Fish-Lyman Company ran an ad in *Junior Home Magazine* for Margaret Evans Price paper dolls. The ad stated that the company offered 12" paper dolls and 7" paper dolls. The 12" dolls were already cut out and mounted on cardboard, and the smaller dolls were to be cut out. The ad has an array of all the dolls in their different costumes. Actually, there are four 12" dolls and four small 7" dolls, but each is pictured many times wearing a different costume (see illustration). The ad also ran in *Child Life*, in December 1922.

Three months later, in March 1923, the company ran another ad for these paper dolls in *Child Life*. In this ad, it stated it would send a complete assortment of twelve 12" dolls plus smaller dolls, for a total of 34 possible combinations. Counting up all the dolls pictured in the earlier ad of September 1922, there are 34.

In the 1920s, The Fish-Lyman Company president was Clinton G. Fish, and the company was a multigrapher and printing company.

No. 1 Lucinda Lee, 1920, $75.00.   No. 2 Lora Lou, $75.00.   No. 3 Baby Darling, $75.00.

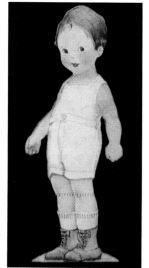  

No. 4 Junior, 1920, $75.00.

Junior Home Magazine ad, September 1922.

Fish-Lyman Co., continued:

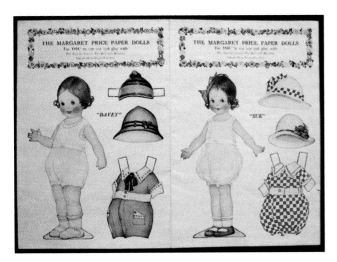

The Margaret Price Paper Dolls, Sue and Davey, 1920, $50.00.

The Margaret Price Paper Dolls, Priscilla and Baby Cuddles, 1920, $50.00.

Foster and Stewart Publishing Corporation

Brazil and Israel, $15.00 each.

Our World Cut-Outs, 1946:	Greece
	Holland/Netherlands
Africa	India
Arabia	Israel (pictured)
Australia	Japan
Brazil (pictured)	North American Indians of the Western Plains
China	Rural Mexico
Eskimos of Alaska	Switzerland
France	Turkey

The 16 sets listed contain paper dolls, outfits, animals and buildings.

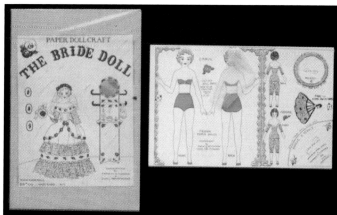

The Bride Doll, 1955, $40.00.

Little Miss (Old) Fashion and Baby Sister, $40.00.

New Orleans Antebellum Paper Dolls, 1955 (not pictured)
Little Miss (Old) Fashion and Baby Sister. This set was sold at F.A.O. Schwartz Toy Store
    and is the same set as Grandmother's Dolls.
Grandmother's Dolls, 1955. These are the same dolls as Little Miss (Old) Fashion & Baby Sister.

Friendship Press

China, 1932, $35.00.

Friendship Paper Dolls, 1933, $35.00.

Mexico, 1935, $35.00.

Japan, 1934, $35.00.

Samuel Gabriel Sons & Co./Gabriel Industries, Inc.

Samuel Gabriel Sons & Co. of New York, New York, was established in 1907. In the 1930s, the company was sold to American Colortype of Chicago, who had been doing most of the printing for Sam Gabriel for many years.

In 1957 the Samuel Gabriel Division of American Colortype was sold to Jerome M. Fryer and Morton J. Levy of Levy and Fryer, Inc. a national sales representative business that had been formed in 1950. The name of Samuel Gabriel Sons & Co. was changed to Gabriel Industries, Inc.

In 1961 Levy and Fryer, Inc. merged into Gabriel and in 1965 Gym-Dandy Inc. and Hubley Mfg. Co also merged into Gabriel, In the years to follow, many companies' toy lines were acquired; the chemistry and erector sets of A.C. Gilbert in 1967 and the Samsonite toy line in 1972. Kohner Bros., Inc., a manufacturer of toys and games, followed in 1975, and the Child Guidance line was acquired in 1978 from Questor Corporation. Also in 1978 Gabriel Industries merged with CBS Toys, a division of CBS, Inc. The next year, Gabriel Industries condensed and reorganized its products into four brand lines; Child Guidance®, Gabriel® Toys and Games, Gym-Dandy®, and Wonder®. A wood gym line was added in 1981 under the brand name Creative Playthings® and in 1982 Ideal Toys was purchased. The name Gabriel was dropped at this time, and the company became known as CBS Toys.

Among the first paper dolls published by the company was a series called Dolly Dear, Dolly Delight, and Dolly Darling. They were numbered #1, #2 and #3 respectively and dated 1911. A few of the early paper dolls came in envelopes. Later there were paper doll books, but the majority of the paper dolls came in boxed sets. The letter "D" that preceded the stock numbers stood for "Doll", and when a number was prefixed by the letter "T" the item was a toy. The 800 and 900 numbers did not use a letter preceding the numbers, and when the firm became known as Gabriel Industries, Inc., the letters were dropped altogether.

If a catalog date is included where the paper doll is pictured, this is only to aid in dating the paper doll and does not necessarily mean the paper doll was new in that catalog. Paper doll sets were often carried in the catalogs for many years. All the known paper dolls for Samuel Gabriel and Sons and Gabriel Industries are listed. The pictures will follow the list.

1 Dolly Dear Series, Dolly Dear, 1911
1 Merry Marjorie (D119)
1 Daisy Dell (not pictured, same as Laurette on page 16)
1 Dolly Dimple Series, Affectionate Alice
2 Dolly Dear Series, Dolly Delight, 1911
2 Dolly Dimple Series, Baby Betty
2 Handsome Harold (D119)
3 Dolly Dear Series, Dolly Darling, 1911
3 Graceful Gertrude (D119)
4 Sweet Sallie (D119)
5 Pretty Pauline (D119)
6 Jolly Jack (D119)
10 The Darling Series, Darling Dick
11 The Darling Series, Darling Daisy (not pictured)
12 The Darling Series, Darling Dot
D78 My Doll Jack (D134 Toddler Twins)
D79 My Doll Jill (D134 Toddler Twins)
D87 Dainty Doll (D114 Our America, doll of Linda)
D88 Darling Doll (D114 Our America, doll of Rita)
D89 Grace, 6" doll in glassine env. (in 1925 catalog)
D89 Edith, 6" doll in glassine env. (in 1925 catalog)
D89 Mabel, 6" doll in glassine env. (in 1925 catalog)
D89 Nancy, 6" doll in glassine env. (in 1925 catalog)
D90 My Dolly Series of New Dressing Dolls, Sister Nan
D90 My Dolly Series of New Dressing Dolls, Brother Bob
D90 My Dolly Series of New Dressing Dolls, Cousin Kate
D90 Betsy McCall Biggest Paper Doll, 32" doll
D91 Young Fashions (D122 Mother & Daughter)
D91 Class Mates (D138 All My Dollies)
D92 Sweetheart Doll, Elsie (box set or glassine envelope)
D92 Sweetheart Doll, Helen (box set or glassine envelope)
D92 Sweetheart Doll, Alice (box set or glassine envelope; not pictured, see 876 doll of Alice)
D92 Sweetheart Doll, Dorothy (box set or glassine envelope; not pictured, see 876 doll of Dorothy)
D92 Young Moderns (D122 Mother & Daughter)
D92 Chums (D138 All My Dollies, not pictured)
D93 Polly Pert (D135 Sisters)
D94 Suzie Sweet (D135 Sisters)
D95 Mabel and Her Costumes
D95 Nellie and Her Costumes
D96 Louise and Her Costumes
D96 Dolly and Her Dresses (D106 Junior Shop, doll of Betsy)
D100 Dolly Sheets to Cut Out (877)
D100 My Wardrobe Dolls
D100 School Mates, four sheets and cover bound as a book
D104 Cloth Dresses to Sew for Polly Pet
D104 Best of Friends (two dolls from D114 Our America)
D105 Play Paper Dolls (D115 Paper Doll Bazaar)
D106 Junior Shop (clothes from D138 All My Dollies, dolls new)
D106 Dresses to Sew for Mary Ann (not pictured, contains one doll from D108)
D107 The Twinnies

D107 Betty Jane (D136)
D108 Mary Alice (D136)
D108 Cloth Dresses to Sew for My Twin Dollies
D109 Doll Dresses to Color (4 dolls from #896 Fancy Dress Dolls)
D109 Doris Dainty (D137 The Twins)
D109 Susan Sweet (D137 The Twins)
D111 Sweet Sue Doll (not pictured, D126 Dollies in Style)
D111 New Moving Eye Doll, Ruth (in 1925 catalog, picture not available)
D111 New Moving Eye Doll, Susan (in 1925 catalog). A patent date of 1919 is on the stand but does not necessarily mean the paper doll was produced in 1919.
D112 Moving Eye Dolly Baby Betty, 1920
D112 Moving Eye Dolly Toddling Tom, 1920
D113 The Twinnies, 1921
D113 Little Orphan Annie (includes doll of Sandy)
D114 My Complete Sew-Dress Box
D114 Our America
D114 Wide Awake and Fast Asleep Doll, Merry Marjorie, 1920
D114 Wide Awake and Fast Asleep Doll, Pretty Polly, 1920
D115 Winnie Winkle and Her Paris Costumes
D115 The "Ever New" Doll (D127 Surprise Dollies)
D115 Paper Doll Bazaar
115 Ballerina Dolls, 1956
D116 Fashion Model
D116 Dollies à la Mode (896)
D116 Tots and Teens (not pictured)
D116 Up-To-Date Dollies
116 "Pony Tail" Paper Doll, 1959
D117 Carol and Her Dresses
D117 Junior Fashions (D114 Our America)
D117 Dollies and Their Wardrobes
117 Angel Face
D118 Dolly Adorable, doll body with three interchangeable heads (D129)
D118 School Days
D118 Paper Doll Play (contents same as D118 School Days)
D118 The Dimple Doll Family (small box set with six American Colortype dolls)
118 Snap-On Paper Dolls, 1958
D119 Dollyland, box with six dolls in envelopes: #1 Merry Marjorie, #2 Handsome Harold, #3 Graceful Gertrude, #4 Sweet Sallie, #5 Pretty Pauline, #6 Jolly Jack.
D119 Dollyland, 1920, box with six dolls. (The dolls are from 877.)
D119 Sew-Easy Doll, paper doll with cloth clothes to sew
D119 Sew-Easy Doll, Dainty Dot
D120 Sew-Easy Dolls, two paper dolls with eight outfits to sew
D121 Frances and Her Frocks
D121 The Dainty Dolly Series of Dressing Dolls, Fanny and Her Frocks. (Not pictured; doll and dresses have "No. 5" on back.)

D121 The Dainty Dolly Series of Dressing Dolls, Gladys and Her Gowns

D121 Babyland "Peggy," 1921

D121 Babyland "Bobby," 1921

D122 Mother and Daughter Dolls

D122 Wide Awake and Fast Asleep Doll, Alice

D122 Wide Awake and Fast Asleep Doll, Dorothy

D123 Happy Faces Dressing Dolls, one doll with extra heads (D128 Quick Change Dolls)

D123 The Sweetheart Series, Tommy Todd (same as Richard by American Colortype)

123 Little Audrey

D124 Just from Paris (D135 Debutantes)

D124 My Dolly, Doll Sheets, 1925, four sheets and cover bound as a book (D90)

D125 Just from College (D135 Debutantes)

D125 Betty is Going Away to Boarding School (D116 Up-to-Date Dollies)

D126 Dollies in Style

D126 The Dimple Doll Family, three dolls from Dainty Dollies 876, not always the same three dolls.

D127 Surprise Dollies

D127 The Winkle Family

D128 On the Campus. (These dolls are the same as D134 The Younger Set.)

D128 Quick Change Dolls

D129 Turn and Turn About Dollies, two 12" doll bodies, six changeable heads.

130 Vicki-Velcro Paper Doll

D130 Indians and Cowboys, stand-ups (four sheets bound together)

D131 Soldiers and Sailors, 1927, four sheets and cover bound as a book (not pictured)

D131 Quartet of Dolls, four dolls from D138 All My Dollies

131 Vicki and Valerie, Velcro dolls

D132 Wedding Party. This is a smaller version of D139 Bridal Party, same dolls.

D133 The Twinnies

D134 Toddler Twins

D134 The Younger Set. This set has the same dolls and clothes as D128 On the Campus, but this box for The Younger Set is the larger size box set (not pictured).

D135 Sisters

D135 The Debutantes

D136 Best of Friends

D137 The Twins and Their Trousseau

D137 The Costume Party (issued with two different box covers, same contents)

D138 All My Dollies

D138 My Mamma Doll, 10" doll with crepe paper and patterns. (Doll cries when pressed.)

D139 Bridal Party

D139 Dolls with Williamsburg Colonial Dress, 1940 and 1955

D140 Along Our Road, stand-up houses, four sheets bound together

D140 Dress Our Dolls, dolls and clothes same as D100 My Wardrobe Dolls.

D141 Our Happy Family, 1929, four sheets bound as a book

D143 The Doll Series, four sheets bound together with cover

D144 Let's Build Our Camp, 1930, six sheets bound as a book; log cabin, paper dolls

T147 Little Pet's Play House; a playhouse, furniture, and paper dolls

T148 The Christmas Eve Playhouse

D149 My Dollies Pastime Cutout Sheets, four sheets and bound as a book

T154 Dolly's Dressmaking Shop

D165 Animal Cut Out Sheets, stand-up animals, four sheets bound together

D172 Foreign Friends

D172 Little Americans from Many Lands, 1929

T199 Doll Furniture, eight sheets of furniture in box set

T227 Fitting Funny Figures, seven figures to put together like a puzzle

250 Little Audrey, 36" paper doll

292 Pony Tail (116)

293 Angel Face (117)

294 Ballerina Paper Dolls (115)

300 Shirley Temple, snap on paper doll, 1958

301 Shirley Temple, magnetic doll, 1961

303 Shirley Temple, magnetic doll, same doll as 301 except larger and new clothes

304 Shirley Temple, doll with "real" hair

305 Shirley Temple, 40" lifesize doll

826 Dolls and Clothes to Cut Out and Paint (not pictured)

867 My Dolly's Crayon Book, 1917

876 Three Little Maids From School

876 Dainty Dollies, 1919

877 My Book of Darling Dollies, 1920

886 Smart Fashions, four dolls from 896

887 My Book of Darling Dolls, six dolls from 896

894 Town and Country

895 Modern Dolls a Plenty (896 Dollies à la Mode)

896 Dollies à la Mode

896 Fancy Dress Dolls

963 Dress Me

T1500 Play By Myself Series, 1953, three dolls from D118 School Days (not pictured)

Funny Folks in Fur and Feather, Doggy Dude

Funny Folks in Fur and Feather, Cock-A-Doodle Doo

Funny Folks in Fur and Feather, Mrs. Dickory Dock

Funny Folks in Fur and Feather, Bre'r Rabbit

Funny Folks in Fur and Feather, Cat (name not known)

Funny Folks in Fur and Feather, Duck (name not known)

A very early series of Gabriel paper dolls is called Funny Folks in Fur and Feather. The paper dolls are packaged in small 5½" x 8½" boxes, and there are six in the series. The boxes are not dated. Three of the sets, Doggy Dude, Cock-A-Doodle Doo, and Mrs. Dickery Dock, are shown here. The doll's name is printed on its back, and each outfit and hat is identified on the back with the doll's name ond outfit number. The other dolls in the series are Bre'r Rabbit, a cat, and a duck.

Funny Folks in Fur and Feather, Doggy Dude, $200.00.

Funny Folks in Fur and Feather, Cock-A-Doodle Doo, $200.00.

Funny Folks in Fur and Feather, Mrs. Dickory Dock, $200.00 (with box).

Dolly Dear Series No. 1, Dolly Dear, 1911, $100.00.

Dolly Dear Series No. 2, Dolly Delight, 1911, $100.00.

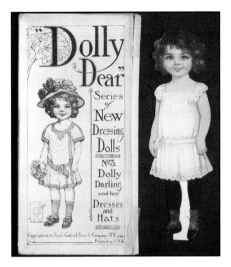 

Dolly Dear Series No. 3, Dolly Darling, 1911, $100.00.

Darling Series No. 10, New Dressing Dolls, Darling Dick, $100.00.

Box for No. 10.

Darling Series No. 12, Darling Dot, $100.00.

Dolly Dimple Series No. 1, Affectionate Alice, $100.00.

All dolls in the Dolly Dimple Series have their numbers printed on their backs. The clothes have the same number plus a letter (A, B, C, or D).

Dolly Dimple Series No. 2, Baby Betty, $100.00.

Dolly Dimple Series No. 3, $100.00.

Dolly Dimple Series No. 4, $100.00. The missing hat on the far right can be seen with D111 Susan.

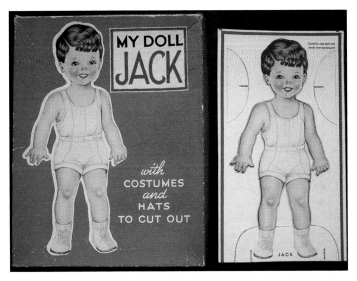

D78 My Doll Jack, $35.00.

D79 My Doll Jill, $35.00.

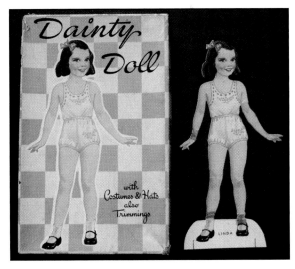

D87 Dainty Doll, $35.00.

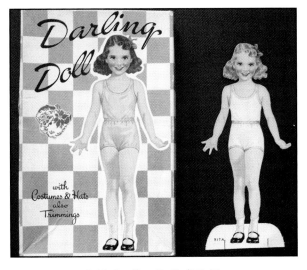

D88 Darling Doll, $35.00.

D90 Betsy McCall, Biggest Paper Doll © 1955, Samuel Gabriel Sons and the McCall Corporation, $60.00.

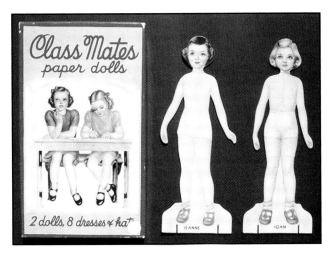

D91 Class Mates, $35.00.

D90 My Dolly Series of New Dressing Dolls, Cousin Kate, $90.00.

D90 My Dolly Series of New Dressing Dolls, Brother Bob, $90.00.

D90 My Dolly Series of New Dressing Dolls, Sister Nan, $90.00.

D91 Young Fashions, $35.00.

D92 Young Moderns, $35.00.

D92 Sweetheart Doll, Elsie, $60.00 (box set).

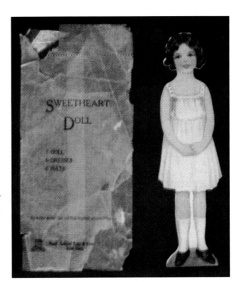

D92 Sweetheart Doll, Helen (glassine envelope set), $45.00. The number D92 has been torn off the bottom right corner of the envelope.

D93 Polly Pert, $35.00.

D94 Suzie Sweet, $35.00.

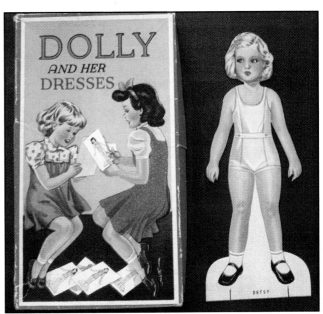

D95 Nellie; D95 Mabel; D96 Louise; $100.00 each, if complete with their boxes and four dresses and hats each. (Louise is missing two dresses.) The dolls, dresses, and hats have the name of the doll on the back. The dresses and hats also have letters A, B, C, or D.

D96 Dolly and Her Dresses, $35.00.

117

D100 My Wardrobe Dolls, $60.00.

D100 School Mates, $60.00. Four sheets and cover, bound as a book.

D100 School Mates, Georgia.

D100 School Mates, Eleanor.

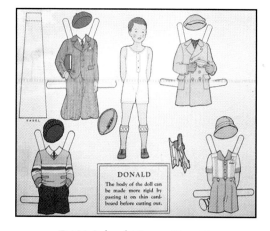

D100 School Mates, Donald.

D100 School Mates, Phyllis.

D100 Dolly Sheets, 1922, $75.00. Four sheets and cover, bound as a book.

D100 inside page of Grace.

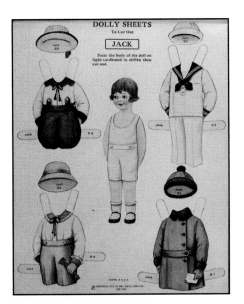

D100 Inside page of Jack.

D100 Inside page of Ruth.

D100 Inside page of Nancy.

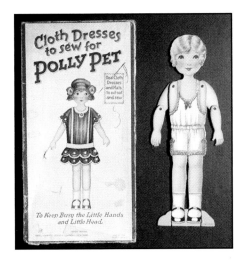

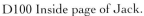

D104 Cloth Dresses to Sew for Polly Pet, $50.00.

D104 Best of Friends, $50.00. (Dolls may vary.)

D105 Play Paper Dolls, $50.00.

D105 Play Paper Dolls and one page of clothes.

D106 Junior Shop, $50.00.

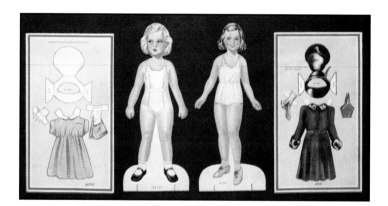

D106 Junior Shop dolls and two outfits.

D107 The Twinnies, $80.00. No date, listed in 1933 catalog.

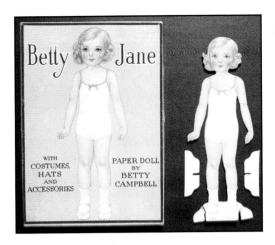

D107 Betty Jane, $35.00.

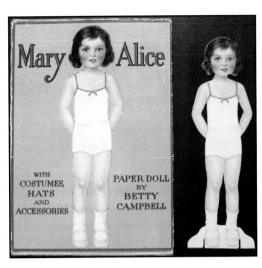

D108 Mary Alice, $35.00.

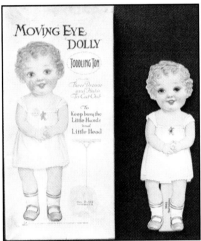

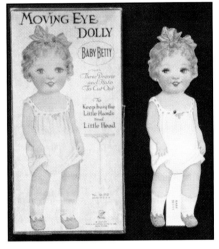

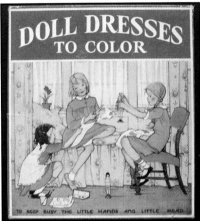

D112 Moving Eye Dolly, Toddling Tom, 1920, $75.00.

D112 Moving Eye Dolly, Baby Betty, 1920, $75.00.

D109 Doll Dresses to Color, $50.00.

D108 Cloth Dresses to Sew for My Twin Dollies, $65.00.

D108 inside contents

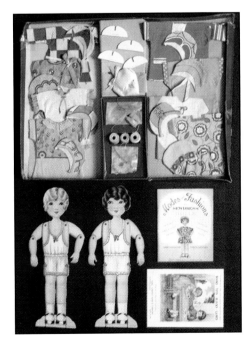

D113 Little Orphan Annie, $150.00.

Samuel Gabriel Sons & Co./Gabriel Industries, Inc.

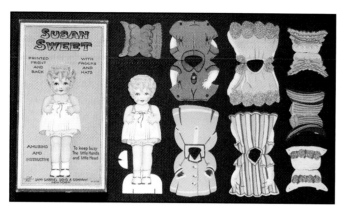

D109 Susan Sweet, $75.00.

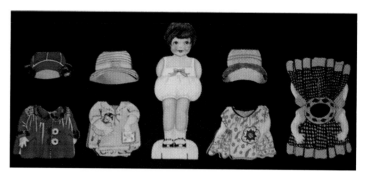

D109 Doris Dainty, $75.00.

D111 Moving Eye Dolly, Susan, $75.00.

D113 The Twinnies, 1921, $85.00.

D115 The Ever-New Doll, $50.00.

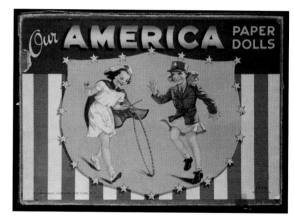

D114 Our America, $60.00.

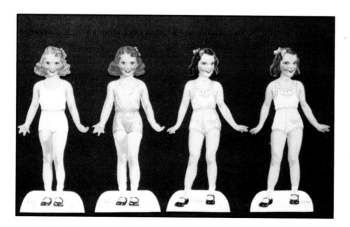

D114 Our America, the four dolls from the set.

D114 My Complete Sew-Dress Box, $65.00 (for picture of the dolls, see D108).

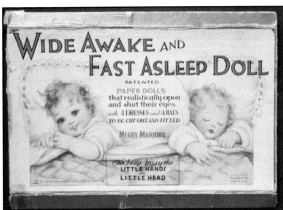

D114 Wide Awake and Fast Asleep Doll, Merry Marjorie, $100.00.

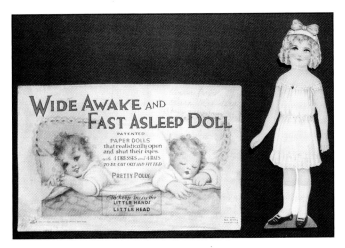

D114 Wide Awake and Fast Asleep Doll, Pretty Polly, $100.00.

D115 Paper Doll Bazaar, $60.00.

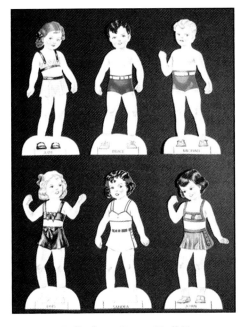

D115 Dolls from Paper Doll Bazaar.

D115 Winnie Winkle and Her Paris Costumes, $200.00. No date, but appeared in 1933 catalog.

D116 Fashion Model, $25.00.

D117 Carol and Her Dresses, $45.00.

D115 Ballerina Dolls, 1956, $35.00.

D116 The Up-to-Date Dollies, $100.00.

D116 Dollies à la Mode, $65.00 box set (six dolls from 896 with this same title).

117 Angel Face, $25.00.

D117 Dollies and Their Wardrobes, $75.00. The box is missing from this set. The dolls' names are Mabel and Nancy, and the names are printed on the back of each doll.

116 Pony Tail, $24.00.

D117 Junior Fashions, $65.00.

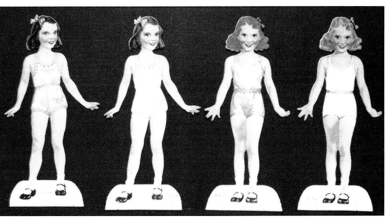

D117 Junior Fashions dolls.

D118 School Days, $50.00.

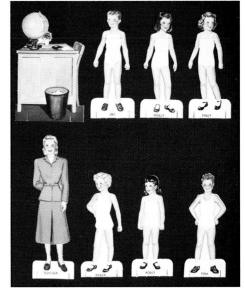

D118 Children and teacher from School Days.

D118 The Dimple Doll Family, $75.00 (includes six American Colortype paper dolls).

D118 Dolly Adorable, $50.00. (Shown in 1933 catalog.)

118 Snap-On Paper Dolls, 1958, $25.00.

D118 Paper Doll Play, $45.00.

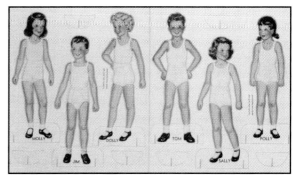

D118 Paper Doll Play, inside contents.

D119 Sew-Easy Doll, $35.00.

D119 Sew-Easy Doll, Dainty Dot, $35.00.

D119 Sew-Easy Doll, $35.00.

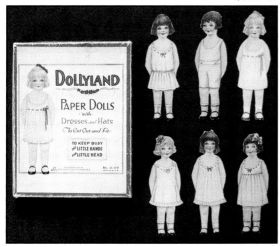

D119 Dollyland, 1920, $90.00.

D119 Dollyland, $90.00. Small box set with six paper dolls in individual envelopes shown here and on page 128.

D119 Dollyland, Merry Marjorie, envelope #1.

D119 Dollyland, Handsome Harold, envelope #2.

D119 Dollyland, Graceful Gertrude, envelope #3.

D119 Dollyland, Sweet Sallie, envelope #4.

D119 Dollyland, Pretty Pauline, envelope #5.

D119 Dollyland, Jolly Jack, envelope #6.

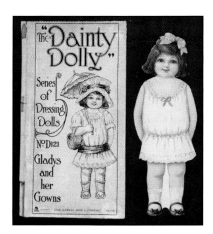

D121 Gladys and Her Gowns, $125.00. Gladys is 14" tall and has "No. 4" printed on her back. Her outfits are numbered on the back: 4A, 4B, 4C, and 4D. She is in the Dainty Dolly Series of Dressing Dolls.

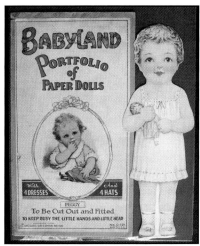

This little boy, the same size as Gladys and with outfits 6A, 6B, 6C, and 6D, has been found without his folder, so his name is not known. $125.00 if complete.

D121 Babyland, Peggy, 1921, $90.00.

D121 Babyland, Bobby, 1921, $90.00.

D121 Babyland, inside contents for Bobby.

D120 Sew-Easy Dolls, $65.00.

D120 box contents.

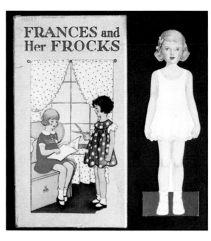

D121 Frances and Her Frocks, $60.00.

D122 Wide Awake and Fast Asleep Doll, Alice, $90.00.

D122 Wide Awake and Fast Asleep Doll, Dorothy, $90.00.

D122 Mother and Daughter Dolls, $40.00.

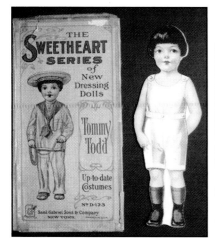

D123 The Sweetheart Series, Tommy Todd, $75.00.

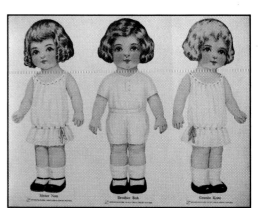

D124 My Dolly Doll Sheets, 1925, $60.00.

D123 Happy Faces, $60.00.

D123 Little Audrey, $50.00.

D126 The Dimple Doll Family, $75.00. (Dolls are from 876 Dainty Dollies and may vary.)

D124 Just from Paris, $60.00.

D125 Just from College, $60.00.

D125 Betty is Going Away to Boarding School, $95.00. The doll and clothes originated from D116 Up-to-Date Dollies.

D127 The Winkle Family, $200.00 if complete.

D127 The Winkle Family.

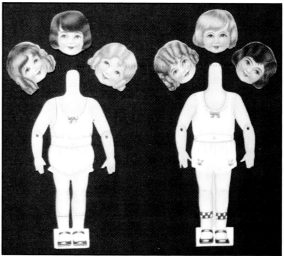

D129 Turn and Turn About Dollies, $80.00.

D126 Dollies in Style, $80.00.

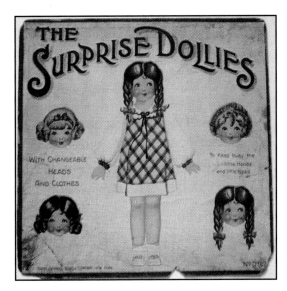 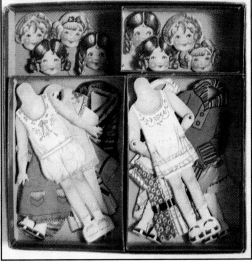

D127 Suprise Dollies and inside contents, $80.00.

D128 Quick Change Dolls, $80.00.

D128 On the Campus, $60.00.

130 Vicki Velcro® Paper Doll, $25.00.

131 Vicki and Valerie Velcro Dolls, $35.00.

D131 Quartet of Dolls (D138 All My Dollies), $60.00.

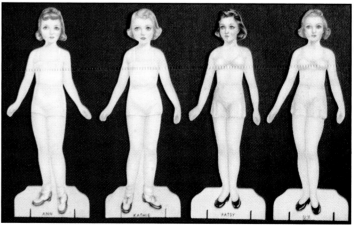

D131 dolls from Quartet of Dolls.

D132 Wedding Party, $65.00.

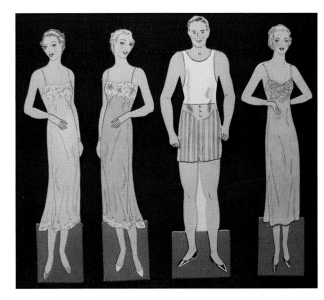

D132 Dolls from Wedding Party.

D133 The Twinnies, $75.00. Some sets have been found to contain the dolls from set D107.

D135 The Debutantes, $90.00.

D135 Sisters, $75.00.

D135 Sisters, inside contents.

D134 Toddler Twins, $65.00.

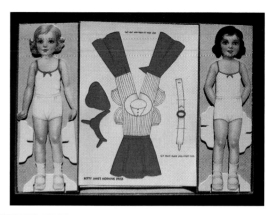

D136 Best of Friends,
$75.00.

D137 The Costume Party, $90.00. Original cover;
shown in 1933 catalog.

D137 The Costume Party, $90.00. Newer cover;
shown in 1940 catalog. Contents the same in both sets.

D137 Costume Party, box contents.

D138 All My Dollies, $75.00.

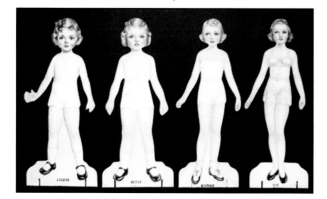

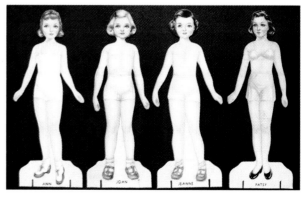

Dolls from D138 All My Dollies.

Dolls from D138 All My Dollies.

D137 The Twins and Their Trousseau, $80.00.

D138 My Mamma Doll, $100.00.

D139 Dolls with Williamsburg Colonial Dress, 1940, $45.00. A reprint of this set was done in 1955; contents were the same.

D139 Bridal Party, $85.00.

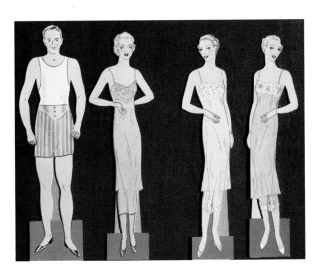

D139 Bridal Party dolls.

D141 Our Happy Family, 1929, $75.00.

D141 Our Happy Family, Jean and Nanny.

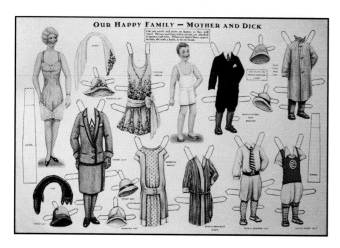

D141 Our Happy Family, Mother and Dick.

D141 Our Happy Family, Father and Chubby.

D144 Let's Build Our Camp, 1930, $75.00.

Page of Paper Dolls from Let's Build Our Camp.

D140 Dress Our Dolls, $65.00.

D143 The Doll Series, Toys and Joys for Girls and Boys, $80.00.

D143 inside page.

D143 inside page.

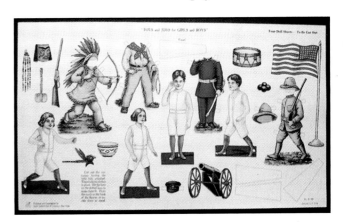

D143 inside page.

D143 inside page.

T147 Little Pet's Play House, $125.00.

D149 My Dollies Pastime Cutout Sheets, 1920, $50.00. The above book contains eight dolls. There are four pages, with two dolls on each. Each doll has two outfits and two hats. The dolls are as follows: Elsie, Helen, Dorothy, and Alice from 876 Dainty Dollies, 1919; Cousin Kate, D90; Sister Nan, D90; Baby Betty, D112; and Toddling Tom, D112.

T147 Little Pet's Play House, outside of house.

T147 Little Pet's Play House, inside of house.

T148 The Christmas Eve Play House, $125.00, partial cut set, some toys not shown.

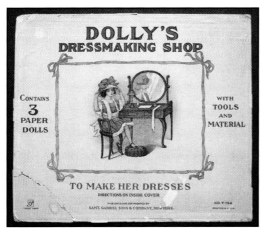

T154 Dolly's Dressmaking Shop; dolls of Nellie and Mabel are here, doll of Louise is missing. $75.00 if complete.

D172 Little Americans from Many Lands, 1929, $50.00. Cover on left, Franz from Switzerland on right. This is the book edition. The set can also be found in a box edition.

D172 Foreign Friends, $50.00 box set. Contents same as D172 Little Americans from Many Lands.

D172 Selma from Sweden on left , Sigrid from Norway in middle, Sonia from Russia on right.

D172 Keith from Scotland on left and Cecile from France on right.

D172 Mina and Hendrick from Holland.

D172 Carlotta from Germany.

Matsue from Japan.

D172 Angelo from Italy.

D172 Manuel from Mexico.

D172 Eileen from Ireland.

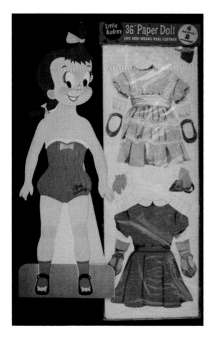

250 Little Audrey, $45.00. ©Harvey Famous Cartoons, no date.

292 Pony Tail, $20.00.

293 Angel Face, $20.00.

294 Ballerina Paper dolls, $20.00.

300 Shirley Temple, 1958, $35.00.

301 Shirley Temple, 1961, $50.00.

303 Shirley Temple, no date, $60.00.

304 Shirley Temple, $75.00.

305 Shirley Temple, $85.00.

867 My Dolly's Crayon Book and inside pages, 1917, $60.00.

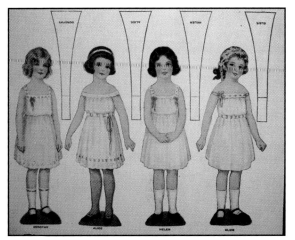

876 Dainty Dollies, 1919, $75.00. The dolls, left to right, are Alice, Helen, Dorothy, and Elsie.

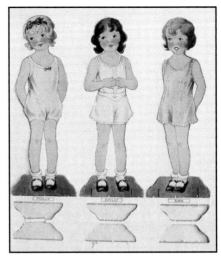

876 Three Little Maids from School, $80.00.

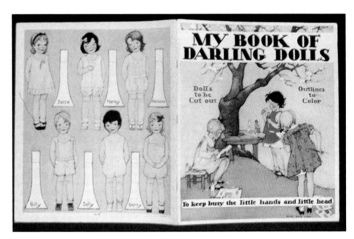

877 My Book of Darling Dollies, 1920, $75.00.

887 My Book of Darling Dolls, $65.00. No date, but listed in 1933 catalog.

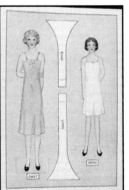
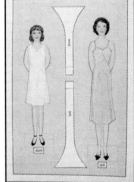

894 Town and Country, $90.00.

894 Town and Country, inside front and back covers.

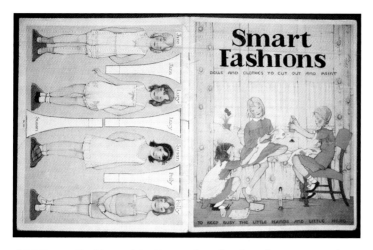

886 Smart Fashions, $65.00. No date, but listed in 1933 catalog.

895 Modern Dolls a Plenty. This book has the same dolls as 896 shown below. No date, but listed in the 1933 catalog, $90.00.

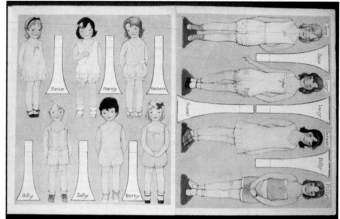

896 Dollies à la Mode, $90.00.

963 Dress Me Book, $60.00.

896 Fancy Dress Dolls, $75.00.

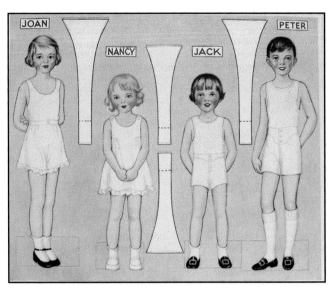

896 Fancy Dress Dolls, inside front cover.

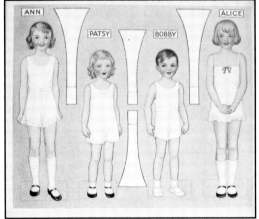

896 Fancy Dress Dolls, inside back cover.

Dolly Delight, Ruth, 1920, $35.00.

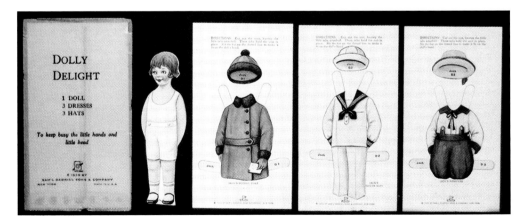

Dolly Delight, Jack, $35.00.

C.R. Gibson Company

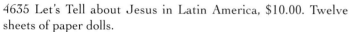

4635 Let's Tell about Jesus in Latin America, $10.00. Twelve sheets of paper dolls.

4936 Bible Think and Do, book 1, $10.00.

The following two books are not pictured:

4634 Let's Tell Others about Jesus
4939 Bible Think and Do, book 2 (stand-ups, no paper dolls)

Goldsmith Publishing Co.

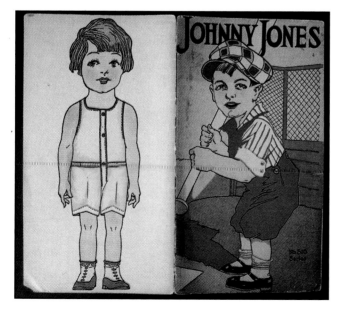

516 Johnny Jones, 1922, $30.00.

516 Daisy Dolly, 1922, $30.00.

516 Pansy Prattle, 1922, $30.00.

2005 Daisy Dolly, 1930, $30.00.

2005 Johnny Jones, 1930, $30.00.

2005 Billy Blue, 1930, $30.00.

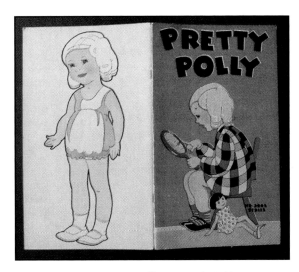

2005 Pretty Polly, 1930, $30.00.

Charles E. Graham and Company

This company was located in both Newark, New Jersey, and in New York. Charles E. Graham and Company evolved from the Graham and Matlack Co., which produced children's books in the early 1900s.

02 Teeny Weeny Dollies Series, Pretty Dollies (two dolls from 0225 Snuggly and one doll from 0225 Cuddly)
02 Teeny Weeny Dollies Series, Beauty Dollies (two dolls from 0225 Cuddly)
02 Teeny Weeny Dollies Series, Cutey Dollies (two dolls from 0225 Cuddly and 0225 Snuggly)
02 Teeny Weeny Dollies Series, Dearie Dollies. This book has the same covers as Snuggly Dolls 0225, but is a much smaller book.
0209-B Busy Little Fingers, box set with four books. Only one book is a paper doll book, 0214 Tiny Dolls.
0212 Dearie Dolls (four dolls from 0225 Snuggly)
0212 Lovey Dolls (one doll from 0225 Snuggly, three dolls from 0225 Cuddly)
0214 Tiny Dolls. (Dolls on cover from 0225 Cuddly; inside pages are similar to paper dolls in *Little Folks Magazine* in the 1920s.)
0214 Dimple Dolls. (Dolls on cover from 0225 Snuggly; inside pages are similar to paper dolls in *Little Folks Magazine* in the 1920s.)
0219 Kiddie-Kolored Kut-Outs, box set with stand-up dolls, dollhouse, and farm
0220 Cutting Things Out, box set with paper dolls (not pictured)
0220 Peek A Boo Tiny Dolls to Dress (12 dolls from 0225 Cuddly and 0225 Snuggly, reduced in size)
0221 Three Bears Kut-Outs and Here is Goldilocks, box set with stand-up figures
0221 Tiny Twinkle, Tubby Twinkle
0222 Kozy-Korner Kottage (includes house, furniture, and dolls; no outfits)
0223 Dimple Dressing Dollies (12 dolls from 0225 Cuddly and 0225 Snuggly)
0223 Snuggly Dolls with Dresses (not pictured, see 0225)
0223 Cuddly Dolls with Dresses (0225)
0224 The Doll's House to Color and Cut-Out (includes house, furniture and dolls; no outfits)
0224 Trit and Trot, Dolls to Dress. (For picture of the dolls, see 0238 Bubble Dressing Dolls.) Trit & Trot do not have movable eyes like the Bubble Dolls have.
0225 Cuddly Dolls with Dresses
0225 Snuggly Dolls with Dresses
0227 The Pitty Pats (dolls same as 0221)
0228 Tippy Toes (0229)
0229 Curly Locks
0237 Lula-Bye-Bye Doll to Dress
0238 Bubble Dressing Dolls
0239 Beauty Dolls to Dress
0239X Beauty Dolls with Moving Eyes (0239)
0242 Scissor's Play Paper Dolls (Graham & Matlack Co; includes paper dolls from the Lion Coffee series of paper dolls)
0243 Scissor's Play Mother Goose (Graham & Matlack Co; includes paper dolls from the Lion Coffee series of paper dolls)
801 Dolly's Cottage (includes house, furniture, and dolls; no outfits)
0902 Teeny Weeny Dolls. This is a box set with four small paper doll books (like the 02 series), but these books all have the number 0902.

Paper Dollies to Cut Out (Graham & Matlack Co. Paper Dolls from Lion Coffee)
Scissors Play Paper Dolls Mother Goose Sets Nos. 1, 2, and 3 in envelopes (Graham & Matlack Co. Paper Dolls from Lion Coffee)

02 Teeny Weeny Beauty Dollies, $20.00. Front and back cover.

02 Teeny Weeny Beauty Dollies, inside pages.

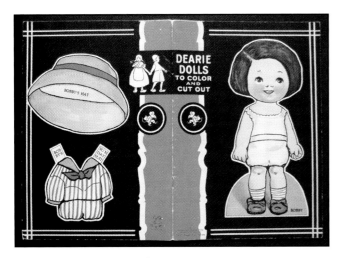

0212 Dearie Dolls, $50.00. Front and back cover.

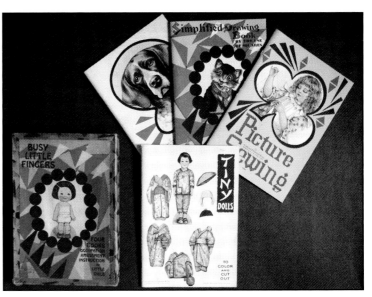

0209 Busy Little Fingers (box with one book of paper dolls), $50.00.

0212 Lovey Dolls, $50.00.

0214 Dimple Dolls, $30.00.

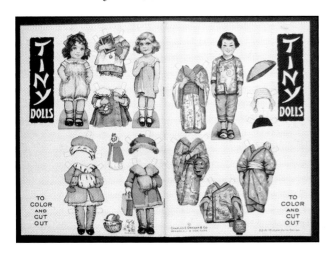

0214 Tiny Dolls, $30.00.

0221 Tubby Twinkle and Tiny Twinkle, $75.00. (Tiny is on the front cover and Tubby is on the back.)

151

0220 Peek-A-Boo and inside pages, $25.00.

0223 Cuddly Dolls, $65.00. (This is a reprint of 0225 with new covers; inside contents the same.)

0223 Dimple Dressing Dollies, $65.00 (contains 12 dolls from the 0225 books).

0225 Snuggly Dolls, $75.00. Dolls are Peggy, Kate, Bobby, Dorothy, and Amanda.

0225 Cuddly Dolls, $75.00.

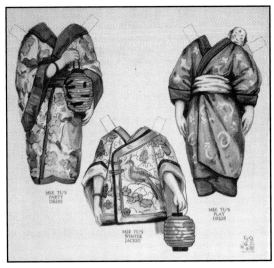

0225 Cuddly Dolls, back cover.

0225 Cuddly Dolls, Jack.

0225 Cuddly Dolls, Mary Jane and Ida May.

0225 Cuddly Dolls, Billy, Betty, and Anne.

0227 The Pitty Pats, $60.00.

0228 Tippy Toes, $75.00.

0229 Curly Locks, $85.00. The girl paper
doll and her outfits are identical to a girl
doll and her outfits in a book called Dearie
Dolls, published by M. T. Sheahan in 1915.

0237 Lula-Bye-Bye, $75.00.

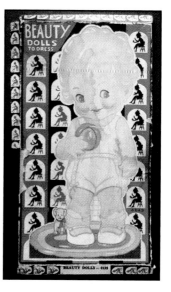

0239 Beauty Dolls to Dress, $85.00.

0238 Bubble Dressing Dolls, $75.00.

0243 Scissor's Play Mother Goose and one inside page, $35.00.

0902 Teeny Weeny Dolls, $75.00. Box set that includes small paper doll books like the 02 books, but these are numbered 0902. The two books shown are Teeny Weeny Dearie Dollies and Teeny Weeny Cutey Dollies.

C1001 Lil' Pearl, 1940, $100.00.

C1002 American Family, 1940, $50.00.

C1003 Nurse and Twins, 1940, $60.00.

C1004 Six Playtime Dolls, 1940, $40.00.

C1010 Five Flying Americans, 1940, $60.00.

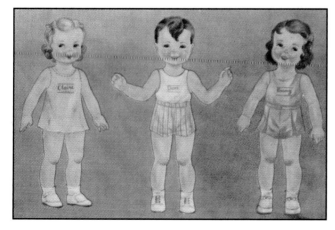

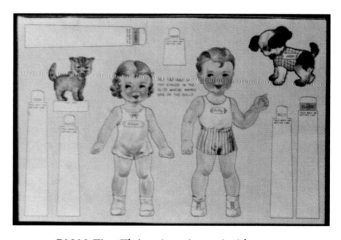

C1010 Five Flying Americans.

C1010 Five Flying Americans, inside cover.

C1015 Super Market, 1940, $50.00.

C1005 Mother and Daughter, 1940, $50.00.

C1011 Shipmates, 1940, $60.00.

 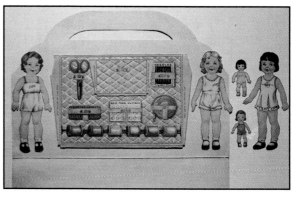

C1018 My Paper Doll's Sewing Kit, 1940, $60.00.

N2009 Suzie Sweet, 1940, $40.00.

N2010 The Doll's Birthday Party, 1940, $40.00.

Other paper doll books (pictures not available):

C1006 Abigail and Butch, 1940
C1009 The Old Lady in a Shoe, 1940

Hamming Publishing Company

The Dolls That *You* Love, 1910, $100.00. Original copyright by L. W. Walter Co. in 1910. The dolls are the same as those in Mother's Darlings and Nurse Marie.

Mother's Darlings and Nurse Marie, 1910, $80.00.

Hart Publishing Company

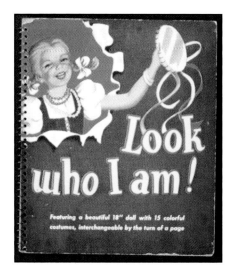

Look Who I Am! 1952, $25.00. 18" doll, spiral. bound book, costumes change as pages in book are turned.

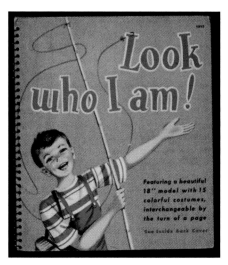

1017 Look Who I Am! $25.00.

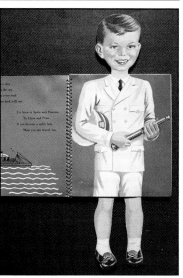

Harter Publishing Company

H-100 Rag Doll Sue, 1931, $85.00.

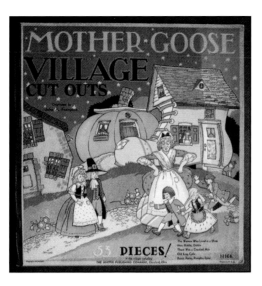

H-164 Mother Goose
Village, 1935, $30.00.

H-015 Historic Hattie, 1931, $125.00.

H-169 This is the House That Jack Built, 1935, $85.00. Front cover and inside page with paper dolls.

E. I. Horsman Company

New Puss in Boots Paper Doll, $95.00.

Teddy Bear Paper Doll. (Not pictured; see Selchow & Righter Co., page 279.)

House of Dolls

Magic Doll, $25.00.

House of Giftcraft

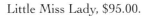
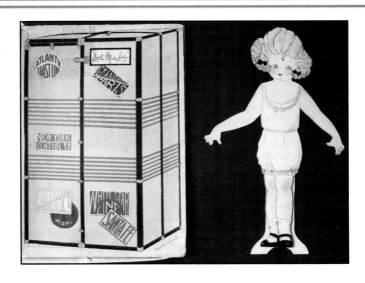

Little Miss Lady, $95.00.

Howell, Soskin Publishing, Inc.

The Martha Washington Doll Book, 1945, $40.00. A reprint of this book was published in 1976 by Century House Americana Publishers.

Nancy and Jane, 1945, $25.00.

Hubbell-Leavens Co., Inc.

Tommy Tom, $65.00.

Polly Dolly, $65.00.

Dolly Dimple (not pictured; see Stecher Lithographic Co.)
Billy Boy (not pictured; see Stecher Lithographic Co.)

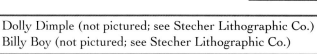

162

International Paper Goods

60 Fun Farm Frolics, 1932, $60.00.

60 Fun Farm Frolics dolls.

George W. Jacobs and Company

Dorothy Dimple and Her Friends, Paper Dolls of Many Nations, © 1909 Bodley Press Associates, Springfield, Massachusetts. Six sheets in envelope.

Paper Dolls of The World, ©1909 Bodley Press Associates, Springfield, Massachusetts. Six sheets in envelope.

Polly Pitcher and Her Playmates, Series One, 1917

Polly Pitcher and Her Playmates, Series Two, 1918

The Lettie Lane Paper Family, 1909 (originally published in *Ladies' Home Journal*)

    First Series, six sheets in a doll house folder

    Second Series, six sheets in a doll house folder

    Third Series, six sheets in a doll house folder

Betty Bonnet and Her Friends (originally in *Ladies' Home Journal*)

    First Series, six sheets in folder

    Second Series, six sheets in folder

    Third Series, six sheets in folder

Kitty Clover (originally published in *Ladies' Home Journal* as Betty Bonnet series; not pictured)

    First Series, six sheets in folder

    Second Series, six sheets in folder

Cinderella, 1918

Polly Ann, six sheets in envelope

Fairy Folk, six sheets in envelope

Bobby Bear, six sheets in envelope (not pictured)

Jack-O'-Lantern, six sheets in envelope

Dorothy Dimple and Her Friends, 1919, $100.00 for complete set.

Dorothy.

Sister Sarah.

Dorothy's Japanese Doll.

Clown friend Toby.

Sister Susan.

Neighbor Alice.

Paper Dolls of the World, 1909,
$80.00 for the complete set.

Abdul (Turkish) and Pedro
(Spanish).

Selim (Egyptian).

Dughha-Das (Indian).

Chief Black Cloud (American
Indian).

Katrinka (Dutch).

Aileen (Irish) and MacGre-
gor (Scottish).

The Lettie Lane Paper Family, Series 2 (there were three different series, each with a house folder), 1909, $100.00.

The Lettie Lane Paper Family, inside pages (not all pages shown).

Polly Pitcher and Her Playmates, Series 1, 1917, $60.00.

Polly Pitcher and Her Playmates, Series 2, 1918, $60.00. The folder design is the same as that for Series 1.

Cinderella, 1918 (cut set). $100.00 for complete, uncut set.

Betty Bonnet, Her Family and Friends, second series folder. $100.00 for complete set.

Betty Bonnet third series folder. $100.00 for complete set.

Lettie Lane third series folder (different from third series with house folder). $100.00 for complete set.

Kitty Clover first series folder. $100.00 for complete set.

Polly Ann Cut-Out Paper Dolls. $100.00 for complete set of six sheets and envelope.

Jack-O'-Lantern Cut-Out Paper Dolls. $100.00 for complete set of six sheets and envelope.

Fairy Folk, Cut-Out Paper Dolls. $100.00 for complete set of six sheets and envelope.

The following pictures are the paper doll sheets that belong in the envelopes. Many of the sheets were printed in the *Philadelphia Ledger*, and the Stoll and Edwards Co. also published them.

Jack-O'-Lantern, $20.00.

Little Red Riding Hood, $20.00.

Hey Diddle, Diddle, the Cat & the Fiddle, $20.00.

Ding Dong Bell — Pussy's in the Well, $20.00.

Little Bo Peep, $20.00.

The Ugly Duckling, $20.00.

The Three Bears and Goldilocks, $20.00.

Dear Little, Funny Little, Old Fashioned Polly Ann, $20.00.

A Little French Orphan that Wants a Mother, $20.00.

Betty's School, $20.00.

Flossie's Thanksgiving Party, $20.00.

Tommy Goes to the Circus, $20.00.

Jolly Time, a Little Western Bronco Buster, $20.00.

The Country Mice Are a Very Thrifty Family, $20.00.

The Toyville Army Celebrates the Fourth, $20.00.

A Fire in Dollville, $20.00.

The following are other known paper dolls in the series (pictures not available):

Bobby Bear Has a Birthday Party
Robinson Crusoe
Five Little Piggies
Billy and Kitty Kat Spend A Day at the Seashore
The Little Flower Fairy and Her Flower Clothes
Puss in Boots

The paper dolls in these sets are cardboard with vinyl heads. The clothes are fabric and peel on and off.

Not pictured:

0130 Li'L Holly, 1973
0131 American Man, 1973

2000 Holly, 1971, $15.00.

2001 Ivy, 1971, $15.00.

2002 Glenn, 1971, $15.00.

4000 Marc & Jerie's Wedding Party, $15.00.

4001 Rod & Liza Jet Away, $15.00.

4002 Greg & Noelle on Campus, $15.00.

Jaymar Specialty Co./Great Lakes Press

The Jaymar Specialty Company was started in 1925 by Jay Jaymar. He began by manufacturing doll clothes that were sold in five-and-ten-cent stores.

The Great Lakes Press was established in 1936 and began its long association with Jaymar at the time Jaymar was producing doll clothes. Great Lakes Press made cardboard hangers for Jaymar to hang the doll clothes on. When Jaymar dropped the doll clothes phase of its business, it began manufacturing toy pianos.

Jaymar has been the national distributor for Great Lakes Press since 1939. At that time, Great Lakes formed a division of children's games and jigsaw puzzles, which later included paper doll box sets.

The following is a list of the known paper doll sets by Jaymar:

905 Four Snap-in-Place Stand-Up Dolls
907 Mother and Daughter (not pictured)
909 Wedding Party
913 Jet Airline Stewardess (dolls same as #970)
915 Debby Dolls and Dollies
970 Jet Airline Stewardess
971 Caroline
972 Four Pre-teen Debby Dolls
973 Jackie
974 Mother and Daughter
975 Beautiful Bride
978 Honeybun, Big Doll for Little Girls
980 Debby Dolls
982 Bride and Groom
984 Janie and Emmy
986 2 Debby Dolls, "Complete with 'Mink Fur' material"
988 Four Bridal Party Stand-Up Dolls (dolls same as #909)
992 Debby Dolls and Dollies
994 Winky Winnie
996 Betsey Bates Debby Dolls
1976 Tweedie Goes to the Beauty Parlor
1986 4 Debby Dolls, "Complete with 'Mink Fur' material"

Li'l Abner and Daisy Mae Dogpatch Constuction Set stand-ups

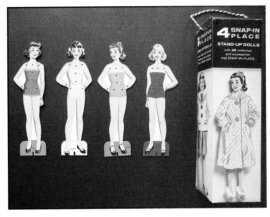

905   4 Snap-in-Place Stand-Up Dolls, $30.00.

909 Wedding Party, $35.00.

913 Paper Dolls, Jet Airline Stewardess, $35.00.

915 Debby Dolls and Dollies, $30.00.

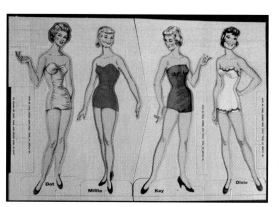

970 Jet Airline Stewardess Paper Dolls, $35.00.

970 Jet Airline Stewardess dolls.

975 Beautiful Bride, $35.00.

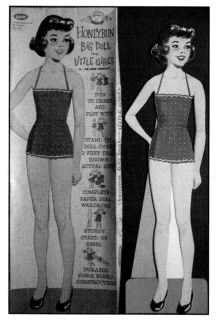

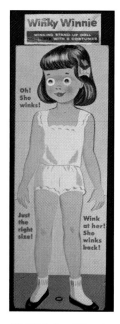

978 Honeybun, Big Doll for Little Girls, $30.00.

994 Winky Winnie, $25.00.

971 Caroline, $30.00.

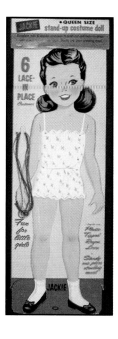

972 4 Pre-teen Debby Dolls, $30.00. (The dolls are the same as 905.)

973 Jackie, $25.00.

974 Mother and Daughter, $30.00.

982 Bride and Groom, $35.00.

984 Janie and Emmy, $30.00.

982 Bride and Groom dolls.

988 4 Bridal Party Stand-Up Dolls, $35.00.

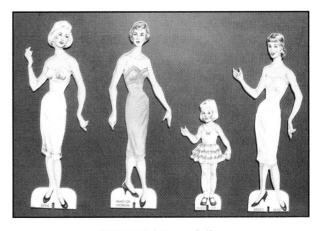

988 Bridal Party dolls.

992 Debby Dolls and Dollies, $30.00.

980 Debby Dolls, $30.00.

996 Betsey Bates Debby Dolls, $30.00.

986 2 Debby Dolls, "Complete with 'Mink Fur' material," $35.00. Set included either 16 or 23 outfits.

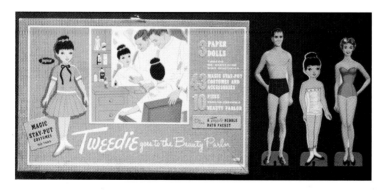

1976 Tweedie Goes to the Beauty Parlor, $65.00.

1986 4 Stand-Up Debby Dolls, "Complete with 'Mink Fur' material," $40.00.

Jenson Publishing Co.

This company was located in Nashville, Tennessee.

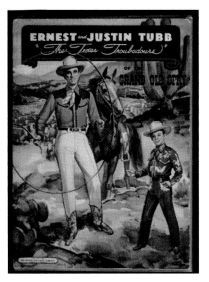 

Ernest and Justin Tubb, 1946, $60.00.

Kaufmann and Strauss

No. 10 Sister Mary, 1915, $75.00.

No. 11 Sister Ruth, 1915, $75.00 if complete.

No. 12 Sister Helen, 1915, $75.00.

No. 13 Brother Jack, 1915, $75.00.

Kotton Kutie, boy, 28"
tall, 1970, $15.00.

Kotton Kutie, girl, 28"
tall, 1970, $15.00.

Kotton Kutie, bear, 28"
tall, 1970, $15.00.

Kotton Kutie sets with smaller 11" dolls (Kathy and Kris) also have the copyright of 1970. Along with Kathy is a small 4¾" doll of Kitty. All outfits are made of cloth. These same sets have also been found with a 1966 copyright by M. H. Troester.

Kingston Products Corporation

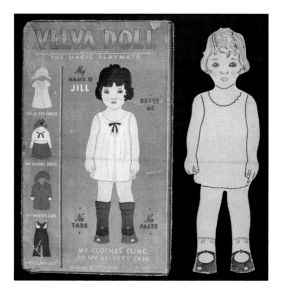

D21 Velva Doll, My Name Is Jill, 1932,
$30.00. Large 17" doll known as "Big Jill."

D20 Velva Doll, My name Is Jill, 1932, 13"
tall, $30.00. Another version of the doll has
been found, so dolls can vary.

D25 Velva Baby and Doll, 1932, $45.00.

VD202 Velva Craft and Velva Doll, 1932. The doll is 13" tall.

D23 Velva Doll, Baby, 1932 (not pictured)

Kits, Incorporated

1050 Lacey Daisy (clothes lace on the doll), 1949, $20.00.

1090 Lacey Dolls Kit (Jan and Lyn), 1954, $20.00.

The Lamp Studio

The Lynda-Lou Doll, $25.00. Costumes snap on and are of fabric.

Landoll Publishing Company

2129 Dollhouse Cut Outs (see Stephens Pub. Co.)
2229 Pajama Party (see Stephens Pub. Co.)
122 Wardrobe Department, 1997
123 Granny's Attic, 1997

Batman and Robin, 1997

E.M. Leavens Company, Inc.

Dolly Dimple, $65.00.

Billy Boy, $65.00.

Billy Boy outfits.

Other known sets (not pictured):

Tommy Tom (see Hubbell-Leavens Co.)
Polly Dolly (see Hubbell-Leavens Co.)

M. H. Leavis

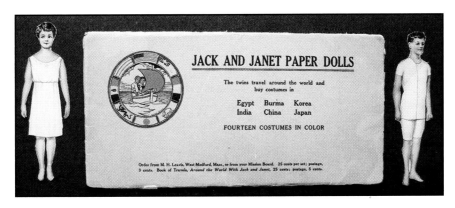

Jack and Janet Paper Dolls, $20.00.

Jack and Janet, twins, travel around the world and buy costumes in Egypt, Burma, Korea, India, China, and Japan. Fourteen costumes in color.

Lido Toy Co.

The Lido Toy Company was well-known and made toy plastic cars, planes, boats, trucks, etc. It also made toy soldiers, horses, and knights. In 1952, it had a Captain Video line of toys.

1092 Glamour Twins, $12.00. Dolls and clothes are of hard plastic. The clothes fit over the dolls and snap in place.

1090 Dolly's Wardrobe (picture not available)

Reuben H. Lilja and Company, Inc.

Mr. Reuben H. Lilja founded his company in 1940. Prior to this, he had worked for Rand McNally and Company in its children's books trade department.

900 Miss America, 1941
901 American Beauties, 1942
902 Miss Hollywood, 1942
903 Jaunty Juniors, 1946
904 Miss Silver Screen, 1946
905 Dress-up, 1947. (Reprint of 901; dolls are redrawn.)
906 Movieland, 1947. (The four dolls are taken from 900, 901, and 902. The dolls are all redrawn.)
907 Sapphire, Queen of the Night Clubs
908 Madame Hattie (reprint of 907 using the two dolls from the back cover)
909 Little Nurse
910 Little Doctor
911 Costume Party
912 Mary Ann Goes to Mexico
913 Country Weekend with Kathy and Jill (also published by Childrens Press)
914 Mother and Daughter (also published by Childrens Press)
915 Around the World with Bob and Barbara (also published by Childrens Press)
916 Patsy (also published by Childrens Press)
917 American Beauties (reprint of 901 using the two dolls from the back cover)
918 Paper Dolls (reprint of 901 using the two dolls from the front cover)
919 Merry Mermaids (reprint of 903 dolls #2 and #4; redrawn)
920 Pretty Penny and Her Pal (reprint of 903 dolls #1 and #3; redrawn)
921 Big Sister (not pictured; reprint of 914)
922 We Three. (The inside pages of this book are from 916.)
923 TV Glamour Girls (not pictured; reprint of 904)
924 Outdoor Fun (reprint of 913, redrawn dolls from front cover)
925 Teen-Age Travel Fun (reprint of 915, redrawn dolls from front cover)
937 Costume Party (not pictured; see 911)
519 Merry Mermaids (not pictured; see 919)
520 Pretty Penny and Her Pal (not pictured; see 920)
620 Pretty Penny and Her Pal (not pictured; see 920)
820 Pretty Penny and Her Pal (not pictured; see 920)

900 Miss America, 1941, $75.00. There are two editions, one with eight pages, the other with six pages. Covers are the same.

901 American Beauties, 1942, $45.00.

902 Miss Hollywood, 1942, $75.00.

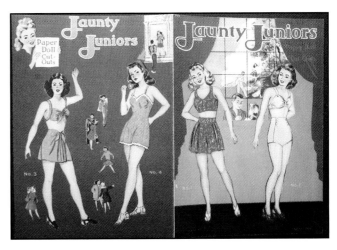

903 Jaunty Juniors, 1946, $45.00. There are two editions of the 903 Jaunty Juniors book. One has six pages of outfits, the other only four. Both have identical covers.

904 Miss Silver Screen, 1946, $75.00. There are two editions of the 904 Miss Silver Screen book. One has six pages of outfits, the other only four. Both have identical covers.

905 Dress-up, 1947, $25.00.

906 Movieland, 1947, $35.00.

907 Sapphire, Queen of the Night Clubs, $100.00.

908 Madame Hattie, $45.00.

909 Little Nurse, circa 1949, $20.00.

910 Little Doctor, circa 1949, $20.00.

911 Costume Party, $20.00.

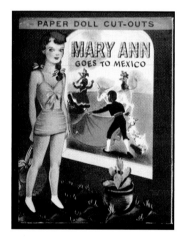

912 Mary Ann Goes to Mexico, $20.00.

913 Country Weekend with Kathy and Jill, circa 1950, $20.00.

914 Mother and Daughter, circa 1950, $20.00.

915 Around the World with Bob and Barbara, $20.00.

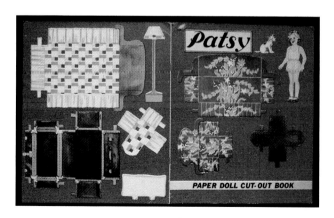

916 Patsy, $20.00.

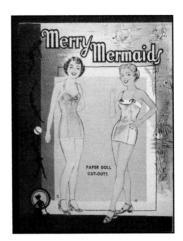

917 American Beauties, circa 1951, $20.00. Front and back covers are alike.

918 Paper Dolls, $20.00. Front and back covers are alike.

919 Merry Mermaids, $20.00.

920 Pretty Penny and her Pal, $18.00.

922 We Three, $18.00.

924 Outdoor Fun, $12.00.

925 Teen-Age Travel Fun, $12.00.

Lisbeth Whiting

189 I'm Debra Dee the Bride, 1963, $25.00.

Another set that may be by the same company is also shown here. The bride, third from left, is named Peaches Plumtree.

Lodewick Creations

This company was based in New York.

Photo Doll, $25.00.

Londy Card Corporation

The Londy Card Corporation was located in Muncie, Indiana. One of the things it was known for was printed shirt cardboard used by laundries and dry cleaners. In 1931, it printed a series of cardboard toy furniture to be put together (refrigerator, breakfast nook, etc.). These cardboard sheets had the number *4* preceding a letter, e.g., 4-J, 4-K, etc. In 1932, the company produced a series of paper dolls. These cardboard sheets had the number *5* preceding a letter. The series consisted of Betty Marie and other members of her family. Other series that are known to exist are an automobile series (with the number *9*) and a train series (with the number *10*).

5F Betty Marie, 1932, $15.00.

5J Big Sister, 1932, $15.00.

5H Little Brother, 1932, $15.00.

9A Automobile, 1932, $15.00.

Other Londy sets are known but not pictured:

5G Betty Marie's Little Sister, 1932
5L Mother, 1932

184

M. S. Publishing Co.

This was a New York company.

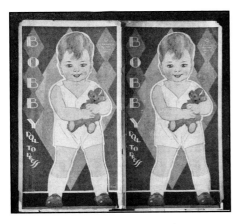

900 Bobby Doll to Dress, $40.00.

901 Miss America Dolls to Paint, Cut Out and Dress, $40.00.

Paper Dolls to Paint and Cut-Out, 1924, $40.00.

Paper Dolls to Paint and Cut-Out, inside page.

Paper Dolls to Paint and Cut-Out, inside page.

Paper Dolls to Paint and Cut-Out, inside page.

Paper Dolls to Paint and Cut-Out, inside page.

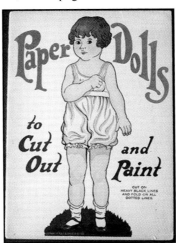

Paper Dolls to Cut Out and paint, 1926, $40.00.

450 Walkie Doll Book, $25.00.

185

Magic Wand Corporation

The Magic Wand Corporation was established in 1960. The name "Craftmaster" appears on some sets.

100 Introducing Wendy and Her Mommy (produced in two editions with different box covers)
101 My Name is Cindy
104 Judy (produced in two editions with different box covers)
105 Butch
106 Bride and Groom
107 Jackie and Caroline. (Produced in two editions. The dolls wear either white or blue and white striped bathing suits.)
108 Sweet Sue
109 Caroline
110 Fireball XL5, Steve and Venus
111 Tressy, 1964 (produced in two editions with different box covers)
112 Tiny Tears with Rock-A-Bye Cradle
114 Bewitched, 1965
115 Tabatha
116 Dolls of the Four Seasons, 1967
117 Granny, 1967
118 Super Twins, 1967
119 Mimi-Mods, 1968
120 Teeny Minis, 1968
121 Black is Beautiful, 1969
201 3 High Fashion Models
204 The First Lady, 1963
1010 Magic Princess, 1964
1011 Paint Me Pretty, 1969
17401 Paper Dolls, 1970 (not pictured)
17402 Paper Dolls, 1970 (not pictured)
17403 Paper Dolls, 1970
90010 Bride and Groom, 1970

Dress Dawn and Her Friends (stock number and picture not available)

100 Magic Wand Paper Dolls, Wendy and Her Mommy, $30.00.

100 Wendy and Mommy (different box cover), $30.00.

101 My Name is Cindy, $25.00.

104 Judy, $30.00.

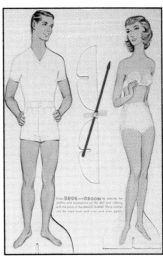

104 Judy (box cover different and doll slightly different from the set on preceding page), $30.00.

106 Bride and Groom, $30.00.

105 Butch, $30.00.

108 Sweet Sue, $25.00.

109 Caroline, $40.00.

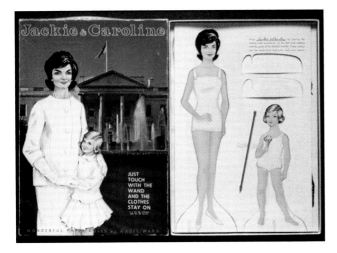

107 Jackie and Caroline, $50.00.

107 Jackie & Caroline (box cover different, and dolls wearing striped swimsuits), $50.00.

110 Fireball XL5, $100.00.

111 Tressy, 1964, $35.00.

111 Tressy (box cover new, doll changed slightly), $35.00.

112 Tiny Tears, $30.00.

114 Bewitched, $65.00.

115 Tabatha, $65.00.

116 Dolls of the Four Seasons, 1967, $12.00.

117 Granny, 1967, $30.00.

118 Super Twins, 1967, $15.00.

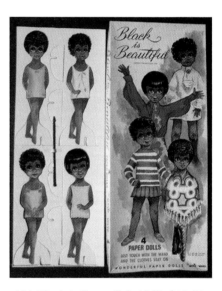

121 Black is Beautiful, 1969, $15.00.

119 Mini-Mods, 1968, $12.00.

120 Teeny Minis, 1968, $12.00.

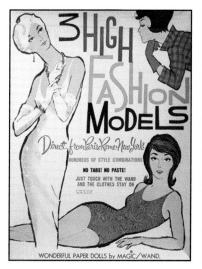

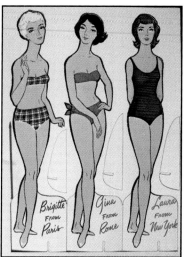

201 3 High Fashion Models, $30.00.

204 The First Lady, 1963, $75.00.

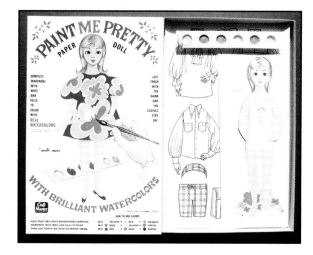

1010 Magic Princess, 1964, $30.00.

1011 Paint Me Pretty, 1969, $30.00.

17403 Paper Dolls, 1970, $12.00.

90010 Bride and Groom, 1970, $30.00.

McLoughlin Brothers

John McLoughlin established his first print shop in 1828 and began publishing children's books shortly afterward. When his two sons, John and Edmund, took over the firm in the late 1840s, the company became known as McLoughlin Bros. The company developed into the foremost producer of children's books in the country. The firm continued to publish until 1920, when it was sold to the Milton Bradley Company. It continued as a division of Milton Bradley until 1944.

McLoughlin Bros. produced paper dolls in abundance, starting in the late 1850s. Its paper dolls that were produced from the turn of the century to 1944 are covered here.

235½ Ideal Doll Book, 1907

236 The New Model Book of Dolls, 1904

239 Our Dollies Model Book, 1909

244 The Dolls' House Model Book (stand-ups; not pictured)

480 Dolls to Cut Out and Dress, 1933 (not pictured)

509 The Playhouse Cut Out Story Book, 1932 (cut/paste book; not pictured)

0510 Dolly and Her Dresses, box (1914 catalog)

515 Play time Circus, 1932 (stand-ups; not pictured)

516 Farm Yard Friends, 1932 (stand-ups; not pictured)

517 The Three Bears Home, 1933 (stand-ups)

521 Fun with Scissors, Crayon, Brush and Pencil (not pictured; no paper dolls)

523 Many Things to Make (2026)

524 Hours of Fun (activity book; no paper dolls)

538 Wide World Costume Dolls (reprint of 236)

540 Fashion Book of Round About Dolls, 1936 (reprint of 545 and 555 Ten Round-About)

540 New Century Dolls (not pictured)

0540 Dolly and Her Dresses, box (1914 catalog)

541 Stand-Up Happy Animal Paper Dolls, 1934

542 Multi-head Paper Dolls, 1933

544 Nursery Rhyme Party Dolls in Costume (235½)

545 Diane and Daphne Round About Dolls, 1933

545 The New Pretty Village (stand-ups; not pictured)

547 Marcella's Raggedy Ann Doll Book, 1940

548 Debbie Dolls, 1937

549 The Little Red School House Kindergarten, 1940

550 Mary and Madge The Round About Dolls

551 Let's Play Paper Dolls, 1938 (reprint of The Sewing Book of the Round About Dolls)

552 The Party of the Paper Dolls, 1938

553 Funny Bunnies, 1938

555 Ten Round About Dolls, 1936

555 Winnies's New Wardrobe, 1939. (Some editions are called Winnie and Her Wardrobe.)

556 Real Sleeping Doll, 1939

557 Big Girl, 1939

558 Finger Fun Dolls, 1939 (not pictured; not paper dolls with outfits)

559 The New Round About Doll Book, 1939

560 Radio Cut-Outs, 1935 (stand-ups; not pictured)

561 18 Little Movie Stars, 1939

700 The Round About Dolls, 1933 (not pictured; reprint of 545 Diane and Daphne)

703 The Fashion Book of Round About Dolls, 1936 (picture not available)

704 Debbie Dolls (not pictured; reprint of 548)

707 Big Girl (not pictured; reprint of 557)

707 Big Sister, 1940 (reprint of 557)

0710 McLoughlin's French Doll Cut-Outs

1020 Raggedy Ann's Gift Box, 1940. This contains Marcella's Raggedy Ann Doll Book 547 and other books.

2026 and 2014 Something to Do for Every Day (not pictured; no paper dolls)

2028 The Dress Parade of the Round About Dolls (not pictured)

2042 Something to Do for Every Day (2026)

2710 Debbie Dolls, 1937. (Reprint of 548. Dolls are in a heavy board-type folder.)

2950 The Fashion Book of Round About Dolls, 1936. (Three-part folder includes two dolls from 545 Diane and Daphne, and four dolls from 555 Ten Round About Dolls. The dolls are heavy statuette-type dolls. Some books are not numbered.)

2951 Fashion Show of Round About Dolls, 1941 (three-part folder)

2952 Round About Dolls On Parade, 1941. (Three-part folder. This is a reprint of The Sewing Book of the Round About Dolls listed further on.)

2953 The Dress Parade of the Round About Dolls, not dated. (Three-part folder with patterns and cloth material to make outfits for the dolls. The paper patterns can be colored and used as dresses also.)

2955 Forward March, 1941 (stand-ups; not pictured)

2991 Fashion Show of Round About Dolls, 1941 (four-part folder)

2992 Round About Dolls on Parade, 1941

7202 McLoughlin's American Army and Navy Cut-Outs. (This contains four sheets of 0205 — A, B, C, and D stand-ups.)

The following have no stock number:

The Dress Parade of the Round About Dolls, no date (three-part folder)

The Fashion Book of the Round About Dolls, 1936. (Not pictured. This is the same as 2950 except this is a four-part folder and has three dolls from 545 — two are alike — and five dolls from 555.)

The Fashion Book of Round About Dolls, 1936 (three-part folder)

The Sewing Book of the Round About Dolls, 1937 (Four-part folder that includes four dolls — two each of two dolls — scissors, crayons, embroidery floss, etc.)

Dolls to Cut Out and Dress, 1929
Our Dollies, 1905. (Not pictured. The contents of this box set are the same as the pieces in book 239.)
New Century Dolls

McLoughlin Bros. numbered sheets:

0100 Young School-age Girl, five outfits and hats
0100 School-age Girl of about 10 years, five outfits and hats
0100 Lady, five outfits and hats
0100 Small Girl, four outfits and hats (not pictured)
0101 Dolls of All Nations (four different sheets)
0102 Bride, four outfits and hats
0102 Teenage Girl
0102 Little Girl
0102 Boy
0103 Dutch Paper Dolls (four different sheets)
0104-B Little Girl (not pictured)
0104-C Bride
0104-D Young Lady, five sports outfits and hats
0105-A Gentleman, four outfits and hats
0105-B Bride, four outfits and hats (not pictured)
0105-C Young Lady, four outfits and hats
0106 Cinderella
0106 Sleeping Beauty
0107 Fairy Tale Characters
0107 Little Women
0109-A Baby
0109-B Little Girl
0109-D Little Girl and outfits
0110-B Two Ladies, six outfits and hats
0110-C Two Ladies, six outfits and hats (not pictured)
0110-D Two Ladies, six outfits and hats
0111-A Two Ladies, six outfits and hats
0111-B Two Ladies, six outfits and hats
0111-C Two Ladies, six outfits and hats
0111-D Two Ladies, six outfits and hats

4009-A Baby, seven outfits, carriage, bathtub (not pictured; see 0109-A)
4009-D Two Little Girls
4010-A Two Girls, six outfits and hats (not pictured)
4010-B Two Ladies, six outfits and hats
4010-C Two Ladies, six outfits and hats
4010-D Two Ladies, six outfits and hats
4011-A Two Ladies, six outfits and hats
4011-B Two Ladies, six outfits and hats
4011-C Two Ladies, six outfits and hats
4011-D Two Ladies, six outfits and hats
4026 Paper Soldiers, Belgian
4026 Paper Soldiers, English
4026 Paper Soldiers, Italian
4036 Fold-Up Furniture

McLoughlin Bros. sheets without numbers:

Celie, 1900 (not pictured)
Edna, 1900
Ethel, 1900 (not pictured)
Katie, circa 1900
Lizzie, circa 1900
Mamie, circa 1900
Nellie, circa 1900

The following is a list of McLoughlin Bros. "Model" books published before 1910. They are books of stand-up toys, not paper dolls.

244 Doll's House Model Book, 1905

Model Book of Animals
Model Book of Furniture, 1904
Model Book of Little Folks' Army
Model Book of Objects
Model Book of Soldiers
Model Book of Trains

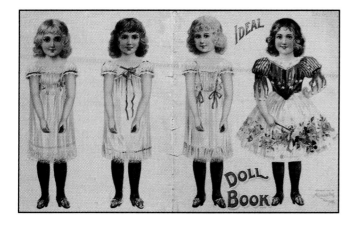

235½ The Ideal Doll Book (some books do not have the number 235½), 1907, $100.00.

The Ideal Doll Book is a beautiful paper doll book with three paper dolls and six pages of costumes. There are two costumes on each page. They include Her Majesty, the Queen; The Gypsy Dancer; The Lady Falconer; Columbine; Winter; Spring; Summer; Autumn; Mary, Mary Quite Contrary; Little Bo Peep; Little Red Riding Hood; and Cinderella.

The dolls in this book actually started out as a line of jointed paper dolls. Three of those early dolls were used as dolls for this book. A fourth doll is shown on the front cover wearing the Columbine costume. The jointed dolls are 10¾" tall and are the exact same size in the book. Notice how the arms hang down, as they did when they were joined to the dolls' bodies with eyelets. It's interesting to see how these jointed dolls evolved from a movable-arm design to a fixed-arm design.

Many of these jointed dolls have been found and are pictured here. The dolls all wear similar dresses with either blue or red ribbons. The dresses with red ribbons can have either long or short ribbons. The dolls' faces are beautiful, and have been found with either type of dress.

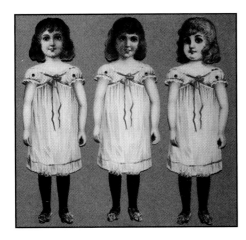

View #1 shows three jointed dolls with long red ribbons.

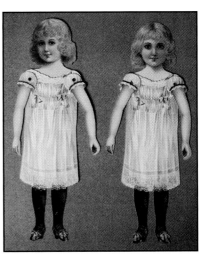

View #2 shows two jointed dolls with blue ribbons.

View #3 shows three dolls with the shorter red ribbons. Notice that the doll in the middle is the same as one of the dolls with the blue ribbons. The doll on the right is the same as the doll on the right in view #1, but one doll has the short red ribbons and the other has the long red ribbons.

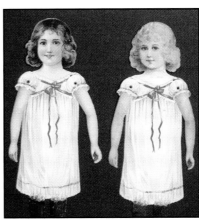

View #4 shows two more of the dolls. The doll on the right is the same as the doll on the left in view #2.

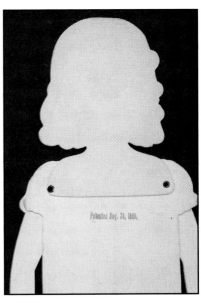

View #5 shows the patent date on the back of one doll.

These jointed dolls have a patent date on their backs of August 24, 1880. This same date is also printed on many Dennison Mfg. Co. jointed paper dolls that were produced in the late 1800s and the early 1900s. A patent search was done, and the patent was issued for toy figures using eyelets in the arms and legs. The patent was not issued to either Dennison or the McLoughlin Brothers, but the patent could be released to companies to use on their toy figures. Although the patent date of August 24, 1880, is printed on the paper dolls' backs, that does not mean that they were published at that time.

236 The New Model Book of Dolls, 1904, $100.00.

236 The New Model Book of Dolls, inside pages.

The New Model Book of Dolls is another beautiful older book of paper dolls. There are six pages of paper dolls. Four of the pages have dolls with foreign costumes. The four pages were also sold by the sheet and were in the 0101 series Dolls of All Nations. (See pictures of these sheets near the end of the McLoughlin section.) The costumes are the same but arranged differently on the sheets. The other two pages in the book contain paper dolls that were also sold on individual sheets dated 1900. It's possible these dolls were also sold as jointed dolls, as they resemble the jointed dolls on page 193 but are of a smaller size.

236 The New Model Book of Dolls,
inside page.

239 Our Dollies Model Book, 1909, $90.00. This book was also published as a box set in 1905.

544 Nursery Rhyme Party Dolls in Costume, $75.00.

544 Nursery Rhyme Party Dolls (with Cinderella on cover).

This is a reprint of the Ideal Doll Book #235½ that was published in 1907. This book was published in Springfield, Massachusetts, so it was published after 1920. The book has the same costumes as the Ideal Doll Book, but some are renamed and arranged differently on the pages. The pages are also of a lesser grade of paper.

There are at least three other books with this same title and number. The contents and dolls are the same for all the books. However, each book has a different cover showing a doll wearing a costume from the costume pages. The book on the left has the Queen of Hearts on the cover. Other covers have Little Red Riding Hood, Cinderella, and Little Bo Peep. A picture of the Cinderella cover is shown on the right.

517 The Three Bears' Home, 1933, $80.00. There are no outfits for the dolls.

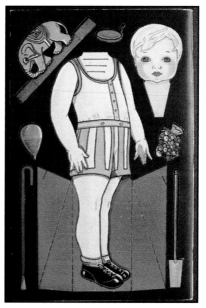

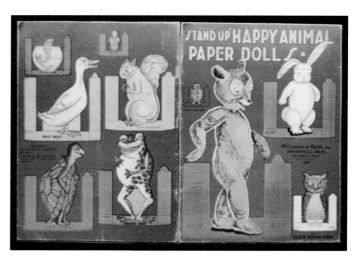

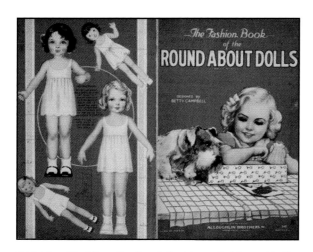

540 The Fashion Book of the Round About Dolls, 1936, $50.00.

541 Stand-Up Happy Animal Paper dolls, 1934, $100.00.

542 Multi-Head Paper Dolls, 1933, $65.00.

545 Diane and Daphne, the Round About Dolls, 1933, $60.00.

547 Marcella's Raggedy Ann Doll Book, © 1940 Johnny Gruelle Co., $75.00.

This book is a reprint of 236 The New Model Book of Dolls that was published in 1904. The six dolls and clothes are the same but are arranged differently on the pages, and the paper is of a lesser grade. This book was published in Springfield, Massachusetts, so it was published after 1920.

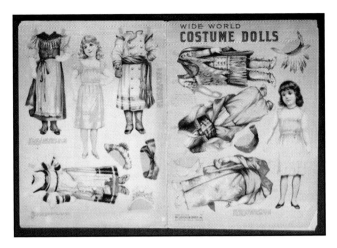

538 Wide World Costume Dolls, $50.00.

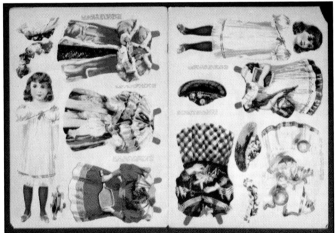

538 Wide World Costume Dolls, inside pages.

549 The Little Red School House Kindergarten, 1940, $100.00.

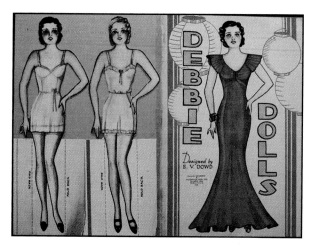

548 Debbie Dolls, 1937, $75.00.

550 Mary and Madge, the Round About Dolls, $50.00.

551 Let's Play Paper Dolls, 1938, $60.00.

553 Funny Bunnies, 1938, $100.00.

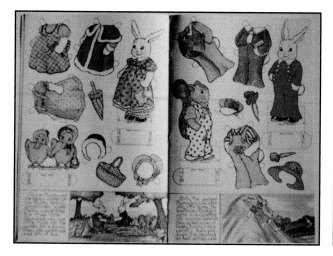

553 Funny Bunnies, inside pages. (Not all pages are shown, just the pages with the paper dolls.)

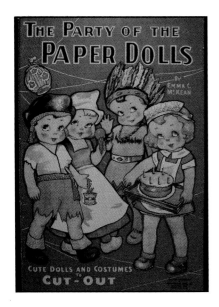

552 The Party of the Paper Dolls, 1938, $60.00.

0710 McLoughlin's French-Doll-Cut-Outs, $150.00. This set contains four of the numbered sheets (0110 sheets B, C, and D, and 0111-D).

555 Ten Round About Dolls, 1936, $60.00.

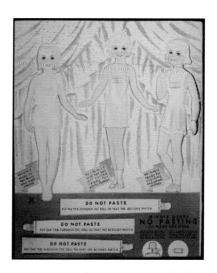

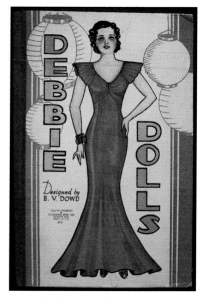

555 Winnie's New Wardrobe, 1939, $60.00.

555 Winnie's New Wardrobe, inside contents.

2710 Debbie Dolls, 1937, $75.00. Includes the same dolls as 548, but these dolls are statuette and are in a heavy board-type folder.

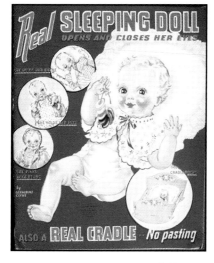

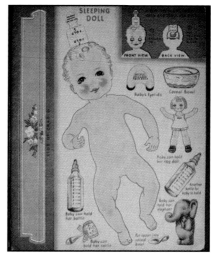

556 Real Sleeping Doll, 1939, $50.00.

557 Big Girl, 1939, $45.00.

559 The New Round About Doll Book, 1939, $65.00.

561 18 Little Movie Star Paper Dolls, inside pages.

561 18 Little Movie Star Paper Dolls, 1939, $100.00.

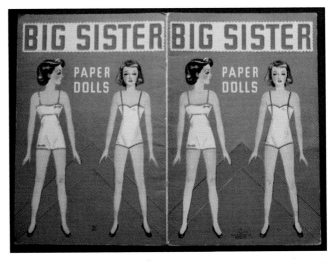

561 18 Little Movie Star Paper Dolls, inside page.

707 Big Sister, 1940, $35.00. Reprint of 557 using two of the four dolls twice.

1020 Raggedy Ann's Gift Box, 1940, $125.00. Contains Marcella's Raggedy Ann Doll book 547 plus coloring books and storybooks.

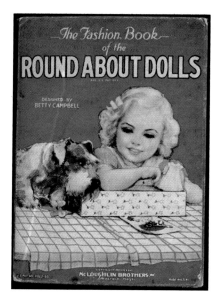

2950 The Fashion Book of the Round About Dolls, 1936, $60.00. Note: Some books are not numbered.

2951 The Fashion Show of the Round About Dolls, 1941, $75.00.

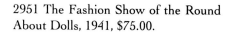

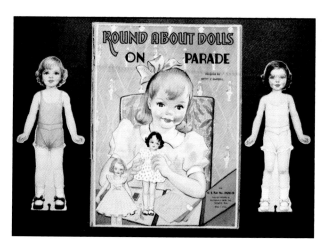

2952 Round About Dolls On Parade, 1941, $75.00.

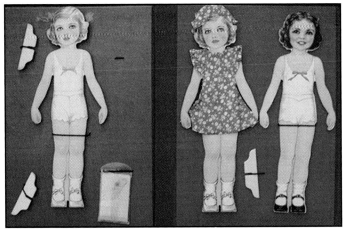

2953 The Dress Parade of the Round About Dolls, $80.00.

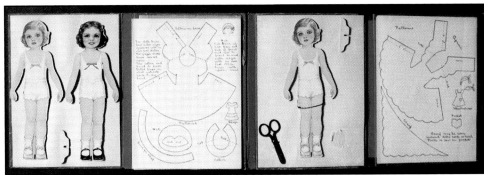

2991 The Fashion Show of the Round About Dolls, 1941, $80.00.

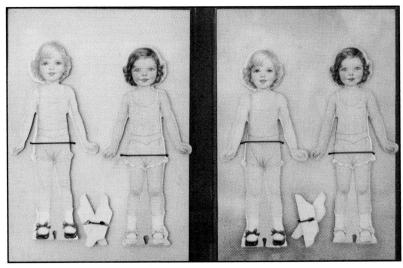

2992 Round About Dolls on Parade, 1941, $80.00.

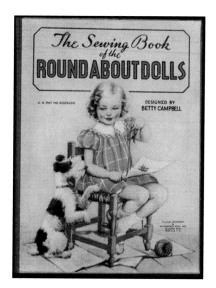
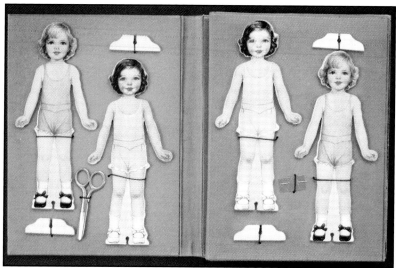

The Sewing Book of the Round About Dolls, 1937, $75.00.

Dolls To Cut-Out and Dress, $30.00. Pictured in the 1930 McLoughlin catalog. This book has the same dolls as New Century Dolls but has fewer pages. There is no date or number on the book, but the catalog number is 189.

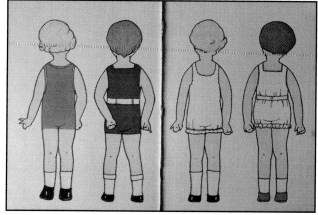

New Century Dolls, $40.00. This book has no date or number, but is shown in the 1930 McLoughlin catalog. The catalog number for the book is 300.

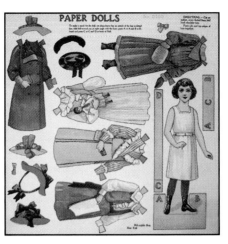

Numbered Sheet 0100, $30.00.   Numbered Sheet 0100, $30.00.   Numbered Sheet 0100, $30.00.

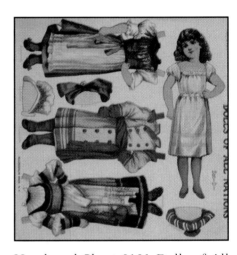

Numbered Sheet 0101 Dolls of All Nations A, $30.00.

Numbered Sheet 0101 Dolls of All Nations B, $30.00.

Numbered Sheet 0101 Dolls of All Nations D, $30.00.

Numbered sheet 0102 Bride, $30.00.

Numbered Sheet 0102, girl, $30.00.

The McLoughlin Brothers catalog for 1914 lists the different series of paper doll sheets as follows:

0100 Paper Dolls
0101 Dolls Of All Nations
0102 New Paper Dolls
0103 Dutch Dolls
0104 Brides
0105 Brides and Bridegrooms
0106 Fairy Tale Dolls, Series 1
0107 Fairy Tale Dolls, Series 2
0108 To 0111 Not Listed

Numbered Sheet 0102, young girl, $30.00.

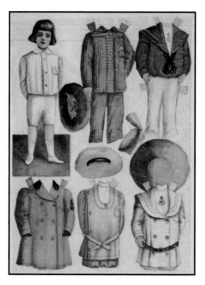

Numbered Sheet 0102 (cut set), boy, $30.00 if uncut.

Numbered Sheet 0103, Dutch Paper Dolls, $30.00.

Numbered Sheet 0103, Dutch Paper Dolls, $30.00.

0104 Set C, $30.00.

Numbered Sheet 0104 Set D, $30.00.

0105 Set A, $30.00.

0105 Set B, $30.00.

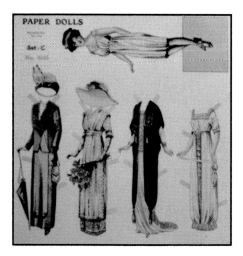

0105 Set C, $30.00.

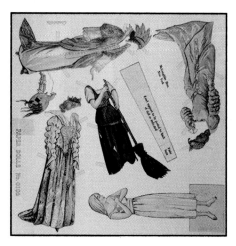

0106 Cinderella, $40.00.

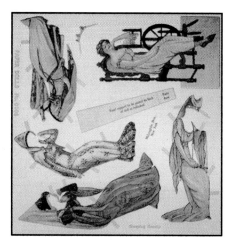

0106 Sleeping Beauty, $40.00.

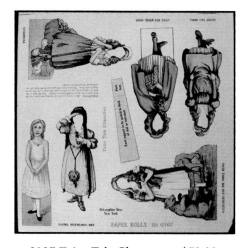

0107 Fairy Tale Characters, $30.00.

0107 Fairy Tale Characters (Little Women, cut set), $30.00 if uncut.

0107 Fairy Tale Characters (partial cut set), $30.00 if uncut.

0109 Set A (baby), $30.00.

0109 Set B (little girl), $30.00.

0109 Set D (two little girls), $30.00.

0110 Set B, $30.00.

0110 Set D (cut set), $30.00 uncut.

0111 Set A, $30.00.

0111 Set B, $30.00.

0111 Set C, $30.00. (Shown is the reprint 4011-C; $25.00 for reprint.)

0111 Set D, $30.00.

4011 Set B is a reprint of sheet 0111 Set B. The address given on this reprint is Springfield, MA, so the date is after 1920. The original 0111 was published while the company was still in New York. The reprint is on poor-quality pulp paper. $25.00.

4009 Set D. This is another example of a reprint sheet. This sheet is the same as 0109 Set D and was published after the company moved to Springfield, MA. $25.00.

Edna, 1900, $35.00.

Nellie, $60.00 if uncut.

Katie, $60.00 if uncut.

Mamie, $60.00.

Lizzie, $60.00 if uncut.

0540 Dolly and Her Dresses, no date, shown in the 1914 McLoughlin catalog, $100.00.

0510 Dolly and Her Dresses, circa 1914, box set with embossed paper dolls and clothes. This doll has the body of Nellie and all of Nellie's clothes. However, the face and hair style are different. This set has been found in the 1914 McLoughlin Bros. catalog. $100.00.

This photo shows another embossed paper doll and her clothes. The doll has the body of Lizzie and all of Lizzie's clothes. Here again, the face and hair style are different. She was also in the box set of Dolly and Her Dresses 0510.

Merry Manufacturing Company

In 1962, the Merry Manufacturing Co. bought out the DeJournette Co. and began to produce its own paper dolls. In addition to paper dolls, the company produced Miss Merry Play Sets such as pretend nail polish and cosmetics sets and nurse kits. For the boys there were Mr. Merry Play Sets; one was the popular Really Neat set, which had play shaving cream, band-aids, a toy razor, and toy blades. By the late 1960s, these sets and the paper dolls came to an end, as the company was sold.

4350 Baby Merry (has bottle and diaper), $35.00.

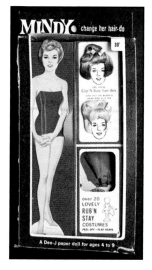

4351 Mindy, 1964, $35.00.

4360 Brenda Lee, $50.00. ©1964 by Brenda Lee & Weston Mfg. Corp. and Merry Mfg. Co.

4361 Linda B, 1964, $30.00.

4362 Jodi, $30.00.

6402 Bride of Frankenstein, $60.00. ©1964 Merry Mfg. Co. and Universal Pictures Co. Inc.

6403 Donna Reed, $50.00. ©1964 Merry Mfg. Co. and Todon of California.

6501 Toni, $30.00.

6504 Wendy Walks, 1965, $35.00.

Lisa, 1964 (cut set), $35.00 if complete in box and uncut.

6502 Jo, $35.00.

6503 Kim, $35.00 if complete in box and uncut.

Miss Merry (number and picture not available)

Milton Bradley Company

The Milton Bradley Company was founded in 1860 in Springfield, Massachusetts, by Milton Bradley. In that year, while working at the Wason Locomotive Car Works, he became interested in lithography and purchased a lithographic press. Since it was the only press in Massachusetts outside of Boston, he began receiving orders in great quantity and was able to start his own business. When business slowed down that first year, Mr. Bradley developed a game called the Checkered Game of Life. He ran it off on his press, and with the help of only one man, assembled and boxed the game. Mr. Bradley took several hundred of the games to New York and sold them to sales managers and news vendors until, by the end of the second day, all were sold. That winter Mr. Bradley produced and sold 40,000 copies of the game. When the Civil War broke out the following spring, Milton Bradley stopped game production to work as a draftsman on plans for the new percussion-lock Springfield rifle.

In the fall of 1861 Bradley went back to game making as he noticed the soldiers needed something to take their minds off the war and their living conditions. He invented a kit called Games for Soldiers. It was a small flat kit and contained nine games: backgammon, Checkered Game of Life, chess, checkers, and five variations of dominoes. From this time foreward, Milton Bradley would remain firmly planted in the game-making industry, and in a few short years he would become the leading manufacturer of games in the country.

In the summer of 1869, Mr. Bradley heard a lecture given by Elizabeth Peabody, founder of the kindergarten movement in the U.S.A. He was so impressed with the kindergarten theory that he agreed to publish a book on kindergarten education based on a method devised by a Mr. Froebel in Germany. The method used supplementary educational material, and Milton Bradley agreed to manufacture these products. For years these materials were a non-profitable part of the business but were something in which Mr. Bradley believed totally, so he continued to manufacture them.

Games, of course, still accounted for the biggest share of production and continued to do so up to present times. For the Milton Bradley Company's 100th anniversary, a modern version of the first Milton Bradley game, Checkered Game of Life, was produced. The new Game of Life reflected modern times, with personal achievement and monetary success, while the original game dealt with the high ideals of morality and happy old age.

One very popular game of 1966 was the game Twister. The company had doubts about its success when the game was presented to it. Twister was not your usual board game. In this game, the participants became the playing pieces and moved from one colored circle to another on a vinyl sheet. To become a successful game it had to be demonstrated, and when the Milton Bradley

Co. persuaded Johnny Carson to play the game with Zsa Zsa Gabor on the *Tonight Show*, the game became an instant hit.

Sometimes a game thought to be too involved or difficult was passed over. Such an incident occurred in the 1930s, when the executives turned down the game of Monopoly. The inventor took his game over to Parker Bros. in Salem, Massachusetts, where the game was accepted and went on to become the largest selling game in the world.

Milton Bradley died in 1911, but the company ran smoothly along until 1932. Then, because of the Great Depression, operations had to be curtailed. By the end of 1941, the company was on the brink of bankruptcy, and to protect their interests, the holders of preferred stock insisted on a reorganiztion. They knew they had to find a president who had the vision of Milton Bradley. Such a man was James Shea, Sr., who left his position in another firm to become the new president of Milton Bradley just one week before the country entered World War II. War rationing of raw materials, including paper, made it next to impossible for Milton Bradley to continue manufacturing its products. So the company turned over a good portion of its facilities to war products. It manufactured gun stocks in its woodworking department, and the company was given a contract with the Coca-Cola Co. to supply game kits for the Armed Forces. This started to put the company back on its feet, and each year after, there was steady growth.

In 1914, the first sets of Bradley's Tru-Life Paper Dolls were published. In the 1914 catalog, three sets were listed and each was listed as new. According to the catalog, the paper dolls were "painted by an American artist from life models." These paper dolls were sold in a variety of sets.

In 1920, Milton Bradley acquired a controlling interest in McLoughlin Bros. of New York. The McLoughlin operation was moved to Springfield, Massachusetts, and became a separate division of the company until 1944. During this time, McLoughlin Bros. published many paper dolls. Some of them were reprinted under the Milton Bradley name.

The Magic Mary paper dolls were first published by the company in 1946. Magic Mary was invented by an engineer in Ohio for his two daughters, who loved paper dolls. He devised a way of hiding a magnet inside the doll and attaching small pieces of metal to the dresses so that they would cling to the doll. After obtaining a patent on his idea in 1943, he tried to interest manufacturers in the doll, but wound up selling the patent to a Mrs. Wright of Cleveland. She took the idea to Milton Bradley, but the executive with whom she spoke rejected it. She then inquired her way to the president's office and was able to stop the president as he came out. Mr. Shea immediately saw the possibilities of the magnet paper doll, and Mrs. Wright had a signed contract before she left. The first Magic Mary was introduced in Milton Bradley's 1946 catalog. The set, 4132, was drawn by Emma McKean. In 1948, a new Magic Mary doll was drawn by Betty Campbell in such a way as to accept the original dresses by Emma McKean plus a few new outfits by Betty Campbell. The number on the new set was 4132-B. It was in 1950 when this same Magic Mary paper doll was used again, but this time all the clothes were drawn by Betty Campbell. The stock number was changed to 4010-1, and three other paper dolls were added to the line: 4010-2 Magic Mary Ann, 4010-3 Magic Mary Jane, and 4010-4 Magic Mary Lou. These three dolls were originally in set 4489A by Betty Campbell. The dolls in the series would change every three or four years, but the names remained the same. The last sets were copyrighted in the 1970s. In 1984 Milton Bradley was acquired by Hasbro, Inc. (James J. Shea, *It's All in the Game*; James J. Shea, Jr., *The Milton Bradley Story*.)

All the known Milton Bradley paper dolls are listed here.	4010-2 Magic Mary Ann, 1962
	4010-2 Magic Mary Ann, 1966
4010-1 Magic Mary, new in 1950 (doll from 4132-B, clothes new)	4010-2 Magic Mary Ann, 1971
4010-1 Magic Mary, 1955	4010-2 Magic Mary Ann, 1972 (same as 1971 set, different cover)
4010-1 Magnetic Magic Mary, 1958	4010-3 Magic Mary Jane, new in 1950 (from 4489A)
4010-1 Magic Mary, 1962. (This is the same doll as the 1958 doll; a few new clothes were added.)	4010-3 Magic Mary Lou, 1955
4010-1 Magic Mary, 1966	4010-3 Magic Mary Jane, 1958
4010-1 Magic Mary, 1971	4010-3 Magic Mary Jane, 1962
4010-1 Magic Mary, 1972 (same as 1971 set, different cover)	4010-3 Magic Mary Jane, 1966
4010-1 Magic Mary, 1972. (This is the same set as the above 1972 set, only the box is smaller and the box cover has been changed slightly.)	4010-3 Magic Mary Jane, 1971
	4010-3 Magic Mary Jane, 1972 (same as 1971 set, different cover)
4010-2 Magic Mary Ann, new in 1950 (from 4489A)	4010-3 Magic Mary Jane, 1975 (new doll, clothes the same as those in 1972)
4010-2 Magic Mary Jane, 1955	4010-4 Magic Mary Lou, new in 1950 (from 4489A)
4010-2 Magic Mary Ann, 1958	

4010-4 Magic Mary Ann, 1955

4010-4 Magic Mary Lou, 1958

4010-4 Magic Mary Lou, 1962. (The doll is in the same pose as the 1958 doll, but is redrawn.)

4010-4 Magic Mary Lou, 1966

4010-4 Magic Mary Lou, 1972 (same as 1971 set, different cover)

4010-1S Magic Mary, 1960. (Doll is like 1958 and 1962 Magic Mary, and set includes a dresser/bedroom wall piece.)

4030 The Animated Cinderella Doll

4042 Two-Gun Pete, new in 1950 (magnetic paper doll)

4043 Bronco Bess, new in 1950 (magnetic paper doll)

4053 Cutie Paper Dolls (two dolls from McLoughlin 552)

4101 The Animated Goldilocks Doll with The Three Bears

4106 Raggedy Ann Cut Out Doll, 1941 (dolls from McLoughlin 547, new clothes)

4109 Animated Alice in Wonderland Dolls

4110 Six Animated Nursery Rhyme Dolls (not pictured, see 4746)

4112-1 Jeans 'N Things, Bells and Beads, 1971

4112-2 Jeans 'N Things, Rags & Jeans, 1971

4132 Magic Mary (drawn by Emma McKean; new in 1946 catalog)

4132-B Magic Mary (drawn by Betty Campbell, clothes from 4132)

4202 Dollhouse (includes a paper doll and clothes; not pictured)

4236 Sunny the Wonder Doll

4279 Bradley's Jointed Doll with Embossed Dresses

4319 Bradley's Tru-Life Paper Dolls (new in 1914 catalog; contains three dolls)

4319 Bradley's Tru-Life Paper Dolls, patented March 21, 1916. (Box cover is the same as above 1914 set, but dolls are new.)

4320 Bradley's Tru-Life Paper Dolls (new in 1914 catalog; contains six dolls)

4321 Bradley's Tru-Life Paper Dolls (new in 1914 catalog, contains 12 dolls)

4330 Annie Paper Doll Kit, 1983

4374 Peggy and Polly, 1934. (Issued under two different box covers. Reprint of Diane and Daphne, McLoughlin 545)

4382 Betty and Barbara, Round About Dolls, 1934 (McLoughlin 545 and 550)

4396 Jean and Joan and Their Friends, 1934 (from McLoughlin 545 and 550)

4414 Three Dolls with Round About Dresses (same set as 4489A, new box cover)

4425 Television Dolls

4441 Patty Duke, 1963

4447 The Twins, Round About Dolls, 1935 (McLoughlin 555 Ten Round About Dolls)

4489 Wood Dolls with Round About Dresses (dolls originally from McLoughlin 545)

4489A Wood Dolls with Round About Dresses (new in 1949 catalog)

4530-1 Magic Mary Fashion Designer, 1985

4530-2 Magic Mary Fashion Designer, 1985

4531 Magic Mary Hair Designer, 1985 (not pictured)

4552 Five Round About Wood Dolls (McLoughlin 555 Ten Round About Dolls)

4716 Cutie Dolls (one doll)

4717 Cutie Dolls (two dolls)

4727 Dollies Dresses to Color and Cut Out

4727 Little Folks Doll's Set. (This has three dolls the same as those in the 1914 set 4319, but this set contains six crayons, and all outfits are to be colored.)

4727 The Mods, 1967

4746 Nursery Rhyme Dolls, 1957 (four dolls)

4785 Sleepy Time Girl. (The doll has eyes that move and is from McLoughlin 545.)

4790 Cutie Paper Dolls (four dolls from the McLoughlin Little Red Schoolhouse 549)

4792 Twinkley Eyes, the Baby Doll Who Looks Around (eyes move)

4815 Magnetic Sue, 1947

4833 Winnie, the Great Big Baby Doll. (Not pictured; the doll is the same as 4792, but its eyes do not move.)

4847 Merrie with the Go-Round Dresses (McLoughlin 545)

4900 Deluxe Magic Mary Dress Designer's Kit, 1959 (doll same as 4010-1 from 1955)

4924 Sweet Lou, circa 1949

4934 Embroidery Dolls, 1959 (like sewing cards)

4938 Raggedy Ann and Andy Dolls, 1959, four doll figures that fit into scenes

4944 New Folding Doll House, listed in 1922 catalog (no paper dolls)

4980 Cut Up Shopping Spree Game, 1968 (includes outfits)

7007 I Wish I Were, 1964, game with paper dolls and outfits

The following is a list of Bradley's picture cut-outs:

8206 Nursery Rhymes (jointed dolls)

8207 Billy Bobtail and His Friends (jointed dolls)

8208 Picture Building with Cut-outs, Folio One

8209 Picture Building with Cut-outs, Folio Two

8210 Poster Patterns

8211 Cut-out Dolls and Animals That Will Stand

8212 Fairy Tales (jointed dolls)

8213 The Family (jointed dolls)

8214 Alice in Wonderland (jointed dolls)

8215 Mother Goose (jointed dolls)

8216 Toyland (jointed dolls)

8219 The Happy Hour Portfolio (some cut-outs are included)

8243 Designs for Beginners in Woodwork

8244 Poster Designs

8249 Bradley's Furniture Cut-outs

8256 Bradley's Window Decorations

8297 Bradley's Character Dolls

8298 The Happy Family, 1923 (five paper dolls to color; includes outfits)

8299 Other Girls and Boys (patterns of dolls in other lands)

The 8300 numbers in the list of Bradley sets below are all stand-ups:

8300 Playtime Circus
8301 Dutch Village
8302 Japanese Village
8303 Eskimo Village
8304 Arabian Village
8305 African Village
8306 Pilgrim Village
8307 Indian Village
8308 Filipino Village
8309 Abraham Lincoln (his home in Indiana)
8360 Hindu Village
8361 George Washington (Mt. Vernon home)
8362 The Landing of Columbus

8363 Santa Claus (village church, children, toys, houses, etc.)
8364 Chinese Village
8365 Mexican Village
8366 Olde James Town
8450 Children's Party (novelty cut-outs for parties)
8451 Children's Gift Shop (designs for gifts children can make)
8452 Little Neighbors of Many Lands, 1926 (stand-ups)
8462 The Orange Industry (stand-ups)
8463 The Date Industry (stand-ups)
8468 Happy Family Dolls
9082 Modern Mother Goose, 1936 (stand-ups)
9251 Walton's Playset, 1974 (stand-ups)

The following have no stock number:

Komical Kut-Outs with Crayons (jointed dolls)
Bradley's Tru-Life Paper Dolls, 1914. (Some sets had no stock number on the box cover.)

4132 Magic Mary, 1946, $45.00. The first Magic Mary.

4132-B Magic Mary, new in 1948, $40.00. The second Magic Mary.

4010-1 Magic Mary, new in 1950, $35.00.

4010-2 Magic Mary Ann, new in 1950, $35.00.

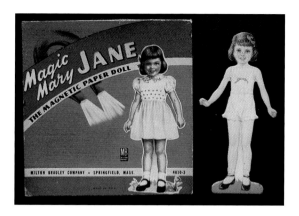

4010-3 Magic Mary Jane, new in 1950, $35.00.

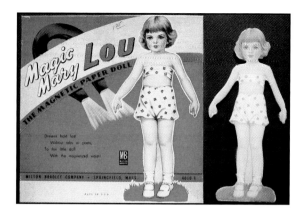

4010-4 Magic Mary Lou, new in 1950, $35.00.

4010-1 Magic Mary, 1955, $35.00.

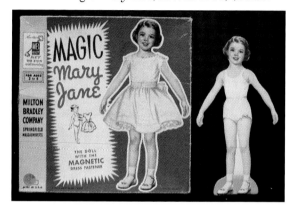

4010-2 Magic Mary Jane, 1955, $35.00.

4010-3 Magic Mary Lou, 1955, $35.00.

4010-4 Magic Mary Ann, 1955, $35.00.

4010-1 Magnetic Magic Mary, 1958, $35.00.

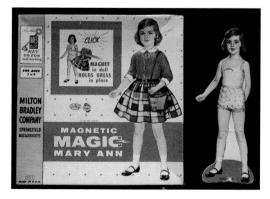

4010-2 Magnetic Magic Mary Ann, 1958, $35.00.

216

4010-3 Magnetic Magic Mary Jane, 1958, $35.00.

4010-4 Magnetic Magic Mary Lou, 1958, $35.00.

4010-1 Magic Mary, 1962, $30.00.

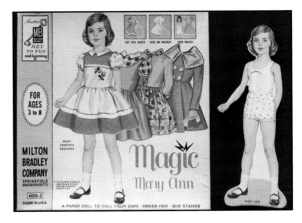

4010-2 Magic Mary Ann, 1962, $30.00.

4010-3 Magic Mary Jane, 1962, $30.00.

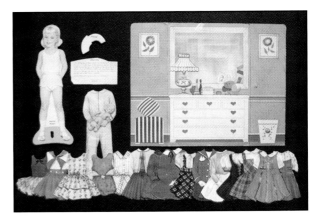

4010-1S Magic Mary, 1960, $40.00. Includes a dresser/bedroom background. Doll is like 1958 and 1962 Magic Mary.

4010-4 Magic Mary Lou, 1962, $30.00.

4010-1 Magic Mary, 1966, $30.00.

4010-2 Magic Mary Ann, 1966, $30.00.

4010-3 Magic Mary Jane, 1966, $30.00.

4010-4 Magic Mary Lou, 1966, $30.00.

4010-1 Magic Mary, 1971, $25.00.

4010-2 Magic Mary Ann, 1971, $25.00.

4010-3 Magic Mary Jane, 1971, $25.00.

4010-4 Magic Mary Lou, 1971, $25.00.

4010-1 Magic Mary, 1972, $25.00.

4010-2 Magic Mary Ann, 1972, $25.00.

4010-3 Magic Mary Jane, 1972, $25.00.

4010-4 Magic Mary Lou, 1972, $25.00.

The 1972 sets were issued in the regular size boxes and also in a smaller size. Dolls and clothes are the same. Magic Mary and Magic Mary Ann are examples of sets with the smaller size boxes.

4010-3 Magic Mary Jane, 1975, $20.00. There is also a 1975 white doll set of Mary Jane (see 1972 set).

4900 Deluxe Magic Mary, 1959, $35.00.

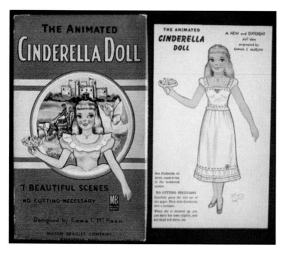

4030 The Animated Cinderella Doll, $30.00.

4042 Two-Gun Pete, new in 1950, $35.00.

4043 Bronco Bess, new in 1950, $35.00.

4053 Cutie Paper Dolls, $40.00.

4101 The Animated Goldilocks Doll, $35.00.

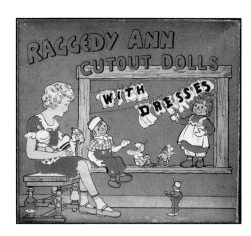

4106 Raggedy Ann Cutout Dolls, ©1941 Johnny Gruelle Co., $100.00.

4106 Raggedy Ann dolls of Betty, Marcella, Raggedy Ann, and Jane.

4109 Animated Alice in Wonderland Dolls, $35.00.

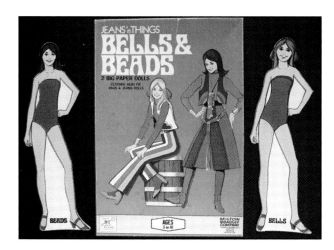

4112-1 Jeans'N Things, Bells & Beads, 1971, $12.00.

4112-2 Jeans'N Things, Rags and Jeans, 1971, $12.00. `

4236 Sunny the Wonder Doll, $25.00. The outfits have tabs that slide under the belt at the doll's waist.

4279 Bradley's Jointed Doll with Embossed Dresses, $80.00.

4321 Bradley's Tru-Life Paper Dolls, 1914, $100.00. This set of paper dolls contains 12 paper dolls. There are four of each size (two blondes and two brunettes). A smaller set, 4320, contains six of these same dolls, two of each size. A still smaller size, 4319, shown on the right, contains three of the dolls, one of each size. The box covers all have the same picture. Note: Some boxes do not have a printed number on the box cover.

4319 Bradley's Tru-Life Paper Dolls, 1914, $75.00.

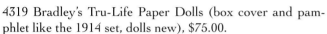

4319 Bradley's Tru-Life Paper Dolls (box cover and pamphlet like the 1914 set, dolls new), $75.00.

4374 Peggy and Polly, 1934, $50.00.

4374 Peggy and Polly, 1934, $50.00. This is another edition of 4374, with a different box cover; contents are the same.

4382 Betty and Barbara, 1934, $50.00.

4425 Television Dolls, $25.00.

4330 Annie Paper Doll Kit, 1983, $15.00.

4396 Jean and Joan, 1934. The dolls are from McLoughlin's 545 and 550.

4414 3 Dolls with Round About Dresses, $40.00. Dolls are the same as #4489A.

4447 The Twins, Round About Dolls, 1935, $35.00.

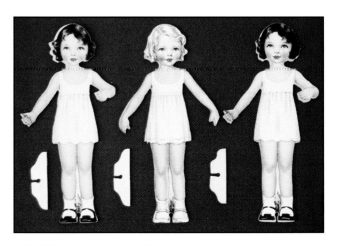

4489 Wood Dolls with Round About Dresses, $60.00.

4489 There are three dolls in the set. Some sets have two blonde dolls and one brunette.

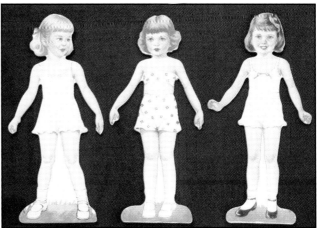

4489A Wood Dolls with Round About Dresses, new in 1949, $60.00.

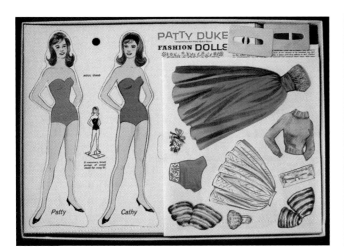

4441 Patty Duke, 1963, $40.00.

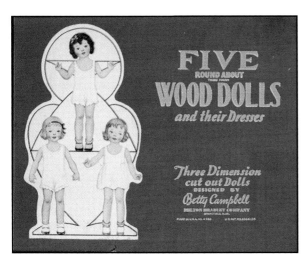

4552 Five Round About Wood Dolls, 60.00.   4552 The five dolls and one page of outfits.

4717 Cutie Dolls (two dolls), $80.00.

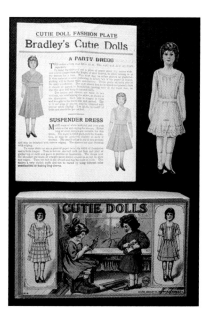

4716 Cutie Dolls (one doll), $75.00.

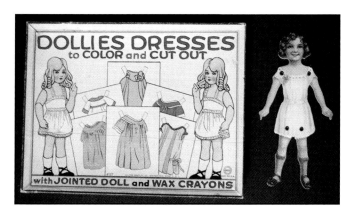

4727 Dollies Dresses, $80.00.

4530-1 Magic Mary Fashion Designer, 1985, $15.00.

4530-2 Magic Mary Fashion Designer, 1985, $15.00.

4727 The Mods, 1967, $15.00.

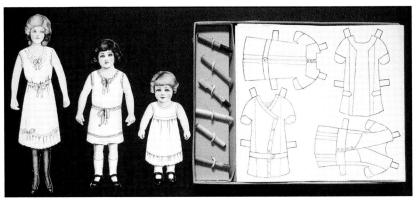

4727 Little Folks Doll's Set, $75.00.

4727 Little Folks Doll's Set dolls, crayons, and one sheet of clothes.

4746 4 Nursery Rhyme Dolls, 1957, $15.00.

4785 Sleepy Time Girl, $35.00.

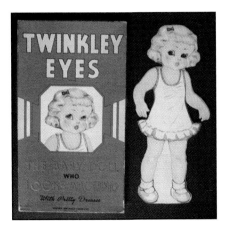

4790 Cutie Paper Dolls, $35.00.

4792 Twinkley Eyes, $30.00. The set of Winnie 4833 is identical to this set, except the eyes on that doll are not movable.

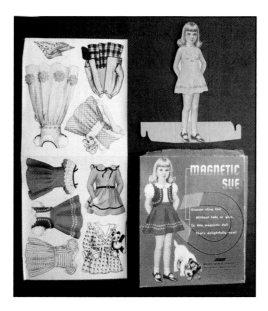

4815 Magnetic Sue, 1947, $35.00.

4847 Merrie with the Go-Round Dresses, $35.00.

4934 Embroidery Dolls, $12.00.

4980 Cut Up Shopping Spree Game, 1968, $25.00.

4924 Sweet Lou, the Doll with the Changing Faces, $35.00. The doll has a revolving wheel that has different faces.

7007 I Wish I Were, 1964, $25.00.

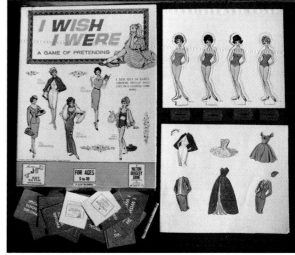
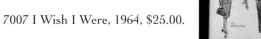

200 Little Miss Hollywood, $30.00. Small box dolls are 6½" tall.

400 Little Miss Hollywood (not pictured) is a medium-size set and contains 9¼" Joy and Sue dolls.

700 Three Little Maids (includes paper doll clothes for Joy and Sue, but either the set did not include the dolls or they were missing from the set), $30.00. The clothes fit the 6½" dolls.

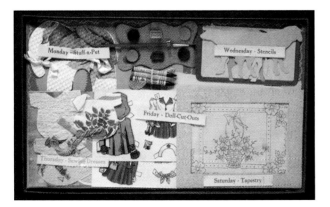

600 Little Miss Hollywood (paper dolls are Joy and Sue), $40.00. Large box dolls are 9¼" tall.

20 Mary Jane. (Even though the title is Mary Jane, the set includes a paper doll of Sue from set 200; the doll is 6½".) This set is not marked with a company name. However, there is strong evidence that it is also from the Minerva Toy Co., as the paper doll of Sue is the same as the 200 Sue paper doll, and the type of inside packaging is the same in both sets. $15.00.

20 Mary Jane (includes a doll of Joy, 6½" from #200, $15.00.

21 Little Princess, $15.00. (Includes the doll of Sue from #200. The name of Geo. Borgfeldt & Co. is printed on the package.)

Mold Trim Products

The Dolly Ballet, 1955 (not pictured; contains ten plastic dolls and sixty costumes) Family (see Trim Molded Products Co.)

John L. Morton & Company

John L. Morton & Co. operated out of Portsmouth, Ohio.

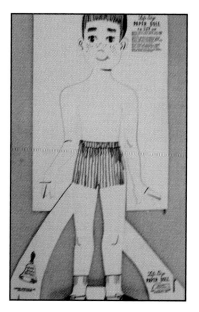

A paper doll of a different girl was also published (picture not available).

Life Size Paper Doll, $18.00.

Life Size Paper Doll, $18.00.

Large box (same box was used for each doll); dolls are 38" tall.

Mother Goose CutOut Picture Book, $75.00.

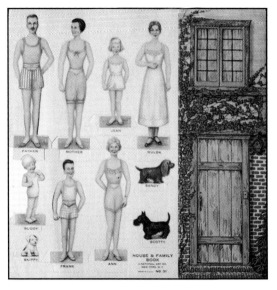

No. 31 House and Family Book, $100.00.

No. 31 House and Family Book, back cover.

No. 31 House and Family Book, center pages of clothes.

No. 31 House and Family Book, one more page of clothes (out of a total of six pages).

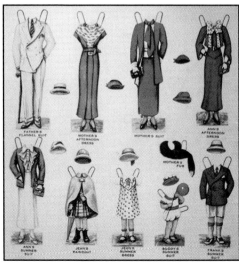

N10-29 Lullaby Twins, $15.00.

N11-29 Wild West Twins, $15.00.

N12-29 Circus Twins, $15.00.

2019 Dilly Dolly (dolls same as Lullaby Twins), $20.00.

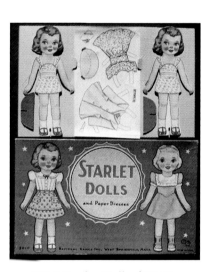

3010 Starlet Dolls, $25.00.

3927 Dilly Dolly Twins (same as Lullaby Twins)

National Syndicate Displays, Inc.

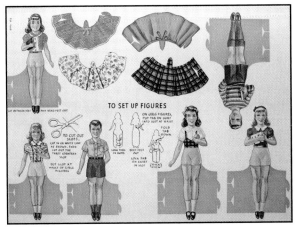

77 "Stand-Up" Cut Out Dolls, 1942, $20.00.

77-1 School Days, 1943, $20.00.

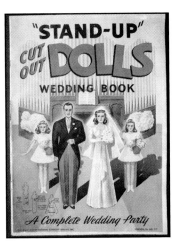

77-2 Birthday Party, 1944, $20.00.

777 "Stand-Up" Cut Out Dolls Wedding Book, $20.00.

Near East Foundation

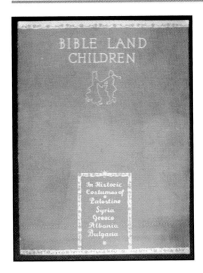

Bible Land Children, 1934, $16.00.

Bible Land Children, inside pages.

Newgood Company

This was a company in Lexington, Kentucky.

Circle Doll, $20.00. This is a different type of paper doll.
As the wheels are turned, the doll gets new outfits.

New York Book Company

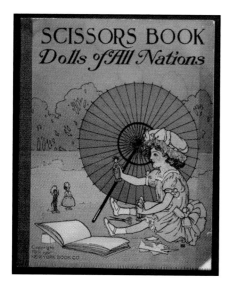

Scissors Book Dolls of All Nations,
1911, $40.00.

Carmencita (Spanish) on the left (uncut page), Elizabeth (American) on
the right (this is a cut set). There are a total of eight paper doll pages in
the book.

Circus Fun, 1920 (includes clown and one outfit; not pictured)

The Nourse Company

The Nourse Company evolved from the Platt and Nourse Company, which had begun as Platt and Peck. When Mr. Platt left the Platt and Nourse Company to form a new book company with Arnold Munk, the Nourse Company operation lasted for a few years before it was bought out by Platt and Munk. Older books originally published by Platt and Peck and Platt and Nourse continued to be sold by the Nourse Co., along with new original books. Many of the earlier Platt and Nourse books were also reprinted by the Platt and Munk Company.

The following were sold by the Nourse Company:

Beautiful Dolls for Children to Dress, 1915 (see Platt and Peck for picture)
Dollies to Dress Like Father and Mother (see Platt and Munk 225 for picture)
Dolls from Fairyland, 1921 (pictured)
Dolls from the Land of Mother Goose, 1918 (see Platt and Munk 221 for picture)
Dolls in Wonderland, 1921 (pictured)
Mary and Teddy Cut Out Dolls (originally published by Platt and Nourse)
Nayan Dolls No. 1, 1921 (pictured)
Playroom Toys to Cut Out, 1921 (paper toys)
Teddy Bear and his Friends to Dress, 1921 (see Platt and Munk 222, Teddy Bear & His Friends, for picture)
Toy Animals I Can Make (paper toys)
Toy Army I Can Make (paper toys)
Toy Furniture for Children to Build, 1917

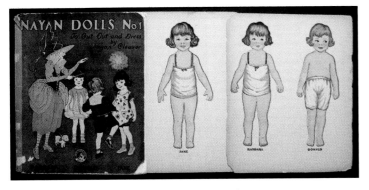

Nayan Dolls No. 1, 1921, $60.00.

Dolls from Fairyland, 1921, $85.00.

Dolls in Wonderland, 1921, $85.00.

Novel Products Corporation

Sue and Sal, the Snap-On Sisters, $20.00.

Nutmeg Press

954 Dress-Ups, $15.00.

Olde Deerfield Doll House

This set of paper dolls depicts a true story, the massacre at Deerfield, Massachusetts, in 1704. There are six paper dolls. Five represent captive children that were carried off to Canada by the Indians. The sixth paper doll is of the Indian Arosen, who later married one of the captives. Included in the set are six very small books that relate to and illustrate in color the true story of each of the characters portrayed.

Two of the children belonged to the family of John Williams. The Williams house is pictured on the front of the folder, and Arosen's wigwam is shown on the back. When cut out and folded, these pieces can be stood up. They measure 9½" x 21¼" each.

Olde Deerfield Doll House, continued:

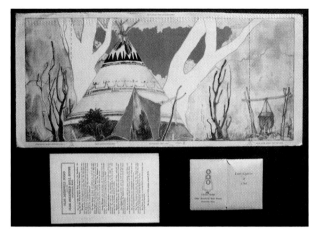

Olde Deerfield Dolls, 1919, $85.00.

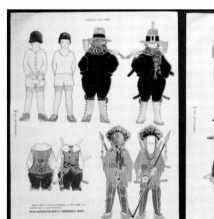

Ottenheimer Publishers, Inc.

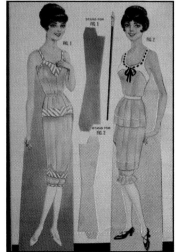
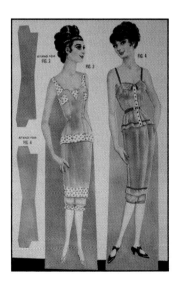

2060-5 My Fair Lady, 1965, $100.00.

2960-2 My Fair Lady, 1965, $75.00.

2961-0 My Fair Lady, 1965, $75.00.

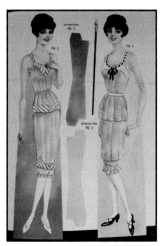

5860-2 My Fair Lady, 1965, $75.00.

J. Ottmann Lithograph Company

The Ottmann Company also published a book of stand-up toys called Buster Brown's Parade.

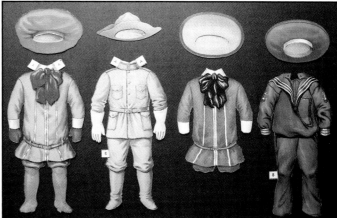

Buster Brown and Tige, $125.00.

Chanticleer Paper Doll (missing two outfits), $200.00 if complete.

Fluffy Ruffles, 1907, $150.00.

Teddy Bear, $100.00. (For Teddy Bear's outfits, see page 279.)

Mary and Her Little Lamb, $200.00.

Mary and Her Little Lamb outfits.

Pachter Company

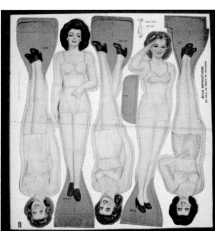

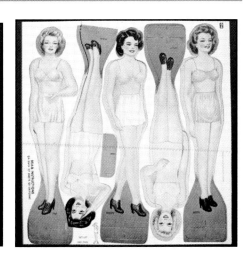

80 Bild-A-Set, 10 Beautiful Junior Girls in Uniforms, 1943, $100.00.

The Pachter Co. also published the #85 Bild-A-Set Constructor Kit in 1943 (a toy making kit).

240

The Little Colonel Doll Book, 1910, $200.00. A hardcover book with 48 sheets of paper dolls and outfits. There are ten paper dolls. All dolls were from the Little Colonel Series of storybooks by Annie Fellows Johnston.

The Mary Ware Doll Book, 1914, $200.00. A hardback book with 48 sheets of paper dolls and outfits. There are ten paper dolls. This is a companion volume to the *Little Colonel Doll Book* listed on the preceding page. All dolls were from the Little Colonel series of storybooks by Annie Fellows Johnston.

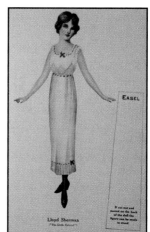

Mary.   Lloyd.

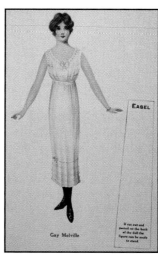
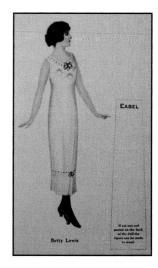

Joyce.   Kitty.   Gay.   Betty.

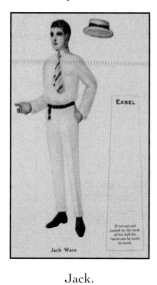
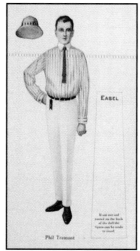

Jack.   Phil.   Rob.   Leland.

Paper Products Mfg. Co.

Dolly's Day by Day Cut-Outs ©1923 and 1924 by Will Pente is one of a series of booklets with a paper doll on the outside cover and another inside on the centerfold. Each has costumes and equipment for carrying out different daily household tasks, such as washing, ironing, baking, cleaning, etc. This booklet has "Sunday — Church" on the covers and "Saturday — Baking" on the inside.

There is also a series of eight handkerchief cards that used these same dolls and clothes. Each is for one day of the week and the eighth is for a birthday. Each of the cards is "©1923 Will Pente." Shown here are the cards for Monday, Tuesday, Wednesday, Thursday, and Friday (Saturday and Sunday are shown in the booklet).

Also shown is the card for the birthday and the reverse side showing the outside of the card. Each handkerchief card has the same front cover, but the cards are in different colors.

Booklet outside cover — Dolly's Day by Day Cut-Outs, Sunday. $60.00.

Booklet inside pages — Dolly's Day by Day Cut-Outs, Saturday.

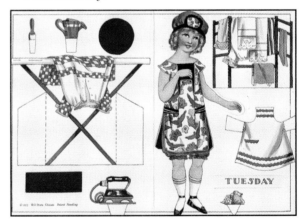

Handkerchief cards — Dolly's Daily Cut-Outs, Monday (left) and Tuesday (right). $50.00 each.

Handkerchief cards — Dolly's Daily Cut-Outs, Wednesday (left) and Thursday (right). $50.00 each.

Handkerchief card — Dolly's Daily Cut-Outs, Friday. $50.00.

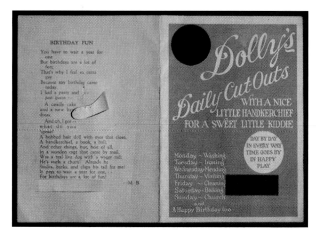 

Handkerchief card — Dolly's Daily Cut-Outs, Birthday. (When card is folded, the doll's face shows through the circle and the word *birthday* shows up in the rectangle.) $50.00.

Parker Brothers, Inc.

George Parker invented and published his first game in 1883, when he was only 16 years old. The name of his first game was Banking. While still in high school he published two more games, and by the age of 18, he had introduced five more games to the public. One of these last five games was a new edition of the old game of Dr. Busby. The game had been invented years before by the Ives Company of Salem, Massachusetts. George Parker bought the rights to the game, and a few years later he bought out the rights to all the old Ives games. One of these games, The Mansion of Happiness, was among the first board games made in America.

In just the five years since he published his first game, the business had grown so large that Parker needed someone to share the responsibilities. When his older brother Charles joined him, the firm became known as Parker Brothers. Eleven years later, in 1898, the oldest brother, Edward, joined the firm.

George Parker spent hour after hour testing each new game the company produced. He would play the games with friends and employees, always alert to how they reacted and how well they were able to understand and follow the rules. He continued to write the rules for all games produced even after the firm had grown into a large corporation.

In 1893 at the Chicago World's Fair, Parker Brothers won the highest award for its games, and at the St. Louis World's Fair a decade later, the company won the grand prize. Parker Brothers has been in the game business for over 100 years now. The list of games produced through the years is endless, but any history of Parker wouldn't be complete without mention of its most popular game, the best-selling game in the world, Monopoly®. The game came on the market in 1935 and was an instant hit with children and adults of all ages. Paper dolls by Parker Brothers made their appearance in 1917. The company catalog that year listed five

244

"Improved Paper Doll Outfits" ranging from 50¢ to $1.50. The dolls had jointed arms and legs. The larger sets included a large girl doll, a medium-sized girl, and a small boy. The smaller sets had only two dolls, the small boy and either one of the girl dolls.

The Improved Paper Doll Outfits were sold by Parker Brothers until 1934. Since the crepe paper outfits found in the Parker sets are similar, and in some cases identical, to Dennison outfits, it may be assumed that Dennison supplied Parker with the printed crepe paper and most likely all the inside paper material in the boxes. Although no Parker sets have been found containing Dennison dolls, the booklet of instructions shows dolls from Dennison set #33.

In the Parker Brothers 1939 catalog, the Magic Dolls of Princess Elizabeth and Princess Margaret Rose are featured. These dolls are of heavy cardboard and have a special surface that allows the cloth clothes to cling to the dolls. Two other magic dolls, Susie and Baby Doll, are also in this 1939 catalog. The Magic Dolls of Princess Elizabeth and Princess Margaret Rose were also sold in England and Canada by Somerville Paper Boxes Limited. It's very possible that Parker Brothers bought the rights from Somerville. More Magic Dolls, including a large 14½" Miss America, were introduced in the 1950s, and still others were introduced in the 1960s.

In 1985 Parker Brothers joined Kenner Products to form Kenner Parker Toys, Inc. Two years later, it was acquired by the Tonka Corp., and since 1991 Parker Brothers has been a division of Hasbro, Inc.

American Miss Magic Doll, 1957
Improved Paper Doll Outfit, 1917, large size with deep double-deck box (not pictured)
Improved Paper Doll Outfit, 1917, large 16" x 10½" size
Improved Paper Doll Outfit, 1917, large 16" x 10" size (not pictured)
Improved Paper Doll Outfit, 1917, small 14" x 9¼" size (not pictured)
Improved Paper Doll Outfit, 1917, small 13¼" x 8¾" size
Lovey and Dovey Magic Dolls, 1951
The Magic Baby Doll (not pictured; listed in 1939 catalog)
The Magic Doll, Susie (not pictured; listed in 1939 catalog)
The Magic Doll (listed in 1947/48 catalog)
Magic Doll, large 14" doll (listed in 1948/49 catalog)
Magic Doll, small 7¼" doll (listed in 1948/49 catalog)
The Magic Doll, for the Little Dressmaker (reprint of the original Susie listed above)
Magic Doll, 1961
Magic Doll, 1961 (different from above)
Magic Doll, 1963
Miss America Magic Doll (listed in 1953 catalog)
Paper Doll Outfit 802, 1917. (Some sets do not have the number 802.)
Princess Elizabeth Magic Doll, 1939
Princess Margaret Rose Magic Doll, 1939

American Miss Magic Doll (box cover), 1957, $35.00.

American Miss Magic Doll (inside).

Improved Paper Doll Outfit (second largest set), 1917, $85.00.

Lovey and Dovey Magic Dolls, 1951, $35.00.

Improved Paper Doll Outfit instruction booklet. Notice the dolls pictured are from Dennison set #33.

The Magic Doll, $45.00. Listed in 1948/49 catalog.

Improved Paper Doll Outfit (smallest set), 1917, $60.00.

The Magic Doll, $35.00. Listed in 1948/49 catalog.

The Magic Doll for the Little Dressmaker, $40.00.

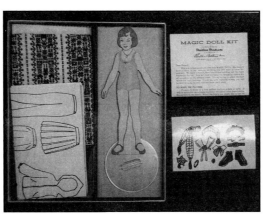

Magic Doll, 1961, $25.00.

Magic Doll, 1961, $25.00.

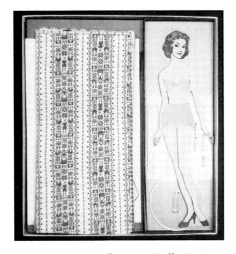

Box contents of Magic Doll, 1961.

Magic Doll, 1963, $25.00.

Miss America Magic Doll (in some sets the doll is dressed in blue), $35.00.

Miss America Magic Doll.

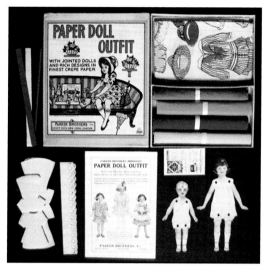

802 Paper Doll Outfit, 1917, $60.00. Some boxes do not have a number printed on the cover.

Princess Elizabeth Magic Doll, 85.00.

Princess Margaret Rose Magic Doll, $85.00.

The Magic Doll, $45.00. Listed in 1947/48 catalog (reprint of Princess Elizabeth).

Pla-Mor Toy Company

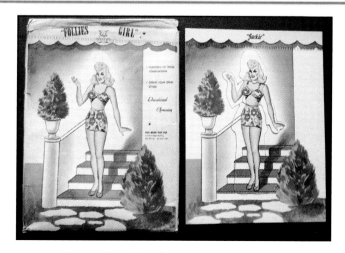

Follies Girl, Jackie, $25.00. Paper doll puzzle.

Platt and Munk Company, Inc.

The Platt and Munk Company was established in 1920. Mr. Platt had previously been a partner in the Platt and Nourse Company and, before that, the Platt and Peck Company, which also published books.

The Platt and Munk Co. published some of the most beautiful books for children, and later, activity sets were included in its line of products. Paper dolls were produced right from the start, though some were reprints of paper dolls previously published by the Platt and Nourse Co.

In the late 1960s, Platt and Munk became a division of Questor Education Products. Four of the company's most recent paper doll sets were reprinted in 1969 by Platt and Munk as a division of Child Guidance Products, Inc., which was a division of Questor. The four sets are Early American Dolls, Betsy Ross, Dolls of Far-Off Lands, and Dolls Across the Sea.

190 Teddy Bear and His Friends, box set that includes three paper doll books. The paper dolls in these books originated in the Nourse Co. book of Teddy Bear and His Friends, 1921 (see 222 Teddy Bear for pictures). The three books are:
190A Bear and Monkey
190B Kitty and Doggie
190C Piggy and Bunny
200 Up-to-Date Dollies
205 Modern Dolls to Cut Out and Dress, box set (dolls same as #210 below)
210 Betty Ann and Her Friends, box set that includes three paper doll books:
210A Betty Ann and Audrey
210B Jean and Tommy
210C Janet and Dick
215 Four Little Friends to Cut Out and Dress (not pictured)
220 Dolls' Open House, 1963
220 Beautiful Dolls for Children to Dress (not pictured, see Platt & Peck)
220B Dolls in Wonderland (not pictured)
221 Dolls from the Land of Mother Goose (reprint of the original Platt & Nourse book)
222 Teddy Bear and His Friends to Dress
224A Early American Dolls, 1963 (four dolls from 242)
224B Betsy Ross, 1963 (four dolls from 242)
225 Dollies to Dress like Father and Mother (reprint of original Platt & Nourse book; not pictured, see Platt and Nourse)
225A Gay Dolls, 1942 (two dolls from 229)
225A New Dolls to Cut Out and Dress (not pictured)
225B Party Dolls, 1942 (two dolls from 229)
225B Pretty Dolls to Cut Out, Color and Dress
225C Pretty Dolls, 1942 (two dolls from 229)
225D Young Miss Dolls, 1942 (two dolls from 229)
226 Dolls from Fairy Land (not pictured, see Nourse Co.)
226A Costume Dolls, 1962 (four dolls from 243)
226B Historical Dolls, 1962 (four dolls from 243)

227A Betty Ann and Her Friends (four dolls from 229)
227B Playtime Dolls (four dolls from 229)
228A Dolls Across the Sea, 1965 (four dolls from 241)
228B Dolls of Far-Off Lands, 1965 (four dolls from 241)
229 Junior Miss Dolls, 1942
230A Playtime Dolls, 1937 (two dolls from 240, date 1937)
230B Betty and Peggy, 1937 (two dolls from 240, date 1937)
230C Janet and Jeanne, 1937 (two dolls from 240, date 1937)
230D Going Abroad Dolls, 1937 (two dolls from 240, date 1937)
235A I'm Growing Up Dolls, 1937 (four dolls from 240, date 1937)
235B Mary Lou and Her Friends, 1937 (four dolls from 240, date 1937)
240 At Home Abroad Dolls, 1937
240 Modern Dolls, 1957
241 Foreign Dolls, 1957
242 Colonial Dolls, 1960
243 Century Dolls, 1960
245 Williamsburg Colonial Dolls, 1967
261 Circus and Animal Cutouts
264 Put Together Pictures, 1955
330 Betty and Jack (see Platt & Nourse, also Platt & Peck Beautiful Dolls)
331 Pretty Dolls to Dress
335 Dorothy and Ruth
336 My Little Dears to Dress
360 The Little Cherubs, 1921
366 Kiddie Dolls, 1922
370 The Little Buntings, 1921
380 Little Blue Bell, 1921. (Not pictured; girl from back cover of 370, see page 257.)
390 Little Boy Blue, 1921
1250 Early American Dolls, 1969 (reprint, see 224A)
1251 Betsy Ross, 1969 (reprint, see 224B)
1252 Dolls of Far-Off Lands, 1969 (reprint, see 228B)
1253 Dolls Across the Sea, 1969 (reprint, see 228A)

205 Modern Dolls to Cut Out and Dress, $65.00. The paper dolls in this set are the same as pictured for 210.

210 Betty Ann and Her Friends, $65.00.

The six dolls from 210 Betty Ann and Her Friends. (The same dolls are also in 205 Modern Dolls.) These six dolls are in three small books inside the boxes. Betty Ann and Audrey are in book 210A, Jean and Tommy are in book 210B, and Janet and Dick are in book 210C.

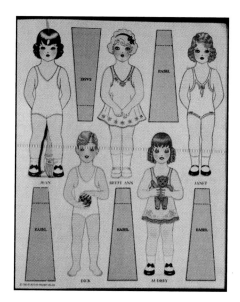

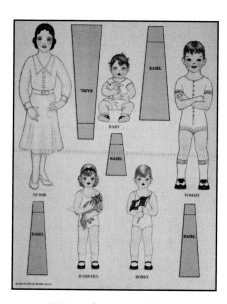

200 Up-To-Date Dollies, circa 1931, $65.00.

200 inside pages of dolls.

200 inside pages of dolls.

220 Dolls' Open House, 1963, $20.00.

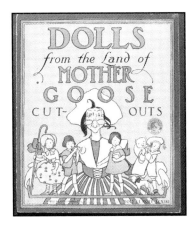  

221 Dolls from the Land of Mother Goose, $75.00.

222 Teddy Bear and His Friends, $90.00.

222 Teddy Bear and His Friends, inside pages of dolls.

224A Early American Dolls, 1963, $20.00.

224B Betsy Ross, 1963, $20.00.

225A Gay Dolls, 1942, $25.00.

225B Party Dolls, 1942, $25.00.

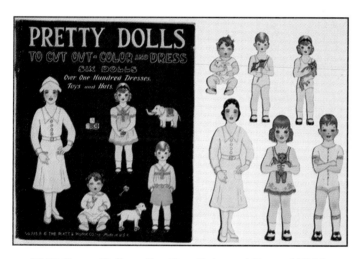

225B Pretty Dolls to Cut Out, Color and Dress, $75.00.

225C Pretty Dolls, 1942, $25.00.

225D Young Miss Dolls, $75.00.

226A Costume Dolls, 1962, $20.00.

226B Historical Dolls, 1962, $20.00.

227A Betty Ann and Her Friends, $40.00.

227B Playtime Dolls, $40.00. The sets of 227A and 227B each contain four dolls from the eight doll set of Junior Miss Dolls 229.

228A Dolls Across the Sea, 1965, $20.00.

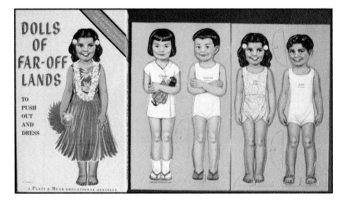

228B Dolls of Far-Off Lands, 1965, $20.00.

229 Junior Miss Dolls.

229 Junior Miss Dolls, 1942, $80.00.

230A Playtime Dolls, 1937, $35.00.

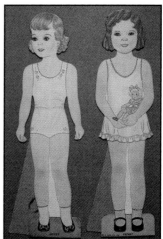

230B Betty and Peggy, 1937, $35.00.

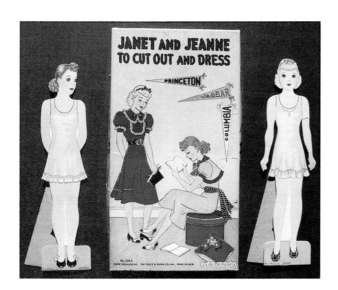

230C Janet and Jeanne, 1937, $35.00.

230D Going Abroad Dolls, 1937, $35.00.

235A I'm Growing Up Dolls, 1937, $60.00.

235B Mary Lou and Her Friends, $60.00.

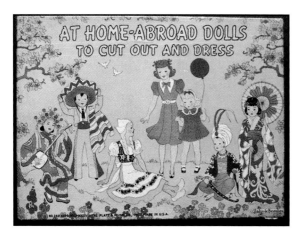

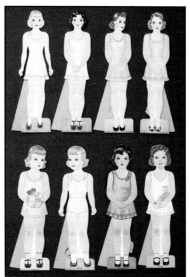

240 At Home-Abroad Dolls, 1937, $100.00.

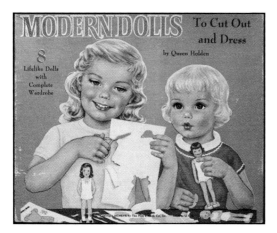

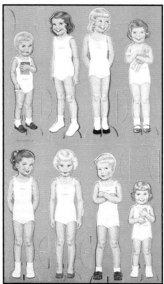

240 Modern Dolls, 1957, $65.00.

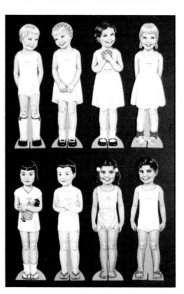

241 Foreign Dolls, 1957, $65.00.

242 Colonial Dolls, 1960, $65.00.

243 Century Dolls, 1960, $65.00.

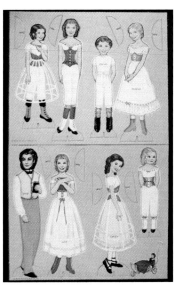

245 Williamsburg Colonial Dolls, ©1967 Williamsburg Restoration, Inc., $35.00.

245 Williamsburg Colonial dolls.

331 Pretty Dolls to Dress, $40.00.

335 Dorothy and Ruth, $40.00.

336 My Little Dears to Dress, $40.00.

360 The Little Cherubs (doll on back cover can vary), 1921, $65.00

366 Kiddie Dolls, 1922, $50.00.

370 The Little Buntings (doll on back cover can vary), 1921, $65.00.

390 Little Boy Blue, 1921, $65.00.

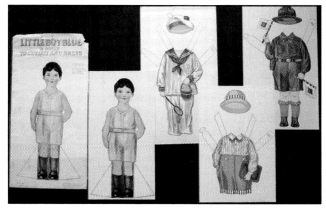

The Platt and Nourse Company

The Platt and Nourse Company emerged from the Platt and Peck Company. Mr. Platt left the company in 1920 and joined up with Arnold Munk to form the Platt and Munk Publishing Company. For a few years the Nourse Company operated alone, but it was eventually bought by Platt and Munk.

Beautiful Dolls for Children to Dress, 1915 (not pictured, see Platt and Peck)
Betty and Jack Dolls to Dress (dolls are from Beautiful Dolls above)
Dollies to Dress Like Mother and Father, 1917
Dolls From The Land of Mother Goose, 1918 (not pictured, see Platt and Munk 221)
Dorothy and Ruth Dolls to Dress (dolls are from Beautiful Dolls above; not pictured, see Platt and Munk)
Mary and Teddy Cut Out Dolls (not pictured)
My Little Dears to Dress (not pictured, see Platt and Munk 336)
Pretty Dolls to Dress (see Platt and Munk 331 for picture)
Table Decorations for Children to Make, 1917 (not pictured)
Toy Furniture for Children to Build, 1917 (not pictured)

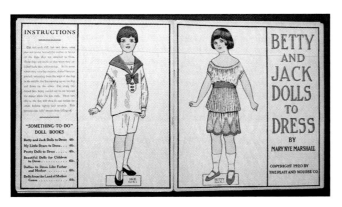

Betty and Jack Dolls to Dress, 1920, $50.00.

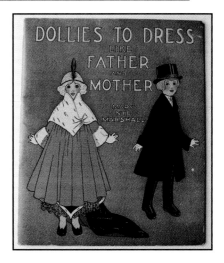

Dollies to Dress Like Mother and Father, 1917, $50.00.

Dollies to Dress Like Mother and Father.

Dollies to Dress Like Mother and Father.

Dollies to Dress Like Mother and Father.

Dollies to Dress Like Mother and Father.

Platt and Peck

Beautiful Dolls for Children to Dress
(includes dolls of Betty, Jack, Dorothy,
and Ruth), 1915, $60.00.

Playtime House

Playtime House produced paper dolls, games, picture puzzles, toys, and blocks. Since this company is no longer in business, there is no way to obtain dates for the following paper dolls. However, it is known that the company participated in the Toy Fair of 1947 in New York, so this bit of information may be useful in dating the sets.

310 Nancy	318 Carol and Ann and Their Baby Twin Sisters
311 Janie	320 Connie and Her Big Woolly Wardrobe
312 Barbara and Her Wardrobe	321 Mary and Jane
312 Betty and Her Wardrobe	341 Janie (311)
313 Dorothy	3151 Three Glitter Dolls and Their Wardrobes.
313 Shirley	(These three dolls are the same as 313 Shirley
313 Irene	and Irene and 314 Peggy, but with new names.)
314 Peggy	3152 Glitter Dolls
316 Three Beautiful Playtime Dolls	

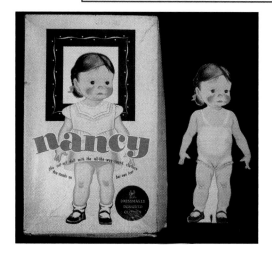

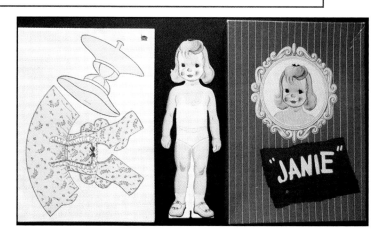

311 Janie, $25.00.

310 Nancy, $40.00.

312 Barbara and Her Wardrobe,
$25.00

312 Betty and Her Wardrobe,
$25.00.

313 Shirley, $20.00.

313 Irene, $20.00.

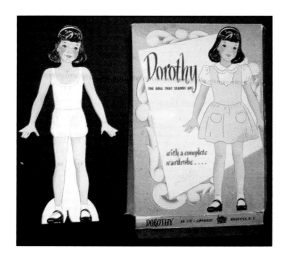

313 Dorothy, $20.00.

314 Peggy, $20.00.

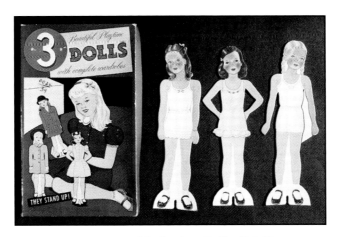

316 3 Beautiful Playtime Dolls, $25.00.

 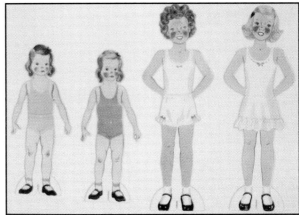

318 Carol and Ann and Their Baby Twin Sisters, $35.00.

320 Connie and her Big Woolly Wardrobe,
$25.00.

321 Mary and Jane, $30.00.

3152 Glitter Dolls, $35.00.

3151 3 Glitter Dolls, $25.00.

Poster Products, Inc.

The Poster Products Company of Chicago, Illinois, manufactured a number of children's activity sets in the 1930s. The four basic sets were called Felt-O-Gram sets 1, 2, 3, and 4. The smallest, set 1, sold for 50¢, and the largest, set 4, sold for $2.50. Each set consisted of a special background board that permitted geometric felt pieces to cling to it. The child could make animals, birds, trees, buildings, etc., with the pieces. The line expanded to include heavy cardboard dolls that felt clothes could cling to.

10 Felt-O-Gram Doll and Her Wardrobe, 1932, $50.00.

12 Felt-O-Gram Twins, 1932, $40.00.

16 Felt-O-Gram Mishe, The Doll of All Nations, 12" doll, circa 1933 (not pictured)

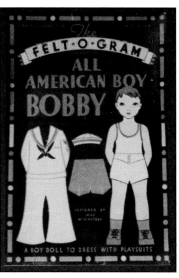

14 Felt-O-Gram, I'm Bebe of All Nations, 1933, $30.00.

20 Felt-O-Gram, All American Boy Bobby, 1934, $40.00.

22 Felt-O-Gram, Black-Eyed Sue, 1934, $30.00.

J. Pressman Toy Corporation

1156 Magnetic Small Fry Fashion Show, $25.00.

1173 High Fashion, 1961, $25.00.

1175 Little Lacey, $15.00.

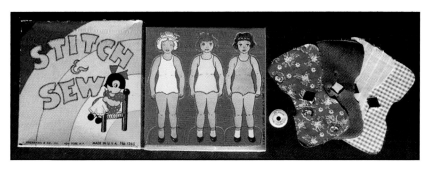

1205 Stitch and Sew, $20.00.

1156 Magnetic Small Fry Fashion Show
1173 High Fashion, 1961
1175 Little Lacey
1205 Stitch and Sew
1209 Stitch and Sew (includes one doll like the Snow White doll in 1214)
1211 Four Sisters Sewing Set
1212 Stitch and Sew
1212 Stitch and Sew (different from above)
1212 Snow White Doll (one doll from 1214)
1214 Snow White Cut Out Dolls
1222 Stitch and Sew (not pictured)
1232 Stitch and Sew
1245 Sewing for Every Girl
2906 Sew and Sew
5956 Magnetic Small Fry Fashion Show (same as 1156)

1209 Stitch and Sew, $20.00.

1211 4 Sisters, $35.00.

1212 Stitch and Sew, $20.00.

1212 Stitch and Sew, $20.00.

1212 Snow-White Cut-Out Doll, $40.00.

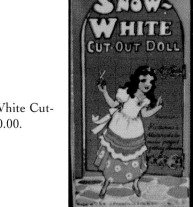

264

1214 Snow White, $50.00.

2906 Sew and Sew, $20.00.

1232 Stitch and Sew, $20.00.

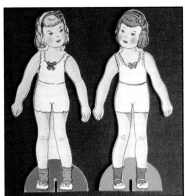

1232 Stitch and Sew, inside contents.

1245 Sewing for Every Girl, $40.00.

1245 Sewing for Every Girl, inside contents. Includes a toy iron and ironing board.

Progressive Toy Corporation

502 Progressive Sewing Set, 1941, $35.00. Two paper dolls, cloth clothes.

502 Progressive Sewing Set, box contents.

252 Progressive Sewing Set, 1941. (Smaller set than 502; has one doll from 502 and same box cover picture.)

G.P. Putnam's Sons

The Princess Diana Paper Doll Book of Fashion, by Clarissa Harlowe and Mary Anna Bedford. A Perigee Book, published by G.P. Putnam's Sons, ©1982 by Clarissa Harlowe and Mary Anna Bedford. Perigee Books is a division of The Putnam Publishing Group, $20.00.

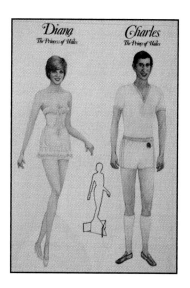

Grosset and Dunlap Publishers is now a division of the Putnam Publishing Group. Some years ago it published the following paper dolls.

C2000 The Bobbsey Twins Play Box, 1954, $50.00.

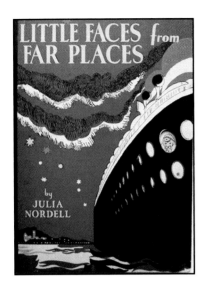

Little Faces from Far Places, 1933, $60.00.

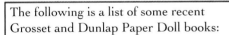

The following is a list of some recent Grosset and Dunlap Paper Doll books:

Supergirl, 1984
The Dolls' Tea Party, 1996
The Dollhouse Family, 1998
My Favorite Dolls, 1999
Girl's From America's Past, 1999
Pretty Ballerinas, 1999
Fairy Tale Princesses, 1999
Timothy Goes to School, 2000

R-R Specialties

Stand-Up American Family, $30.00.

Rand McNally and Company

Rand McNally amd Company was established in 1856 in Chicago, by William Rand and Andrew McNally. It became well known for its printing of railroad items such as timetables, passenger tickets, and maps of rail routes. Today it is best known for printing road atlases.

The company also published a large amount of children's books, and for many years it produced *Child Life Magazine*. In 1976, Rand McNally bought the Saalfield Publishing Co. Many of the more recent Saalfield books were reprinted by Rand McNally, including some paper doll books.

Pictured are the two paper doll books published by Rand McNally in the 1930s, a book from 1928 that contains one paper doll page, and four paper doll books published in 1984.

RM 103 The Make-It Book, 1928, $10.00.

186 Little Friends from History, 1936, $35.00.

211 Let's Play Eskimo, 1937, $25.00.

Puddin', 1984, $10.00.

Stardancer, 1984, $10.00.

Peanut Butter & Jelly, 1984, $10.00.

Mandy, 1984, $10.00.

Random House

The logo "Happy House" is used on all of the following except the Strawberry Shortcake Playhouse.

Annie, 1982; Muppet Babies, 1984; $10.00 each.

Strawberry Shortcake, 1984; The Berenstain Bears, 1984; $10.00 each.

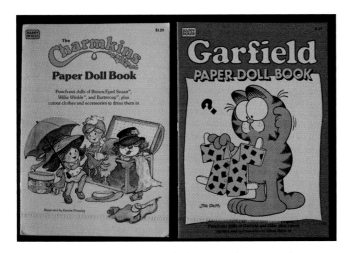

Charmkins, 1984; Garfield, 1984; $10.00 each.

Strawberry Shortcake Playhouse, 1980, $15.00.

Other Random House paper doll books (not pictured):

Star Wars Episode I, Queen Amidala, 1999
Berenstain Bears' New Clothes, 1997
Anne of Green Gables Pop-up Dollhouse, 1994 (has stand-up figures but no outfits)

Rea-Harrison Company

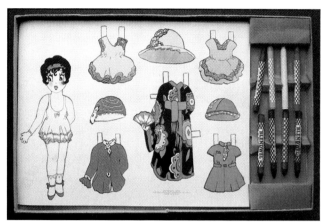

The Betty Belle Paper Dolls, 1929, $65.00.

Reely-Trooly Company

These paper dolls were also sold by the Rust Craft Company of Boston, but there was a change: *Trooly* was spelled *Truly*.

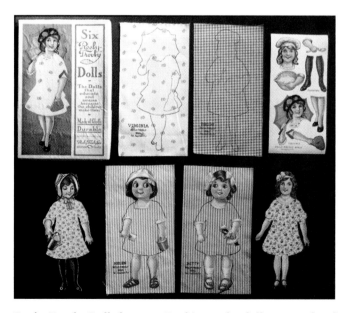

Reely-Trooly Dolls box set. In this set the dolls are made of cloth backing. The picture shows two dolls already finished, two dolls made up but not cut out, and two unfinished dolls. $35.00.

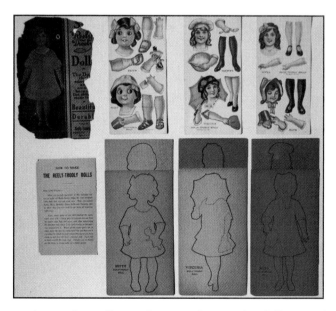

Reely-Trooly Dolls envelope. In this set the dolls are of cardboard. $35.00.

Jumbo Movy-Dols, Marguerite Clark, 1920, $135.00.

Jumbo Movy-Dols, Mary Miles Minter, 1920, $135.00.

Jumbo Movy-Dols, Mary Pickford, 1920, $135.00.

Jumbo Movy-Dols, Lila Lee, 1920, $135.00.

The Regensteiner Corporation

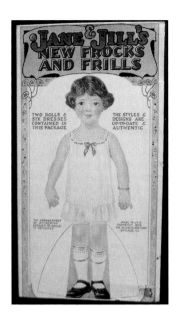

Jane and Jill's New Frocks
and Frills, 1925, $75.00.

The Reilly and Britton Company

In 1917, Will Pente designed and patented his Fold-A-Way Toys. That year, he designed four storybooks, which included paper dolls, outfits, and stand-up figures, for the Reilly and Britton Co. of Chicago, Illinois. The books were small, only 5¼" x 7¼". The cut-outs were on the right side of the page and the story on the left, so that the story would remain when the paper dolls were cut out. That year, Will Pente designed at least two other books of the stand-up toy variety for Reilly and Britton. Shortly after Will Pente designed the books, the company became known as Reilly and Lee; it continued to publish books for many years.

The following is a list of the Reilly and Britton Co. paper doll
and stand-up books that are known but not pictured:

Dolly Blossom's Bungalow, A Book of Fold-A-Way Toys, 1917
Dolly's Breakfast — The Fold Away Can't Break Dishes
The Oz Toy Book, 1915 (includes over 50 stand-up figures)
The Story of Cinderella, 1917
The Story of Little Black Sambo, 1917
The Story of Peter Rabbit, 1917
The Story of the Three Bears, 1917

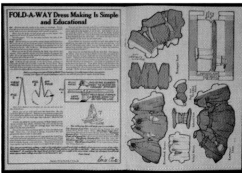

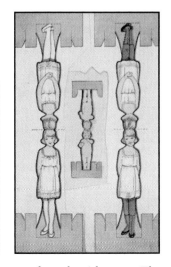

Dolly Blossom and Her Wardrobe, 1917, $75.00. "Reilly and Lee" is printed on the front cover and on the title page. The 1917 copyright is by Reilly and Britton, and all pieces are marked on the back with the Reilly and Britton trademark.

Ritt-Miller Company

Rosebud Art Co., Inc.

Betty, complete wardrobe and trunk, 1932, $60.00.

No. 60 Little Ladies Sewing Set, $35.00. (See Progressive set on page 266 with these same dolls.)

Rogers, Kellogg, Stillson

Gloriana, the Famous Hollywood Star, 1932, $100.00.

Gloriana, the Famous Hollywood Star.

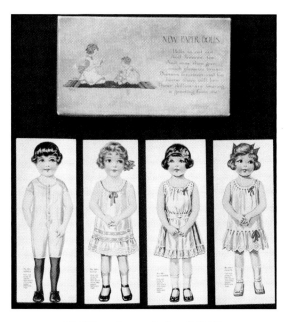

586 New Paper Dolls, $75.00.

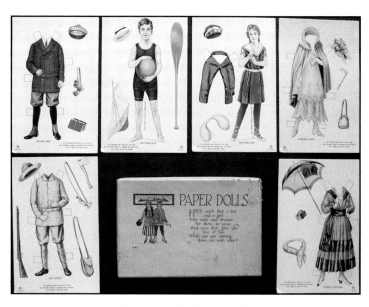

587 Paper Dolls, $100.00.

Scholastic, Inc.

Papa Bear's Party, 1982, $10.00.

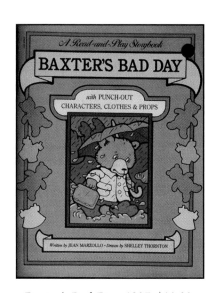

Baxter's Bad Day, 1983, $10.00.

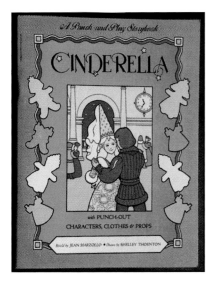

Cinderella, 1984, $10.00.   Doll House Christmas, 1983; Doll House Adventure, 1984; $10.00 each.

B. Shackman Co., Inc.

B. Shackman and Co. was founded in 1898 by Bertha Shackman in Wilkes Barre, Pennsylvania. The business was later moved to New York City, and the four Shackman sons eventually took over the firm. The Merrimack Publishing Corporation is the publishing subsidiary of B. Shackman.

Shown here are just two of the many paper doll books the company has produced.

The Girls of Rosebrooke School, Alexandra, 1999, $10.00. (This is a paper doll of artist Kathy Lawrence's daughter, Alexandra.)

The Girls of Rosebrooke School, Maria, 1999, $10.00. (This is a paper doll of author Mary Young's grand-daughter, Maria.)

There are six paper doll books in the series of The Girls of Rosebrooke School. Other titles, not shown, include Allison, Sabrina, Lianne, and Shannon. All six books are by artist Kathy Lawrence.

S.F. Goodman Mfg. Co.

The S.F. Goodman Manufacturing Company was located in Pittston, Pennsylvania.

Up-To-Date Doll Sets 2, $75.00. The two jointed dolls are the same as those used in the Dennison sets.

Sears, Roebuck and Co.

 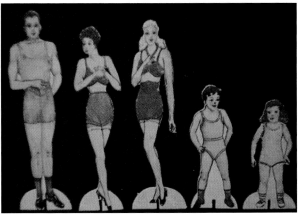

Happi-Time Family and inside contents, $60.00. Although this set of paper dolls does not actually say it was published by Sears, Roebuck and Co., "Happi-Time" is the logo that Sears, Roebuck used on many of its toys for years. (For another Happi-Time paper doll set, see the section about Cardinal Games.)

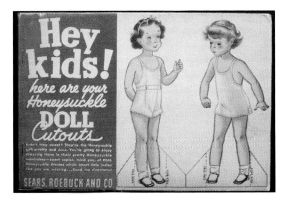

Honeysuckle Doll Cutouts, $20.00. Honeysuckle was the trade name used by Sears for its children's clothes for many years.

Selchow and Righter Company

The Selchow and Righter Company is an offshoot of a business started in 1867 by A. B. Swift. Mr. Swift was a wholesale distributor of toys and games on John Street in New York City. One of the games listed in his first catalog that year was Parcheesi® In 1870, the company was purchased by Mr. Elisha G. Selchow. Mr. Selchow hired a young man named John Harris Righter to help run the business. Righter did such a successful job that he was soon made manager, and he later became a partner in the firm. The company continued to sell large quantities of toys, games, and baseball equipment, and a large assortment of mechanical toy banks. Mr. Righter died in 1909 and Mr. Selchow in 1915, but the company continued to succeed under the name of Selchow and Righter. Like most other toy companies, it experienced only two major slowdowns during the years that followed: one during the Depression of the early thirties and the other during World War II.

After the war, a crossword game was brought to Selchow and Righter for consideration but was turned down. It was not the first time the owner of the game had been turned down, so he decided to set up his own factory and produce the game himself. The name of the game was Scrabble®, and the owner had the name trademarked. He asked Selchow and Righter if they would sell him a small quantity of playing boards, which they agreed to do. A year later, a greater amount of playing boards was ordered, and by 1952, the order was large enough to cause Selchow and Righter to wonder if they had done the right thing in turning down the game. The owner's little factory was beginning to swim in Scrabble tiles, and new orders from customers made the owner realize he could no longer handle it alone. Hence, the game was licensed to Selchow and Righter. The game has now been translated into many foreign languages and also made in Braille.

For many years, the Selchow and Righter Co. was the American distributor for J. W. Spear and Sons of London/Bavaria. It handled all types of Spear games and toys, including toy theaters and paper dolls. A Little Red Riding Hood theater with jointed figures was pictured in the 1924/25 Selchow and Righter catalog. Spear's paper dolls were also featured in that catalog.

Dolly May, $75.00.

Fair Margaret, $75.00.

Flossie, $75.00.

Lady Belle, $75.00.

Mamie, $75.00.

Little Laddie, $75.00.

Teddy Bear, $75.00.

Teddy Bear, inside contents.

Lady Alice, $75.00.

Lady Alice and dresses.

Lady Betty, $75.00.

Lady Betty and dresses.

Lady Irene, $75.00.

Lady Irene and dresses.

Lady Ruth, $75.00.

Lady Ruth with dresses.

Ruth, envelope only, $20.00. This is the later style of envelope. Doll and dresses not available.

Marion, $75.00. This is a later, renamed edition of Lady Irene. Clothes are new.

Marion with dresses.

Margaret, $75.00.

Margaret with dresses.

Katherine, $75.00. This is a later, renamed edition of Lady Alice. Clothes are new.

Katherine with dresses.

Dolly Dorothy (envelope missing), $75.00 (if complete).

Katie (envelope and outfits missing), $75.00 (if complete).

Some of the Selchow and Righter paper dolls were published in both a small size of about 9" and a larger size of about 12". Some of the early sets have numbers on the clothing tabs. Lady Alice and Dolly Dorothy have 1-1, 1-2, and 1-3. Lady Betty and Lady Ruth have 2-1, 2-2, and 2-3. Dolly May and Fair Margaret have 3-1, 3-2, and 3-3. Mamie and Little Laddie have 4-1, 4-2, and 4-3. Flossie and Lady Belle have 5-1, 5-2, and 5-3. Lady Irene has 6-1, 6-2, and 6-3.

Our Favorite Dolls, $125.00.

Our Favorite Dolls, $125.00.

Each of the Our Favorite Dolls folders is yellow, brown, and white. The name Selchow and Righter appears on each, and down at the bottom of the folder in smaller print is "American Litho. Co." Amlico also produced these dolls, and it's more than likely that Amlico stands for American Litho. Co.

J. W. Spear & Sons

The following paper dolls of J. W. Spear and Sons of London/Bavaria were distributed in the United States by Selchow and Righter and are listed in its catalog. 1924/25.

Daisy and Her Dresses, in 7" x 7" box	Peggy, 7" doll in 7" x 8" box
Dolly Dimple, 6¾" doll in 7" x 3¾" box, with four costumes (pictured)	Peggy, same as above, only 9¾" doll in larger box
Dolly Dimple, 10" doll in 11½" x 6½" box, with four costumes	Peggy and Her New Outfit, in 9¾" x 11" box, with four dresses, four hats, five playthings
Dolly Rosycheeks and Her Pretty Dresses and Hats, in 11" x 14¼" box (pictured)	
Dorothy, in 9¾" x 11" box, with four dresses, four hats, and five playthings	The following are Spear's Character Dolls with removable heads:
Joan, in 11" x 14¼" box, with four dresses, four hats, and four miscellaneous items	Joan, 13" doll in 11" x 14" box, complete outfit, several heads
	Our Baby, 12½" doll in 14" x 12" box, with complete outfit, several heads
Little Dick, 7" doll in 7" x 8" box (pictured)	One Doll, in 9¾" x 11¼" box, with four dresses, four hats, and six heads
Little Dick, same as preceding, only 9¾" doll in larger box	

Dolly Dimple (small 6¾" doll), $75.00.

Dolly Rosycheeks, $125.00.

Little Dick and His New Outfit (small 7" doll), $75.00.

Daisy and Her Dresses, $75.00. Daisy is 10¼" and the box is 11¼" x 9¾". The doll on the right is a J. W. Spear & Sons "character doll" with three changeable heads; she was found in the box with Daisy. Printed on her back is "Spear's Original Character Doll No. 5484."

Dolly Bright Eyes, $100.00. (These dresses are also in the Dolly Dear set shown in the Dutton section.)

Other Spear & Sons paper dolls (not pictured):
Dolly's Wardrobe
Dolly Dimple's Wardrobe
Dolly Dear, character doll with six changeable heads
Alec and His New Outfit

Simplex Toys

Simplex Toys was a company based in New York.

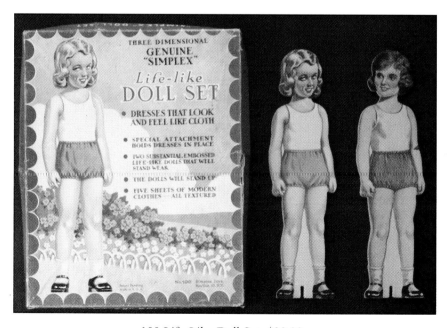

100 Life-Like Doll Set, $20.00.

R. I. Sherman Mfg. Co.

The R. I. Sherman Manufacturing Company operated out of Boston, Massachusetts.

The following paper dolls are in a set of four. They were given away free with the purchase of a 10¢ package of Diamond Finish Starch. The doll envelopes are numbered 1, 2, 3, and 4, and each includes one doll, one dress, and one hat. The dolls are not marked, but on one tab on each outfit there is the letter *B* in a diamond and the number 544. Each envelope is printed with "The R. I. Sherman Mfg. Co."

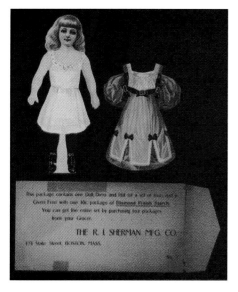

No. 1.

No. 2.

No. 3.

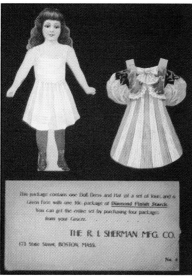

No. 4.

Two paper dolls.

Shown are two paper dolls, on the lower right, similar to No. 2 and No. 4, but which have different faces. They have the word *copyright* printed on their backs, but no other information. Outfits for these two dolls were not available.

Dolls of the Nations, 1909; left, France; right, Germany; $25.00 a sheet.

Dolls of the Nations; left, Holland; right, Italy; $25.00 a sheet.

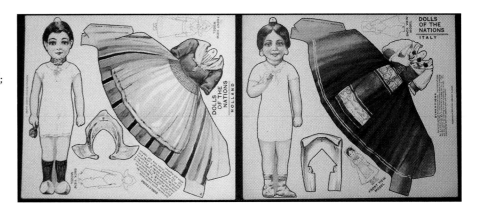

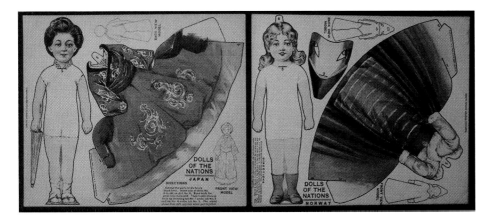

Dolls of the Nations; left, Japan; right, Norway; $25.00 a sheet.

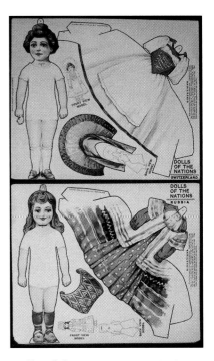

Dolls of the Nations; top, Switzerland; bottom, Russia; $25.00 a sheet.

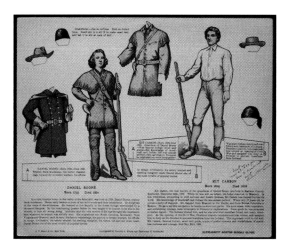

Daniel Boone and Kit Carson, $30.00 a sheet.

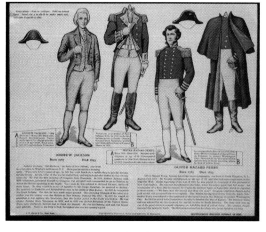

Andrew Jackson and Oliver Hazard Perry, $30.00 a sheet.

Pocahontas and John Smith, $30.00 a sheet.

Priscilla and John Alden, $30.00 a sheet.

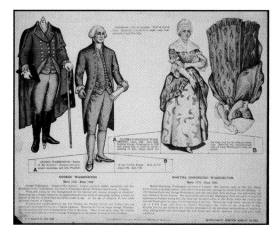

George Washington and Martha Dandridge Washington, $30.00 a sheet.

Queen Isabella of Spain and Christopher Columbus, $30.00 a sheet.

25 Magnetic Margie, $20.00.

53 Magnetic Missy, $20.00.

67 Magnetic Marcia, $20.00.

171 Combat Joe and 160 Combat Jim, $30.00 each.

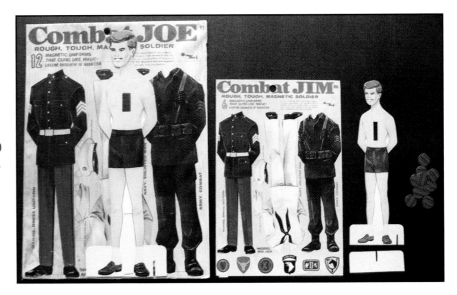

116 Magnetic Troll, 1965, $20.00. ©Uneeda Doll Company, Inc.

The following four paper dolls, issued in 1999, are not pictured:

Japan Magnetic Dress-up Keiko
Italy Magnetic Dress-up Sophia
Germany Magnetic Dress-up Leisl
Mexico Magnetic Dress-up Francisca

Spertus Publishing Co.

600 New York World's Fair "Make A Model" (stand-ups; not pictured)

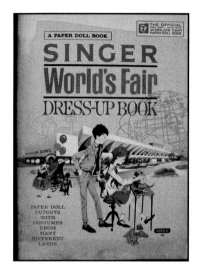

700 Singer World's Fair Dress-up Book, 1963, $15.00. The date 1961 also appears on title page.

700 Peter and Wendy Dress Up for the New York World's Fair, title page with the paper dolls.

700-59 Dress Up for the New York World's Fair, $15.00. (Inside pages same as 700.)

Standard Brands, Inc.

Charlie McCarthy's Radio Party, 1938, $50.00. Includes stand-up figures (but no outfits) of Charlie McCarthy, Edgar Bergen, Dorothy Lamour, Nelson Eddy, Don Ameche, and Robert Armbruster.

The Betty Lou series, a series of 12 sheets; each contained the same doll of Betty Lou, but each had a different title and different clothes.

Some other titles in the series are:

Betty Lou Goes to Europe
Betty Lou as a Nurse
Betty Lou as a Pilot
What Betty Lou Found in Grandmother's Trunk
Betty Lou Plays House
Betty Lou Goes to the Beach
Betty Lou in Her Garden

Betty Lou Goes to a Mother Goose Party, $35.00.

Betty Lou Takes Dancing Lessons, $35.00.

Betty Lou as the Flower Girl at a June Wedding, $35.00.

Standard Publishing Company

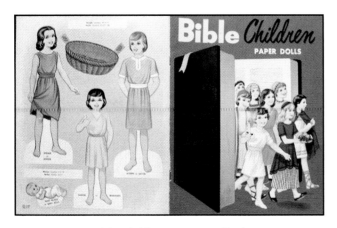

2590 Bible Children Paper Dolls, $15.00.

2591 Children of God's World, $15.00.

Stanton and Van Vliet Co.

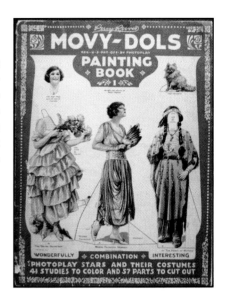

Percy Reeves Movy-Dols Painting Book I, 1919, $200.00. This book contains eight movie star paper dolls in color and the same eight stars in black and white to be colored, for a total of 16 pages of paper dolls. The eight stars include May Allison, Douglas Fairbanks, Charlie Chaplin, Elsie Ferguson, Mary Pickford, Norma Talmadge (pictured on the cover of the book), Marguerite Clark and Geraldine Farrar. The title page has "Stanton and Van Vliet Co. Publishers Chicago." The front cover of the book has, in very small print, "Walton and Spencer Co. Chicago, Ill." For pictures of the eight paper dolls, see the Walton and Spencer Company.

The Magic Circus, 1918, children and circus stand-ups (not pictured)

Stecher Lithographic Co.

In 1871, Frank A. Stecher and his partner, John Mensing, began the Lithographic and Chromo Company in Rochester, New York. In 1886 the firm was incorporated as the Stecher Lithographic Company.

Mr. Stecher died in 1916, but the company continued to flourish, and in 1933 it merged with Traung Label and Lithograph Company. In 1965 the company merged with Schmidt Lithograph Company to form the Stecher-Traung-Schmidt Corporation. The company was sold to the International Paper Corporation in 1983.

100 Bettina and Her Playmate Rosalie, $90.00.

732 Boy and Girl Cutout Doll Book, 1932, $75.00.

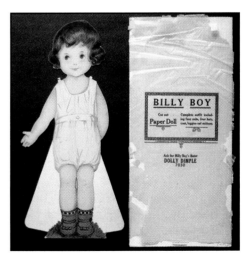

7029 Billy Boy, $70.00. (For a picture of Billy Boy's outfits, see page 178.)

7030 Dolly Dimple, $70.00.

Some dolls of Billy Boy and Dolly Dimple have "©1915 Stecher Litho. Co." printed below the doll's feet.

The following books are not pictured:

38 Betty's Painting and Cut Out Book, 1926 (stand-ups)
38 Betty's Painting Book, 1917
16 Betty's Painting Book (a smaller version of the above book)
(The #16 and #38 Painting books from 1917 have some of the same figures as the 1926 book, but they aren't made to stand up.)

The Stecher Lithographic Co. also published paper dolls of Polly Dolly and Tommy Tom. See the Hubbell Leavens Co. and the E.M. Leavens Co. for pictures of these paper dolls.

Stephens Publishing Company

135 Circus Day, 1946, $15.00.

136 June Bride, 1946, $25.00.

137 The Scissors Bird Paper Dolls, $15.00.

155 Filmland Fashions, $30.00.

156 Playtime Fashions, $30.00.

165 Playhouse Dolls, 1949, $18.00.

166 Sweetie-Pie Twins, 1949, $15.00.

175 Patty's Party, $15.00.

176 Triplet Dolls, $15.00.

177 Glamour Models, $15.00.

178 Movie Starlets, $15.00.

181 Little Sweethearts, $15.00.

183 6 Good Little Dolls, $15.00.

182 Cheerleader Teen-Age Doll Cut-outs, $15.00.

184 Glamour Parade, $15.00.

2129 Doll House Cut Outs, $15.00.

2229 Pajama Party, $15.00.

The Doll's House That Glue Built, 1910, $125.00.

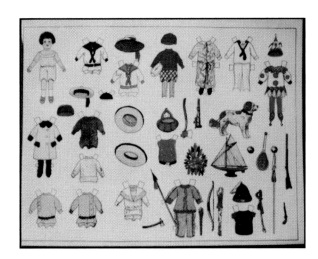

The Doll's House, inside pages.

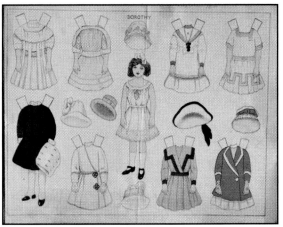

The Treasure Trunk of Dollies, 1912, $125.00.

Treasure Trunk, inside pages (not all pages are shown).

The following books are not pictured:
The Air Ships That Glue Built (cut and paste book)
The Children's Store, 1910 (stand-ups)
Famous Queens and Martha Washington, 1895
The Farm That Glue Made, 1909 (cut and paste book)
The Fun That Glue Made, 1907 (cut and paste book)
The House That Glue Built, 1905 (dollhouse book, cut and paste book)
The Kewpie Kutouts, 1914. (Paper dolls are reprinted from the *Woman's Home Companion*.)
Prince and Princess Paper Dolls, 1895
The Railway That Glue Built, 1908 (cut and paste book)
The Ships That Glue Sailed, 1910 (cut and paste book)
A Year of Paper Dolls, 1894

Stoll and Edwards Co., Inc.

Sunshine Cut-Outs (Every Day series), 1926, $80.00.

Sunshine Cut-Outs (Every Day series).

Sunshine Cut-Outs (Sports series), 1926, $80.00.

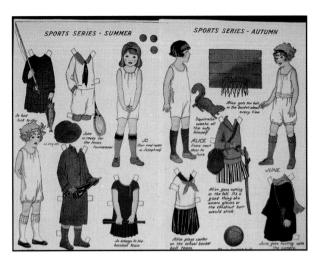

Sunshine Cut-Outs (Sports series).

Sunshine Cut-Outs (Vacation series), 1926, $80.00.

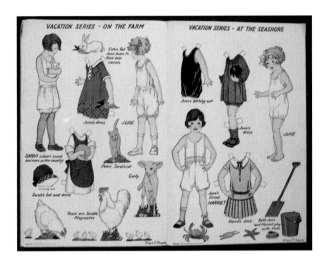

Sunshine Cut-Outs (Vacation series).

We Are the Wardrobe Paper Dolls, 1921, $80.00.

Betty Bonnet, 1915 (not pictured; originally appeared in *Ladies Home Journal*; see Geo. W. Jacobs & Co.)

Kitty Clover, 1918 (not pictured; originally Betty Bonnet in *Ladies Home Journal*; see Geo. W. Jacobs & Co.)

Polly Pitcher and Her Playmates Series One, 1917 (see Geo. W. Jacobs & Co.)

Polly Pitcher and Her Playmates Series Two, 1918 (see Geo. W. Jacobs & Co.)

Jolly Time Series (not pictured; see Geo. W. Jacobs & Co.)

Fairy Folk Series (not pictured; see Geo. W. Jacobs & Co.)

George Sully and Company

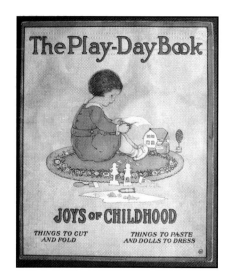

50 The Play-Day Book, 1919, $75.00.

50 Play-Day, inside page.

50 Play-Day, inside page.

50 Play-Day, inside page.

51 Dolls to Make and Dress
52 Play-Day Cut Outs
60 The Bird-Toy Book
61 Bird Cut Outs Series 1
62 Bird Cut Outs Series 2
70 The Animal Toy Book
71 Animal Cut Outs Series 1, 1919
72 Animal Cut Outs Series 2, 1919

The paper dolls in 50 Play-Day Book include the same dolls as those in 51, plus a doll named Sue (and her garden). She was also in the book Play Day Cut Outs (52).

Suntex Corporation

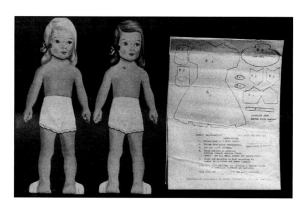

Li'l Miss Designer Kit (dolls with plastic clothes), 1953, $15.00.

Terri Lee Company

Terri Lee in 3-D (not all her clothes are shown), $150.00.

Thermoloid Corporation

Career Girl Fashion Art Set No. 1, $25.00.

Career Girl Fashion Art Set No. 2, $25.00.

Career Girl Fashion Art Set No. 3, $40.00.

Career Girl Fashion Art Set No. 3, inside contents.

Charles Thompson Company

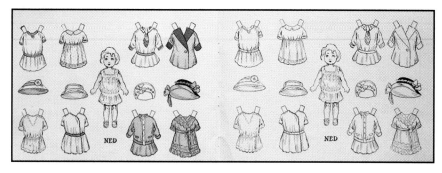

Forget-Me-Not Paper Dolls, 1912, $75.00. Forget-Me-Not and Primrose Paper Dolls have paper doll pages in color and duplicate pages in black and white to be colored.

Forget-Me-Not Paper Dolls, inside contents, two of many pages.

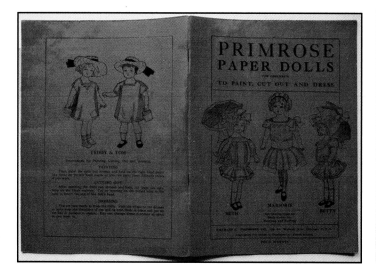

Primrose Paper Dolls, 1912, $50.00.

Primrose Paper Dolls, inside page.

Primrose Paper Dolls, inside pages.

Real Life in Dolly Land, $100.00.

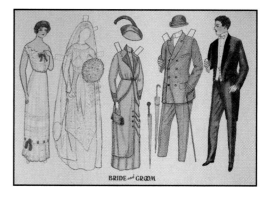

Real Life in Dolly Land, inside page.

Real Life in Dolly Land, inside page.

Real Life in Dolly Land, inside page.

Real Life in Dolly Land, inside page.

Real Life in Dolly Land, inside page.

Torme Products Co.

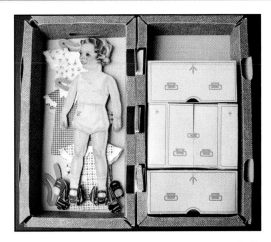

2 "Dress-Me" Dolls, 1935, set no. 9, $25.00.

Suitcase set, with "B" on the paper doll, $50.00.

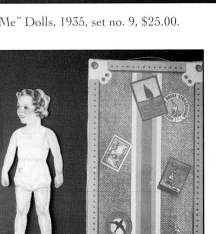

Suitcase set with trunk closed.

Totsy Mfg. Co.

The heavy cardboard paper dolls pictured here had stands that were on the sides of the right legs and shoes. The stands were perforated so that they could easily be removed. "The Totsy Mfg. Co." was printed on the stands. The paper dolls were each sold with a cloth dress that could also fit a real doll of the same size. $15.00.

Shown here is a large 20" baby paper doll that was sold with a dress that could have been used for a real doll or the paper doll. $25.00.

Toy Factory

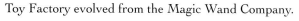

Toy Factory evolved from the Magic Wand Company.

101 Denim Dolls, 1974, $10.00.

102 Lori, 1974, $10.00.

103 Little Darlin's, 1974, $10.00.

104 Wizard of Oz, 1975, $35.00.

105 Fonzie, 1976, $20.00.

106 Kotter, 1976, $25.00.

107 Barbarino, 1976, $25.00.

108 Sweathogs, 1976, $25.00.

109 Amy, $15.00.

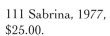

110 Jill, 1977, $25.00.

111 Sabrina, 1977, $25.00.

112 Kelly, 1977, $25.00.

303

1515 Doll House Dress Shop, 1938 – 1941, $25.00. Dolls are 4½" tall.

1517 5 American Queens, 1938, $25.00.

1530 Magic Sewing Set (with transfer patterns), 1938, $35.00.

1531 Style Show Sewing Set, 1936, $35.00. This set was produced with three, four, or five 6½" dolls. (See 4320 for all five dolls.)

1565 Little Traveler's Sewing Kit, 1940, $35.00. (1941 date inside, 1939 on doll's cardboard.)

1565 Little Traveler's Sewing Kit, 1941, $35.00. Dolls are 5½" tall and box is 7" x 12".

4101 Angela Cartwright, 1960 (not pictured; dolls same as #3450)
4106 Pam and Jeff, 1964 (not pictured; same as 4102)
1391 Little Traveler's Trunk, 1941
1561 Little Traveler's Sewing Kit, 1940

The Transogram company also published walking paper dolls. Instead of feet on the doll, there is a revolving wheel on the back of the doll that has feet printed on it. As the child moves the doll across a flat surface, the doll appears to be walking. The dolls do not have extra outfits.

3450 Angela Cartwright, 1960, $50.00.

4101 5 Model Miss Cutout Dolls, 1961, $35.00. The dolls in this set are identical to the five dolls in the Angela Cartwright set. The doll in the middle was Angela and is named Penny in this set.

3574/5 Little Traveler's Sewing Kit, 1947, $30.00. (Dates of 1941 and 1951 inside.) Box is like 3575 but smaller, and dolls are like those in 1515.

4102 Pam and Jeff, 1963, $30.00.

4320 Little Traveler's Sewing Kit, 1941, $35.00. The dolls are 6½" tall and the box is a larger size, 7½" x 14".

3575 Little Traveler's Sewing Kit, 1947 date on box, 1952 date inside, $30.00.

4101 Cutie Cut Ups, 1964, $35.00. These dolls were also used in the Angela Cartwright set.

Treasure Books

T-153 My Own Dolls to Color and Dress, 1952, $20.00.

T-167 The Dress-Up Doll Book, 1953, $20.00.

353 Dolls Around the World, 1960, $25.00.

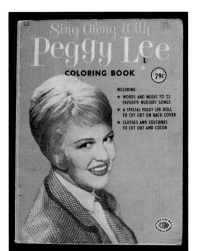

370 Sing Along With Peggy Lee, 1961, $60.00.

2901 Dress-Up Dolls, 1960.

The following sets are not pictured:

250 My First Learn and Play Book, 1954 (includes stand-ups on the back cover)
255 Busy Days, 1954 (includes two pages of paper dolls in black and white)
265 Nine Cut-out Dolls (T-153 and T-167)
265 Dolls to Cut Out (reprint of T-153)
323 Ballerina Doll Coloring Book, 1958 (includes four pages of paper dolls in black and white)
326 Bobbsey Twins Doll Coloring Book, 1958 (paper dolls from C2000, see G.P. Putnam's Sons)
350 The Little Nurse's Coloring and Cutout book, 1960 (includes paper doll in black and white)
2906 Shari Lewis and Her Puppets, 1961 (not paper dolls)
2907 Doll House, 1961 (activity book with stand-ups)
3750 Dolls to Cut Out and Color, 1957 (reprint of T-153)
9544 Scissors and Coloring Fun (reprint of T-153)
T-151 Fun and Play for Every Day, 1952 (includes two pages of paper dolls in black and white)
T-166 The Merry Mailman, 1953 (includes stand-ups on the back cover)
T-172 Let's Visit the Zoo (includes stand-ups on the back cover)

Trim Molded Products Company

B101 Creative Cut-Outs, 5 Stand-Up Plastic Ballet Girls, $10.00.

C102 Creative Cut-Outs, The Doll House Family, $10.00.

Tuttle Press Co.

The Tuttle Press Company was located in Appleton, Wisconsin.

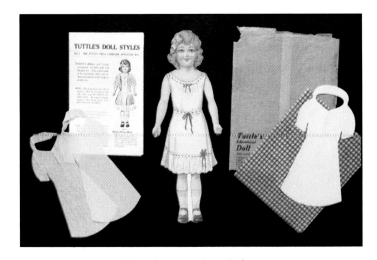

Tuttles Educational Doll, $35.00.

Ullman Mfg. Co., Art Publishers

This company was founded in 1887. It merged with Standard Toykraft (Avalon) in the 1900s.

1022 Paradise of Paper Dolls, $50.00.

713 The Life of Gloria Stanley Told in Paper Dolls, $150.00. The paper dolls in this set are the same as those in Gloria Stanley Dolls on page 310.

944 Priscilla Crayon Outfit with Paper Dolls, $50.00. Two other paper doll sheets (from the Winnie Weston's set 1011) were also included in this set.

1011 Winnie Weston's Dolls and Their Wardrobe, $60.00.

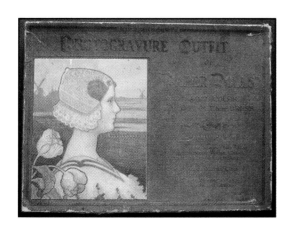

1022 Photogravure Outfit of Paper Dolls, 1920, $50.00.

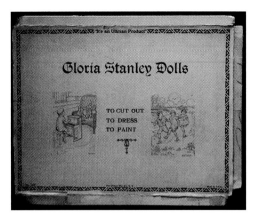

7241 Gloria Stanley Dolls, $150.00 if complete. Shown above and below are four of six known sheets.

Not pictured:

745 Gloria's Dolls, box set with paints and crayons. Includes the same paper dolls as 713 and 7241.

Universal Toy and Novelty Mfg. Co.

The Universal paper dolls were sold in sets or by the sheet.

Dotty Dimple's Dolls, $100.00.

Maude's Sport Suits, $20.00.

Paper Toy Dolls, $20.00.

Flossie's Robes, $20.00.

Dotty Dolls, $80.00.

Dotty Dolls, $20.00.

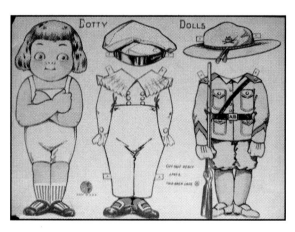

Dotty Dolls, $20.00.

This sheet is sometimes found with
the name Sunshine Sue. $20.00.

$20.00.

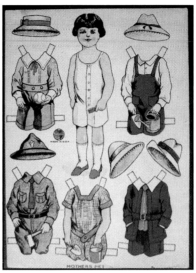

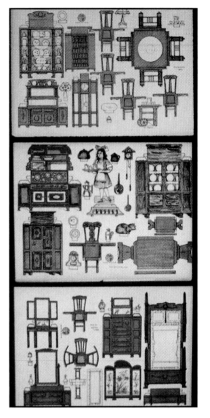

Tommy Tucker, $20.00 each. The sheet on the right is the same as the Tommy Tucker on the left but it was printed in reverse.

Mother's Pet, $20.00.

Not pictured:

Mary's Trousseau

Furniture Sheets, $10.00 each.

Vogue

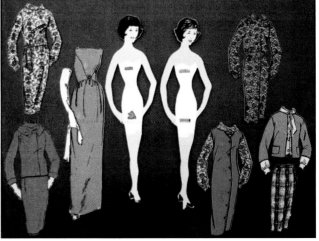

Vogue's Magnetic Board Kit, $40.00. This was used by Home Economics teachers in their classes. Clothes in the sets could vary.

P.F. Volland & Co.

P.F. Volland & Company of Chicago (Joliet), Illinois, was known for its exceptionally fine books for children and for its greeting cards. One line of books that is particularly well known is the Raggedy Ann series by Johnny Gruelle (*Raggedy Ann in Cookie Land*, *Raggedy Ann's Magical Wishes*, etc.). These books were later reprinted by the Donohue Company in Chicago and, more recently, by the Bobbs-Merrill Company.

A set of six paper dolls was also published by the company, with the title of Paper Playmates and Their Frocks. They were issued either in a glassine envelope with all six dolls, or as two sets in small boxes with three dolls in a box. Shown is the set with the glassine envelope.

There was also a set of greeting cards issued, each card with a doll from the six-doll set. Shown is the card with the baby and its two outfits. The baby fits in the basket. The card is 4400 and is copyrighted 1915.

Paper Playmates and Their Frocks, $100.00.

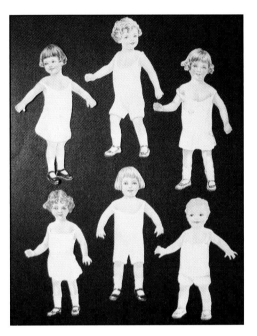

The six dolls from Paper Playmates.

1915 Greeting Card with baby paper doll, $35.00.

Walton and Spencer Co.

The Walton and Spencer Company was in Chicago.

Percy Reeves Movy-Dols Photoplay Stars in Cut-Outs, 1919, $200.00. This is a portfolio type of folder that contains eight pages of movie stars. The pages are on two large fold-out sheets with four paper dolls on each sheet. Each page is dated 1919 for the paper dolls 1 – 4, and the date of 1920 is on the paper dolls 5 – 8. Each page states "Published by Percy Reeves, 1245 State Street, Chicago." In small print at the bottom of the folder is printed "Walton and Spencer Co. Chicago."

1) Mary Pickford.

2) Elsie Ferguson.

3) Norma Talmadge.

4) Charlie Chaplin.

5) Geraldine Farrar.

6) May Allison. 7) Marguerite Clark. 8) Douglas Fairbanks.

These paper dolls were also produced by the Stanton and Van Vliet Company of Chicago, as a combination paper doll and painting book.

Warren Paper Products

Built-Rite Division

Warren Paper Products was established in 1921 in Lafayette, Indiana. It began as a manufacturer of cardboard containers for items such as candy, jewelry, etc. In the early 1930s the company began producing doll houses of paper board. Toy forts and toy gas stations also were made at that time, and in the 1940s they added stations and towns for train sets, furniture for the doll houses and farm sets. All the sets were of paper board and were made to be put together easily.. Paper dolls, doll houses and other toy sets were produced by the Built-Rite Division of Warren Paper Products. Paper dolls were introduced in the early 1950s and were produced up until 1970. In 1990, Rose Art Industries purchased the Warren Company.

Currently the company produces a nice line of picture puzzles and games.

Following the list of the company's paper dolls is a list of its early toy sets and doll houses, which have become quite collectible. Since the paper dolls were not dated, catalog dates are given when known.

15 Cindy and Lindy (1955 and 1956 catalogs)	359 TV Paper Doll set, Talent Show (1957 and 1958 catalogs)
15 Debby and Dotty (1955 and 1956 catalogs)	460 Magic Press-On Paper dolls (in small playing card size box, in 1961 and 1962 catalogs)
33 Ann and Pam (1953 – 1961 catalogs)	
33 Jan and Ann	488 Country and Western
33 Jan and Jean (1953 – 1961 catalogs, two different editions of dolls)	842 The Dress Up Game
	845 Color By Number Paper Dolls
33 Marge and Mary (dolls same as Sandy and Candy)	846 Kiddies Fun Kit (includes a stand-up circus and other paper toys)
33 Sandy and Candy (1953 – 1961 catalogs)	847 Two Big Stand-Up Dolls, Color and Re-Color. (1959 and 1960 catalogs. Later, in the 1963 catalog, the name of the set was changed to Color by Number Doll Set and was thereafter listed in catalogs up to 1970)
33 Toni and Terry	
34 Joan and Bill	
35 Jean and Janet (not pictured; dolls same as Ann and Pam)	
359 TV Paper Doll Set, Barn Dance Jamboree (1957 and 1958 catalogs)	848 Four Merri-Time Dolls with Life Like Fur Garments (1960 – 1968 catalogs)

867 The Dress-Up Game (not pictured; 1963 – 1970 catalogs)
970 Furry Garments (not pictured; 1962 catalog)
2006 Junior Miss (game chest that includes 842 and 359 talent show; 1969 and 1970 catalogs)
2420-1 My Little Pony, 1984 (not pictured)
2425 Charmkins, 1983
8600 The Dress Up Game (842)

Built-Rite doll houses, toy buildings, and stand-ups:

1 Toy Soldiers
2 Trench Set
7 Dollhouse made for *Life Magazine*
7 Toy Garage
8 Doll House
9 Doll House
10 Two Story Doll House
10 One Room Furnished Doll House
11 Playtime Doll House, style 4
11 Playtime Doll House, style 6
12 Playtime Doll House, style 24
14 Trench and Soldier set
14 Play Time Doll House, style 20
15 Toy Garage
16 Toy Fort
17 Gas Station
18 Airport
19 Railroad Station
20 Model Stock Farm, plastic animals
20 Battery Set
20 Railroad Tunnel
22 Army outpost, 20 "action" soldiers
24 Toy Fort Set
25 Toy Fort Set
26 United Airlines Airport Hanger
27 Doll Mansion
27 Barn with Animals
28 Playtime Doll House, style 12
29 Three Car Set
33F Built-Rite Toy House
34 Doll House
35 Modern Doll House
36 Doll House
36F Three Room Furnished Doll House
37 Farm Machinery Set
40 Railroad Accessory Set, suburban
41 Miniature Village, 11 buildings
45 Railroad Set, passenger and freight stations

45 Living Room Furniture
46 Dining Room Furniture
47 Dolly's Roomette, playhouse
47 Bedroom Furniture
49 Kitchen Furniture
51 Bedroom Playroom Set
52 Dining Room Play Room Set
53 Kitchen Play Room Set
55 Miniature Houses
56 Miniature Buildings
57M Miniature Farm Buildings
66 Build Your Own Kitchen
75 Living Room Furniture
76 Dining Room Furniture
77 Bedroom Furniture
78 Kitchen Furniture
98 Motor Set
99 Garage with 6 Cars
99 Garage with 3 Cars
100 Fortress
105 Farm Set, barn and plastic animals, etc.
111 Train Accessory Set
112 American Soldiers
115 Furnished Doll House with Garage
119 Stock Farm Deluxe
119 Built-Rite Farm Set
120 Five Room Suburban Doll House
127 Large Farm
128 Miniature Village & Scenery Set
148 Train Accessory Set
156 Miniature Houses and Buildings
178 Train Accessory Set
201 Guardsmen
204F Doll house
212 Station and Railroad Accessory Set
245 Train Accessory Set
252 26 Piece Fort Set
257 Fort and Soldiers Set
298 Train Accessory Set
415 Doll House and Garage
459 Five Rooms of Toy Furniture
498 Train Accessory Set
556 Miniature Village
1033 Built-Rite Toy House
1075 Built-Rite Cottage
1422 94 Piece Fortress Set
2050 Country Estate Doll House
4132 Nativity Set

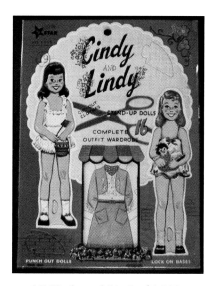

15 Cindy and Lindy, $16.00.

15 Debby and Dotty, $16.00.

33 Jan and Ann, $16.00.

33 Marge and Mary, $16.00.

33 Sandy and Candy, $16.00.

33 Jan and Jean, $16.00.

33 Jan and Jean, $16.00.

33 Ann and Pam, $16.00.

33 Toni and Terry, $16.00.

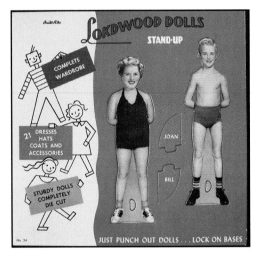

34 Joan and Bill, $16.00.

359 TV Paper Doll Set, Barn Dance Jamboree, $25.00.

359 TV Paper Doll Set, Talent Show, $25.00.

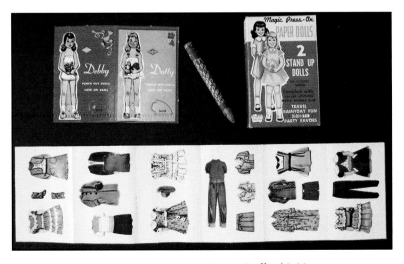

460 Magic Press-On Paper Dolls, $8.00.

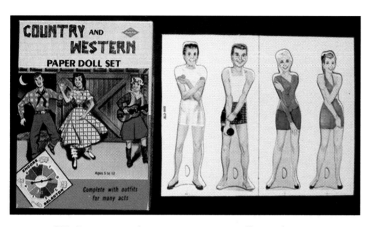

488 Country and Western Paper Doll Set, $20.00.

842 The Dress-Up Game, $30.00.

845 Color by Number Doll Set, $20.00.

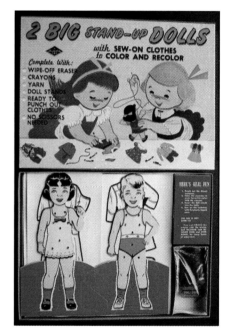

847 2 Big Stand-Up Dolls, $20.00.

848 4 Merri-Time Dolls with Life Like Fur Garments, $25.00.

2006 Junior Miss Game Chest, $40.00.

2425 Charmkins, 1983, $15.00.

The Whitehall Publishing Company of Chicago published sets of children's books, and some sets contained paper doll books. One set, Children's Workshop, was produced in a two-sided folder that contained six small coloring books and six small paper doll "Dress-up" booklets. The paper doll popped up on the front of each booklet and the clothes were on a fold-out of six pages. Another set, which doesn't have a title, is in a box like a small suitcase. It contains the same six paper dolls, but in a different format, and some of the names of the dolls have changed. There are three Double Doll pop-up books with two paper dolls in each book. The paper dolls pop up on the inside of the book, and the clothes are in small separate booklets. The clothes are the same as those in the Children's Workshop set, but there is one less page of clothes for the dolls in this set. Also included in this set are three Copy-Color books, each with a pop-up scene.

Box set with three pop-up paper doll books. (These are Dress-Up Jumbo and Bunny, 1950; Dress-up Puss and Chicky, 1950; and Dress Up Teddy and Dolly, 1950. The doll of Jumbo was also published alone as Mumbo the Elephant Dress-Up, and Puss was done alone as Shuffle On Catsy Dress-Up.) $45.00.

Dress-Up Teddy and Dolly, inside of book showing the dolls and the two booklets that contain their clothes, 1950.

Children's Workshop, folder with six small paper doll booklets and six story/coloring books, with an envelope for each. The six paper dolls include Teddy Bear, Wee Chicky, Raggedy Ann, Funny Bunny, Mumbo, and Shuffle On Catsy. $60.00.

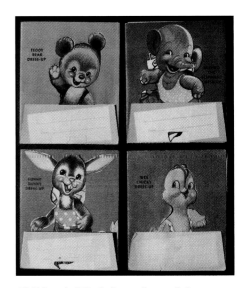

Children's Workshop, four of the paper doll booklets.

Whitehall Pub. Company, continued:

Children's Workshop, Raggedy Ann and her clothes.

Albert Whitman and Company

Brownies from Bingo-Land, 1922, $75.00.

Brownies from Bingo-Land, one page from book.

Other Cut-Out Books by Albert Whitman & Co. (not pictured):

Fairy Cut-Outs from Fairy-Land
Clown Cut-Outs from Circus-Land
Animal Cut-Outs from Ark-Land

One of the most collectible items produced by this company is *The Mary Frances Housekeeper, Adventures Among the Doll People*, 1914. This is a hardcover book with four color pages of paper dolls and four duplicate pages in black and white. There are also 14 pages of paper furniture in color, and again, each of these is duplicated in black and white. This was done to allow removal of the color pages without breaking the continuity of the storybook. The child was also encouraged to use the black and white pages for tracing, to make additional paper dolls and furniture. The story is about a family of paper dolls in need of a house in which to live. There are 253 pages in the book. The child reader learns the art of housekeeping in an enjoyable manner. Included in the book are detailed instructions for making a cardboard dollhouse for the paper dolls.

Other books in the series are *The Mary Frances Sewing Book*, *The Mary Frances Cook Book*, and *The Mary Frances Garden Book*, but these books do not contain paper dolls.

There is a reprint of *The Mary Frances Housekeeper* entitled *Easy Steps in Housekeeping*.

The book pictured is in mint condition, with all paper doll and furniture pages intact, and has the dust jacket.

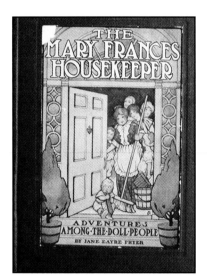  

The Mary Frances Housekeeper, 1914, $200.00 and up.

The Mary Frances Housekeeper, inside pages.

First Days in School, 1942, $50.00.

The John C. Winston Company, continued:

First Days in School, inside pages.

Winthrop-Atkins Co., Inc.

405 Tammy's Magic Mirror Fashion Show, $30.00.

6310 Martha Ann, $20.00.

6310 Patty Anne (not pictured)

6685 Pebbles, 1974; 6686 Bamm-Bamm, 1974; $15.00 each.

6687 Pebbles and Bamm-Bamm, 1974; 6688 Wilma and Fred, 1974; $15.00 each.

6689 Betty and Barney, 1974; 6690 Yogi and Cindy, 1974; $15.00 each.

9600 Heidi, 1971, $15.00.

9601 Alice In Wonderland, 1971, $15.00.

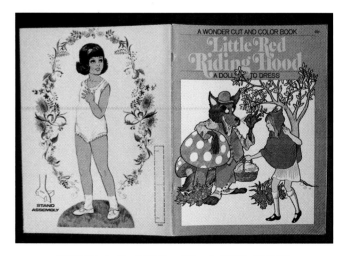

9602 Little Red Riding Hood, 1971, $15.00.

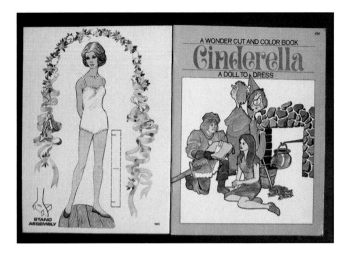

9603 Cinderella, 1971, $15.00.

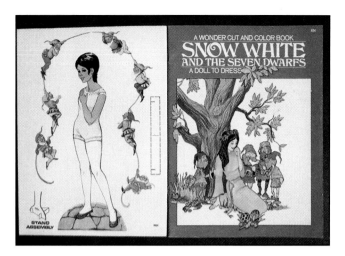

9604 Snow White, 1971, $15.00.

9605 Bride and Groom, 1971, $15.00.

2509 Hansel & Gretel, $15.00.

2509 Hansel & Gretel (back cover).

The World Publishing Company

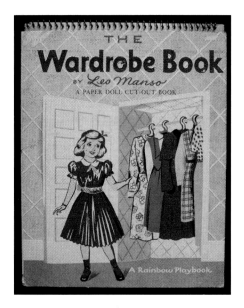

R-501 The Wardrobe Book, 1952, $35.00.

R-501 The Wardrobe Book, inside page of dolls.

World Syndicate Publishing Company

1265 Brownies to Cut-out Crayon and Paint (some pages printed in color), 1930, $75.00

Other known paper doll sets (not pictured):

1201 Little Elves (elves, clothes, and animals to cut out and color), 1930
1202 Fairyland Sprites (with outfits to color and cut out), 1930
1266 Fairies from Fairyland (original © by Albert Whitman, 1922), 1929

Unknown Publishers

These paper dolls have become known to paper doll collectors as the "American Beauties" paper dolls. Envelopes have been found with the following titles: American Beauties, Rosebud, Tiny Ladies, and Little Tots.

American Beauties No. 1, $75.00. The envelope is missing but is similar to that for No. 2. It shows the doll wearing the first dress to the right of the doll.

American Beauties No. 2, $75.00.

Rosebud Series A, $75.00.

Rosebud Series B, $75.00. Envelope B is exactly the same as that for series A, but is printed in green ink.

Extra dress. This dress and hat match the style of outfits and hats for those of Rosebud B, and may belong to her. However, it would give her four dresses and hats instead of three like the other dolls have.

Tiny Ladies, $75.00. The clothes for this doll are the same as those in the Rosebud Series A. Note that both dolls are holding boxes of candy.

Tiny Ladies, $75.00.

Little Tots, $75.00.

Little Tots, $75.00.

The origins of the following two paper dolls have been a mystery for many years. No publisher or title has been found as yet.

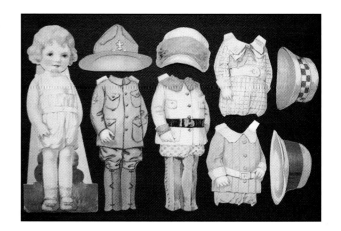

 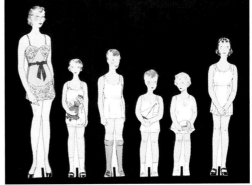

1672 Reelwood "Stand-ups" Dolls and Cut-outs, $40.00. No publisher given, just "Sandusky New York" printed on box.

Additional Companies

Addison-Wesley Pub. Co.
  Humphrey Robot, 1983

Alchemy II, Inc.
  The World of Teddy Ruxpin Fan Club
  Press-out Book, 1986

Alphabet Soup
  Paper Boys, 1984

Amav Industries
  6015 Lace-up Wardrobe Dolls, 1988

A.M. Lockwood, Cleveland, Ohio
  "Stand-ups" dolls and cut-outs #22, box set

Andrews McMeel Publishing
  Child's Play, A Paper Doll Book, 1997
  Child's Play featuring Ann Estelle, A Paper
  Doll Book, 1998

Artamo Co.
  12" walking paper doll with patterns to
  make cloth clothes.
    (The patent for the doll is held by the
    Transogram Co.)

Athena Publishing Company
  Antique French Doll Paper Dolls, 1975
  Antique German Bisque Paper Dolls, 1977
  Dolls of the 1930s, 1976
  The Antique Dolls Go to a Paper Doll
  Wedding, 1976

Atlantic Plastics, Cleveland, Ohio
  07105 Doll-Up-Dolly, 1949

Avon Books (division of Hearst Corp.)
  75127 Gilda Radner, 1979

Bantam Doubleday Dell Publishing Group
  Anne of Green Gables, 1994

Bellerophon Books
  Queen Elizabeth I Paper Dolls to Color, 1972
  Royal Family Paper Dolls, 1982
  Henry VIII and His Wives Paper Dolls to
  Color, 1972
  Great Women Paper Dolls, 1974 (reprinted
  in 1977)
  Infamous Women Paper Dolls, 1976
  Paper Dolls of the French Revolution, 1993

Betty's Store
  Betty Boop Goes to Hollywood, 1984

Binny and Smith, Inc.
  7516 Fashion Dolls, 1981

Brightside Toys — The Gates Group
  Kabuki Dolls With Costumes to Color and
  Cut Out, 1983

Breyer Animal Creations, Division of Breyer
  Molding Co.
  My English Horseshow, 1971
  My Welsh Ponies, 1973
  My Western Horseshow, 1972 (contains
  paper dolls to color)

Cader Books (Three Rivers Press)
  Mad About Martha, 1996
  Bad as I Wanna Dress — Dennis Rodman,
  1997

Candlewich Press
  Maisy's Pop-Up Playhouse, 1995 (with mouse
  paper doll)

Chicago Historical Society
  Fashion Paper Dolls from the Costume
  Collection

Child's Welfare Co., Chicago
  Pastime Occupations
  Susie & her twin Bobbie

Collins and World Publishing Co.
  Paper Dolls of the Middle East, 1978

Colorgraphics, Inc., Chicago, IL (subsidiary
  of the Meyercord Co.)
  900 Sculpture-ettes, 1942
  925 Sculpture-ettes, 1943

Congdon and Weed, Inc.
  Monster Paper Dolls, 1983

Creative Child Games (Playmore and Wald-
  man Publishing Corp.)
  29019 My Beautiful Paper Doll Set, 1992
    (contains four small paper doll boxes
    with numbers 19501, 19502, 19503, and
    19504)

Creative Imaginations, Inc.
  Mary Engelbreit's Ann Estelle's Friend
  Sophie, 1999
  Ann Estelle's Friend Michael, 1999

Creative Toys
  Lace-Up/Dress-Up (no number)
  My Dolly 2350
  Jack and Jill 5016

Crest Industries Corp.
  Fashion Fun Dress-Up Paper Doll Set

Cross Publishing Co.
  Curly-Top Visits the Holy Land. (This is a
  reprint of the DeJournette set with this
  same title.)

Current, Inc.
  A Sugarplum Dream, 1990
  Beatrice Bunny, 1991
  Boy Paper Doll, no date
  Butterfield Bear, 1989
  Characters with Heart, no date, circa 1980
  Easter Bears, no date, circa 1997

8 Lace on Teddy Bears, no date
Elizabeth's Castle Adventure, 1992
Friends Around the World, no date, circa 1994
Frontier Friendship Paper Dolls, 1989
Getaway Dolls, 1983
Girl Paper Doll, no date
Heather Honey Paws, 1989
Lace-me-ups, no date, circa 1979
Lucy and Company Paper Doll Set, no date, circa 1994
Miss Victoria Rose, no date, circa 1991
Paper Play set, 1983
Playtime Pals, 1982
Thanksgiving Bears, no date, circa 1996
When I Grow Up, 1980

Deluxe Game Corporation, New York
The Little Dressmaker (suitcase style box set with five paper dolls and sewing items to make cloth clothes for the dolls.)

Discovery Toys, Inc.
Pajama Party, 1991, 1992

Dollar Tree Dist.
21622 Paper Doll Glitter Fun

Dol-Lee-Dolls
Mary Lee, 1951 (a paper doll known as a "Ribbon Doll")

Doll-E-Inlay, Grand Rapids, MI
101 Girl Puzzle, 1954 (a tray type puzzle of a girl with two extra dresses)
103 Boy Puzzle, 1954 (a tray type puzzle of a boy with two extra suits)

Doubleday & Co., Inc., Dolphin Books
This Year's Girl, 1985
U.S.A. Fun and Play, 1966

Dover Publications, Inc.
This is just a sample of the many paper dolls books this company produces.
Fashion Paper Dolls from "Godey's Lady's Book" (1840 – 1854), 1977
Pavlova and Nijinsky, 1981
Kate Greenaway, 1981
Great Empresses and Queens, 1982
Peter Rabbit Paper Dolls, 1982
Curious George, 1982
Carmen Miranda, 1982
Peter Rabbit Toy Theater, 1984 (includes paper dolls)

Dress Yourself Doll Co.
For this paper doll set, the child would send in a picture of herself and receive a paper doll with her face. Clothes for the paper doll were also included.

Eberhard Faber Toy and Game Co. (Div. of Eberhard Faber Pen & Pencil Co.)
5261 Fashion Designer (includes a 10" paper doll)

Eclipse Books
California Girls Paper Dolls, 1988
Paper Dolls From The Comics, 1987

Eukabi Publishers
American Indian Dances, 1952
Kachina Dolls, 1952

Evergreen Press
Antique German Bisque paper dolls, 1977
Louisa May Alcott's Little Women paper dolls, 1981
Antique French Dolls paper dolls, 1975
Dolls of the 30s paper dolls, 1976
The Antique Dolls go to a Paper Doll Wedding, 1976
A Paper Doll from the Caroline Burford Danner Costume Collection, 1990
A Royal Romance, 1983

Famus Corporation
Patty's Playmates (same paper dolls and clothes as Paper Playmates by the M. Shimmel Sons, Inc.)

Foundation Desk Co., Inc., Chicago, IL
The Juvenile Artist 1923, 1924 (large book of activities for children, includes 4 paper dolls)

Fun World
8626 Fancy Nancy's Fashion Boutique (paper doll with a cloth dress that will fit an 11½" "fashion doll")

Gates Group
Genevieve, the Velvet Touch paper doll, 1985
Mark Twain's Tom Sawyer and Becky Thatcher Velvet Touch paper dolls, 1986

Getherease, Inc.
Costumes of Splendid China, 1993

Golden Gate International Exposition
Treasure Island Twins, 1939

Hallmark
It's Fun to Pretend, 1981

Harper Festival (Division of Harper Collins)
My Book of Little House Paper Dolls, 1995 (Big Woods Collection)
My Book of Little House Christmas Paper Dolls (Christmas on the Prairie), 1996
My Book of Little House Paper Dolls (A Day on the Prairie), 1997
My Little House Christmas Sticker Book (Santa Claus Comes to the Prairie) includes paper dolls, 1997
Growing Up with Dick and Jane, 1996, includes stand-up figures
Little Princess Paper Dolls, 1999
Narnia Paper Dolls, 1998
Secret Garden Paper Dolls, 1998

Hasbro, Inc.
Cut-It-Out! Project Set, 1993
Wendy the weather Girl

Henry Heininger Co. (Dodge Publishing Co.)
The Happy Family Movie Dolls

Hermann HDKF Co.
My Hanky Doll — A Hanky Book with Cut-Outs (paper dolls), 1949. There are different editions, with different paper dolls.

Higley Press
Sammy and Sue Go Visiting
Sammy and Sue Go to Church

Hobby House Press
A Fashion Doll's Paper Doll Diary, 1988
Aimee, 1996
American Colonial Brides, 1980
Danielle, 1996
Effanbee Presents Storybook Paper Doll, 1979
Effanbee Presents Through the Years with Gigi, 1830 – 1900 Paper Doll, 1979
Effanbee Presents Currier and Ives Paper Doll, 1979
Effanbee's Wee Patsy Paper Dolls & Playhouse, 1996
Folk Art Paper Dolls, 1989
Historic French Costumes, 1991
Katy Keene, 1988
Katy and Gloria in "Meow Meow" Paper Dolls, 1992
Katy Keene Hollywood Premiere Paper Dolls, 1994
Katy Keene Swimsuit Illustrated paper Dolls, 1995
Katy Keene Romance Paper Dolls, 1996
Katy Keene Movie Premiere Paper Dolls, Featuring Movie Star "Errol Swoon," 1996
Paper Dolls in the style of Mucha, 1993
Sis the Candy Kit, 1989

Illuminations, Inc.
05401 Mary Elizabeth, 1987
05402 Allison, 1987
05403 Nicole, 1987
05404 Jonathan James, 1987
05405 Emily, Thomas, Baby Gwen, 1987
05406 Mrs. Charlotte, Mr. Edward, 1987

Imperial Toy Corporation
Petticoats and Pantaloons, 1979

Interlyth, New York
Make Believe Theatre (includes paper doll actors with costumes)

J. Olson
Stand Me Up Dolls, 1951

JBJ Quality Products, Inc.
Bonita's Closet, 1983
Bonnie's Closet, 1983

Jak Pak, Inc.
0134 Wendy's Wardrobe (some sets have the number 301)

Jane Gray Co., New York
The Rainbow Party, 1916

Kenner
254G Kenner's New Fashion Fun, Sparkle Paints, 1968 (includes paper doll and outfits)

Kunen Publishers, Inc.
  The Paper Doll Jigsaw Puzzle Book, 1949

Lah-Ti-Da Creations
  Life Story Paper Doll, Debbie, 1977
  Life Story Paper Doll, Felicia, 1978

Lakeside Toys (Div. of Lakeside Industries, Inc., Minneapolis, MN)
  Betsy McCall Fashion Designer, 1961
  Barbie and Skipper Fashion Designer, 1965

La Velle Mfg. Co.
  Little Dressmaker, 1922
  No. 14 Kolorit Set, circa 1923. Includes six paper dolls, four sheets of clothes, paints and crayons.

Learning Works
  LW361 Paper Doll Party, 1996
  LW363 Design A Paper Doll You, 1996
  LW373 Paper Doll Christmas, 1997
  Jewish Paper Doll Book, 1997

Lechtman Printing Co., Kansas City, MO
  Dollie Dolls, 1933

Lee Publications
  M560-PD Magnetic Paper Dolls Set 2, Fashion Show (in tin box)

Lillian Vernon
  LV 4389 Paper Doll Kit, 1988

Little Brown & Co.
  Dress Your Bear, Seven Bears to Cut Out and Dress, 1994

Macmillan
  Newt! 1995

Makatoy Co., Chicago
  100 stencil outfit for making paper dolls

Make Pretend, Inc.
  7002 Amish Doll Set, 1994; 7003 Early American Doll Set, 1994
  7005 Pilgrim Doll Set, 1994
  Victorian Doll House, 1994 (includes paper dolls)

M&R (Toy) Mfg. Inc.
  11106 Country Kids Paper Dolls
  11107 Party Time Paper Dolls

Martha Pullen Company, Inc.
  Heirloom Paper Dolls, 1991

Mayfair Novelty Co., New York
  Doll Cut Outs (paper doll sheet with a girl and boy)

McKim Studios, Independence, MO
  World Traveler Dollies (light cardboard sheets of paper dolls)

Meritus Industries, Inc.
  79002 Ginny, 1984 (Vogue Dolls)

Merrimack Publishing Corporation (A subsidiary of B. Shackman, Co. Inc.)

This is just a sample of the many paper dolls that this company has produced:
  50810 Bonnie, an Old Fashioned Bunnie, 1986
  30326 Circus Teddy Bear, 1983
  8467 The Hopper Family, 1989
  90374 History of Little Fanny
  3052 Kate Greenaway
  30243 Kitty Cucumber, 1983

Michel and Co.
  Betsy Rose

MJ Studios, Inc. (Nickel Press)
  Deluxe Native American Princess Paper Doll Set, 1995
  Deluxe Victorian Paper Doll Set, 1995

My Ladye Faire Doll Co.
  Evening Gown Series 1, 2, 3, 4 and 5

Neptune Plastics, Inc.
  898 Be A Li'l Miss Designer (see Suntex Corporation)

New American Library
  The Official J.A.P. Paper Doll Book, 1983 (John Boswell Associates)

North American Bear Company, Inc.
  Muffy Vanderbear Collection (cardboard display piece with a rotating wheel that changes Muffy's clothes as it turns)

O.B. Andrews Co., Chattanooga, TN
  Betsy, Amy, Dotty, Jill. (Each doll and outfits are packaged separately in small folders.)

O.W. Nelson
  20½" doll in light blue dress
  20½" doll in pink dress. The dolls and their three outfits and hats are marked "O.W. Nelson" on the back. The dolls also are marked "American Lithographic Co. N.Y." These two dolls were also used to advertise Minard's Liniment.

Ohio Art
  33D190 No. 33 Lookin' Pretty, Sports
  34D190 No. 34 Lookin' Pretty, Summertime
  35D190 No. 35 Lookin' Pretty, Everyday

Old Sturbridge Village
  Old Sturbridge Village paper dolls

Our Tiny Treasures, Inc.
  The Elise Doll Designer Fashions, 1984

P&A
  3-206 Victorian Roses and Lace
  4-265 Flower Girls paper dolls

Paper Palace
  Victoria, ©1981

Peck-Aubry
  This is just a sample of some of the many paper dolls this company has produced:
  Anne of Green Gables, 1995
  Barbie (many different nostalgic sets)
  Elvis, the early years, 1996
  Gone with the Wind, 1999

Little Women, 1994 (a reprint of the Peck-Gandré 1993 set)
  Little Women, 1999 (different from above book)
  Secret Garden, 1995

Peck-Gandré
  This is just a sample of some of the many paper dolls this company has produced:
  Alice in Wonderland, 1992
  Dorothy Visit's Oz, 1992
  Goldilocks and the Three Bears, 1988
  Little Women, 1993
  Mein Liebling, 1983
  Nostalgic Barbie, 1989
  Nostalgic Ken, 1989
  Prince Charming, 1987
  Sleeping Beauty, 1987
  Wendy Ann Series, 1993

Penguin Putnam, Inc.
  Amazing Grace, 1998

Petco Press
  Gabby the Goldfish, 1953
  Biffy the Elf, 1953
  Henry the Honeybee, 1953

Pinkham Press
  Triple Joy Book, 1927, includes paper dolls

Playmore Inc., Publishers (also listed under Creative Child Games)
  My Beautiful Paper Doll Set, 1992. (Four small boxes in one large box. The small boxes contains Sports Doll, Beach Doll, Wedding Doll, and Cheerleader.)

Playskool, Inc.
  Dress Up Puzzles, 1981

Pleasant Company Publications (The American Girls Collection)
  American Girls Paper Dolls, 1990 (Kirsten, Samantha, and Molly)
  American Girls: Molly McIntire and Her Old-Fashioned Outfits for You to Cut Out, 1992
  American Girls: Samantha Parkington and Her Old-Fashioned Outfits for You to Cut Out, 1992
  American Girls: Felicity Merriman and Her Old-Fashioned Outfits for You to Cut Out, 1992
  American Girls: Kirsten Larson and Her Old-Fashioned Outfits for You to Cut Out, 1992
  American Girls: 4 American Girls Kit, 1992 (Molly, Samantha, Felicity, and Kirsten)
  American Girls: Molly's Paper Dolls, 1994
  American Girls: Kirsten's Paper Dolls, 1994
  American Girls: Felicity's Paper Dolls, 1994
  American Girls: Addy's Paper Dolls, 1994
  American Girls: Samantha's Paper Dolls, 1994
  American Girls: Josefina's Paper Dolls, 1998

Pleasure Books, Inc., Chicago
  140 Fairy Tale Cut Out Dolls and Furniture, 1936

Pocket Books
  The Royal Baby, 1983

Additional Companies

Prentice-Hall, Inc.
Thirty from the 30s, 1974

Press Pacifica
Hawaiian Royalty Paper Dolls, 1985

Price Stern Sloan, Inc.
Bare Bear's New Clothes, 1986
Santa's New Suit, 1993

Product Sales International, Inc.
Pinafore Pockets Fun Folder, 1991

Puffin Books, Viking Penguin, Inc.
Baby Mouse, 1984
Dressing Teddy, 1986
Teddy's Birthday Party, 1986
Teddy's Holiday, 1987

R.S. Peck & Co.
Playmate Paper Dolls, 1932

Rainfall Educational Toys, Div. of Chariot
Family Publishing
Face to Face with Women of the Bible Paper
Dolls, Deborah and Barak
Face to Face with Women of the Bible
Paper Dolls, Mary, Joseph and Baby Jesus
Face to Face with Women of the Bible
Paper Dolls, Queen Esther and King Xeres

Rayna
Abraham Ak, Annie Ak (Eskimo paper
dolls), 1979

Red Farm Studio
Kim's Paper Doll Coloring Book, 1978
Kim's Cousin Ginger's Paper Doll Coloring
Book, 1982
Kim's Paper Doll Travels Around the
World, 1978
Jeremy and Jennifer Bear Paper Dolls,
1978
Kim's cousins Bobby and Ginger Paper
Dolls coloring book (no date)

Rose Art Industries, Inc.
1760 Cabbage Patch Kids Designer Paper
Doll Set, 1990
1853 Disney's The Little Mermaid, 1991
1945 Disney's Beauty and the Beast, 1992
1451 Disney's Cinderella, 1993
1339 Disney's Pocahontas, 1995

Rosewood Press
Baltic Folk Costumes, 1990

Ruth Weaver
Jacob and Sadie: Amish Paper Dolls, 1994

Schylling, Inc./Magicloth Corporation
This is just a sample of the many sets produced:
Alice in Wonderland, 1995

Curious George, 1995
Gene Set 1, 2 and 3, 1999
Introducing Raggedy Ann and Andy, 1995
Mr. Potato Head, 1997
Wishbone, 1996

Sayre Ross Company
The Wonderful, Magical World of
Marguerite (circa 1968)

M. Shimmel Sons, Inc., Brooklyn, N.Y.
213 Paper Playmates

Shopko
Pinafore Pockets, Fun Folder, Fun With
Paper Dolls, 1991

Shure Products, Inc.
551 Cinderella's Ballroom Dance, 1998
552 Ballet Designers, 1998

Smart Style Paper Doll Co.
Patty, Paul, Bob, and Barbara, 1918.
(These four paper dolls could be bought
as a set or individually.)

Staples-Smith, NY
Carmen and Quita, Pan-American Doll
Dress-Designing Kit, 1942

Steven Riley Company
Paper Doll Bubble Bath (paper dolls on the
box cover, clothes on the packages of
bubble bath inside the box), circa 1950s.
This was available in at least two
different sizes of boxes.

St. Martin's Press
The Paperdoll Book Elvis, 1982
The Simply Devine Cut-Out Doll Book,
1983
The Supreme Court, 1993

T. Mathews Co., New York
#14 Nursery Playmates

Texas Tech University Press
A New Century, 1998
Amanda Goes West, 1983
Amanda's New Life, 1983
Amand's Home on the Range, 1984
Collection by Design, 1999
Fowler Family Gets Dressed, 2000
Heroine of the Limberlost, 1998
On My Honor, Volume One (a paper doll
history of the Girl Scout Uniform), 1994
7 Sisters Follow a Star, 1987
Whene'er You Make a Promise, 1987

Theriault's Gold Horse Publishing
Bebe Louvre, 1999
Blondinette Davranches, 1998

Tomy Corp.
2508 Fashion Plates, 1978

Treasure Chest Publications, Inc.
Kachi A Hopi Girl, 1989
Dolii A Navajo Girl, 1990
Chana An Anasazi Girl, 1991
Bizagolaa An Apachi Girl, 1989

Troubador Press
Fashion Kit Design & Color Paper Doll, 1972
Flashback Fashion Paper dolls, 1983
Gorey Cats Paper Dolls, 1982
Great Ballet Paper Dolls, 1981
Horse Show Paper dolls, 1986
Huggs & Cuddles Teddy Bear Paper Dolls,
1984
Disney's Beauty and the Beast Play set,
1991 (stand-ups)
Disney's The Little Mermaid Play set, 1992
(stand-ups)
Travels with the Happy Bears Paper Dolls, 1985

Universal City Studios
22180 The Bionic Woman, 1978

Univision Inc.
Fashion Dolls, 1973

Utopia Enterprises, Inc., New York
Story Stage Starring Jackie Gleason and
his TV Troupe ©1955 VIP Corporation

Viking (A division of Penquin Books)
Madeline Paper Dolls, 1994

Virginia Wickenden
Hawaiian Paper Dolls, 1940

Waddle We Doo Inc.
10110 Paper Doll Fashion, 1991
10111 Paper Dolls Country, 1991

White Caps Press
Ma Petite Amie, 1990

Williamsburg Restoration, Incorporated
Eighteenth Century Costume Dolls, Ladies
Costumes, 1939
Eighteenth Century Costume Dolls,
Gentlemen's Costumes, 1939
Paper Dolls, Gentleman in 18th Century
Dress, 1939
Paper Dolls, Lady in 18th Century Dress,
1939

Wood Worm
Alaskan Paperdolls, 1995

Index